Ronald Reagan

THE PRESIDENTIAL PORTFOLIO

Ronald Reagan

THE PRESIDENTIAL PORTFOLIO

A HISTORY ILLUSTRATED FROM THE COLLECTION
OF THE RONALD REAGAN LIBRARY AND MUSEUM

Lou Cannon

INTRODUCTION BY Michael Beschloss

PublicAffairs NEW YORK

PublicAffairs books are available at special discounts for bulk purchases in the U.S. by corporations, institutions, and other organizations. For more information, please contact the Special Markets Department at The Perseus Books Group, 11 Cambridge Center, Cambridge, MA 02142, or call (617) 252–5298.

BOOK DESIGN BY EDWIN SCHLOSSBERG INCORPORATED, JENNY DOSSIN, AND JOAN GREENFIELD.

Library of Congress Cataloging-in-Publication Data
Cannon, Lou.
Ronald Reagan: the presidential portfolio/Lou Cannon; introduction by Michael Beschloss.—1st ed.
p. cm.
Includes bibliographical references and index.
ISBN 1-891620-84-3
1. Reagan, Ronald. 2. Reagan, Ronald—Miscellanea. 3. Presidents—United States—Biography. 4. United States—Politics and government—1981–1989. 5. United States—Politics and government—1981–1989—Sources. I. Ronald Reagan Presidential Library. II. Title.
E877.C365 2001
973.927'092—dc21
[B]
2001041677

FIRST EDITION
10 9 8 7 6 5 4 3 2 1

CONTENTS

INTRODUCTION by Michael Beschloss

One reason why the story you are about to read is so captivating is that the culmination is so unexpected. If a visitor to the Ronald Reagan Presidential Library and Museum did not know how the story ends, who would anticipate that exhibit after exhibit, showing the son of a hard-drinking itinerant salesman; the lifeguard on the Rock River; the ostentatiously carefree sports announcer and actor; the depressed man abandoned after World War II by his motion picture audience; the spokesman for General Electric and "twenty-mule-team" Borax; even the two-term California governor would culminate in artifacts, images, and documents that tell us about one of the most important presidents in American history?

A decade after his presidency, we can glimpse the qualities and accomplishments for which future generations are likely to honor Ronald Reagan. They will begin with Reagan's life history, demonstrating the old American ideal that the most seemingly ordinary people among us possess inner strengths, not easily visible, that will let them accomplish extraordinary things if given the chance.

They will note the best aspects of Reagan's personality and character—the modesty that caused him through his successes to be appealingly startled at how far he had traveled in life; the equanimity that allowed him to joke about his near-fatal shooting and write that breathtaking farewell letter to Americans about his Alzheimer's disease; the persistence that kept him faithful to basic principles; the sunny optimism that revived an America demoralized by the Vietnam defeat, the Watergate scandal, and frustration with the failures and the excesses of big government.

Whatever their party or creed, future Americans are likely to be impressed by the political skills that made Ronald Reagan an exceptional leader. He was often exalted as a "great communicator" for his powerful speeches like the one praising "the boys of Pointe du Hoc" on the fortieth anniversary of D-Day or his eulogy for the perished *Challenger* astronauts. More telling were the spontaneous moments when Reagan summoned just the right words to change the American mind—at the 1976 Republican convention, when the defeated candidate gave an impromptu call to arms so stirring that some delegates lamented that they had nominated the wrong man, or in the 1980 debate with Jimmy Carter, when he asked voters whether they were "better off than you were four years ago." Like Dwight Eisenhower, he was self-confident enough to give others the credit when necessary and like Eisenhower, as president, he took the personal invective and poison out of what could have been some of the most bitter partisan battles of our history over economic, foreign, and social policy.

Above all, Reagan did what we should expect more than almost anything else from a political leader—risk his political career for high principle. In 1980, some of his advisers recommended that he pretend to be more benign toward the Soviet Union than he really was in order not to scare away moderate voters. Reagan responded by saying that Americans had the right to know where he stood and that if after telling them, they gave him the presidency, he could claim a mandate to fulfill his campaign promises. Many Americans who disagreed with his foreign policy views voted for him anyway, taking Reagan's boldness and candor as a sign that he would practice strong leadership in the White House.

The result was a president who left an indelible stamp on history. Reagan argued that the Soviet empire was teetering and that if the West poured the pressure on Moscow, we had the chance to end the Cold War in our lifetime. Distasteful as he found large budget deficits, he was willing to swallow them if they were essential to fuel a defense buildup that would impress the Kremlin with the renewed determination of America and the West. A considerable body of post-Soviet evidence suggests that Reagan's defense increases and

threats to build a strategic defense system did much to cause Soviet leaders to sue for peace.

Reagan also championed and defined the conservative movement that took command of American politics in 1980. He was the voice of Americans who were tired of what they saw as Washington-ordered social engineering and excessive meddling with the private sector and who wanted to revise and edit what they considered the excesses of the New Deal, Fair Deal and Great Society. Reagan did what presidents rarely manage to do: he created a political engine that outlived his presidency to carry on his ideas. Each of his successors has labored in his shadow. George Bush the elder worked to convince Reagan Republicans that he was one of them. Bill Clinton felt compelled to assure Americans that "the era of big government is over." George W. Bush cast his candidacy and presidency as a vehicle to fulfill Reagan's unfinished "revolution."

We live today in a country and world that are largely the ones that Ronald Reagan made. Domestically, most Americans now believe that sending power to Washington should be a last resort and that the private sector is the most powerful source of prosperity. Abroad, as Reagan once controversially predicted, the "evil empire" is dead, Europe is united and peoples around the world are turning not to Lenin but to Jefferson.

Few would argue that Reagan was faultless. Future critics will probably wonder why Reagan, with his great heart, did not worry more about the disproportionate price that some Americans paid for "supply-side economics" or hold out more of a hand to African-Americans. They will lament that this otherwise commanding leader could have entangled himself in a scandal like Iran-Contra.

But as the dean of Reagan-watchers, Lou Cannon, has so deftly shown in the text of this book, Americans of the future are likely to see Ronald Reagan as one of the most event-making leaders we have ever had. More than that, they are likely to see him as one of those iconic presidents whose mere image conjures up qualities that come from the best of the American character. When they glimpse that grinning man riding his horse in the California mountains, they will think of optimism, self-discipline, self-reliance, simplicity, humor and the undying belief that there will never be a limit to what Americans can do.

REAGAN'S JOURNEY

On a tile platform behind the Ronald Reagan Presidential Library, framed by dust-brown hills that once were backdrops for Hollywood westerns, a graffiti-splashed fragment of the Berlin Wall thrusts toward the sky. It is a window to the past, to the dangerous years of the Cold War. The window opens on twenty-eight miles of barriers, fortifications, and electrified fences that divided Berlin and extended another seventy-five miles beyond the city. Collectively, they were known as the Berlin Wall. The 6,000-pound segment of the wall at the Reagan Library, ten feet high and three and a half feet wide, is painted with pastel drawings of faded flowers and an enormous butterfly. Its beauty is deceptive, for the wall itself was deadly. One hundred and ninety-one people were killed trying to cross it, more than 5,000 people escaped to freedom over and under it, and many thousands more were held in servitude by its grim presence. On June 12, 1987, President Ronald Reagan stood on the western side of the wall in front of the historic Brandenburg Gate and addressed the leader of the Soviet Union. "Mr. Gorbachev, open this gate!" Reagan said, his voice rising to be heard above the loudspeakers that sought to drown him out on the East German side. "Mr. Gorbachev, tear down this wall!"

Reagan's message resonated throughout eastern Europe—all the way to Moscow. Two and a half years later, the wall was torn down by the German people without objection from Mikhail Gorbachev or resistance from the Communist rulers of East Germany. Although Reagan was no longer president, Berliners were grateful for what he had done for them and for the cause of freedom. In April 1990 they sent him the piece of the wall now preserved at the Reagan Library accompanied by a letter that commended his "unwavering dedication to humanitarianism and freedom over communism throughout his presidency."

Reagan's dedication began long before he went to Washington. During the 1930s, he spoke out against the barbaric denial of freedom in Nazi Germany. Later, he vehemently denounced the evils of Stalinist Russia and other communist regimes. Freedom came naturally to Reagan. It was part of the air he breathed as a boy in small-town Illinois, where once we honored Lincoln. Reagan was born in Tampico, Illinois, on February 6, 1911. He grew to manhood in Dixon, where an arch spanned Main Street in tribute to American soldiers who had died in Europe during the Great War, then known as the "war to end all wars" and now remembered as World War I.

When Reagan was a boy, Dixon was home to aging veterans of the Grand Army of the Republic who had fought in the Civil War. Reagan learned early in life that freedom is worth fighting for and that heroes are precious, but he also learned that war was not to be glorified. When he was twenty, Reagan wrote a short story in which a war-weary U.S. soldier on the western front tells a comrade that this dreadful war will seem "worth fighting" only when it ends.

It was a long journey from the arch on Main Street to the Brandenburg Gate, an odyssey with many adventures. Reagan's heroes have always been heroes, and to those who knew Reagan before he became famous he seemed a hero himself. As a young man, Reagan was a lifeguard on a treacherous section of the Rock River that ran through Dixon. The legend was that he rescued seventy-seven people from drowning, and the wonder of the legend is that it was true. The lifeguard became a radio announcer, a Hollywood film star, a television host, and a spokesman for one of America's best-known corporations. In time he became an inspiring public speaker, a governor of the nation's most populous state, and president of the United States. His path to the presidency was

unique and unlikely, and no one who walked it with him knew what would come at the end of the road. But Reagan was a long-distance runner on the course of freedom. His speech at the Brandenburg Gate had its origins in Illinois, where Reagan as a student at Eureka College in 1933, thrilled to the cadences of President Franklin Delano Roosevelt. "My firm belief is that the only thing we have to fear is fear itself," Roosevelt told a desperate nation in his inaugural address. Reagan loved this speech and delivered its famous peroration on a broomstick microphone in dramatic imitation of FDR. The world would change many times over, and Reagan's politics would change, but he would never forget how FDR had inspired his fellow Americans in time of need.

Reagan believed in the politics of inspiration and in the power of freedom. He believed, in a thoroughly American way, that anything conceived by the mind of man could also be created. These beliefs would propel Reagan along the winding road that began in Illinois and ended in Red Square, where Reagan and Gorbachev together proclaimed a new era that ended the most perilous period in human history.

This is a story of that long journey.

Ronald Reagan

THE PRESIDENTIAL PORTFOLIO

③ A. Bowers   J. Kennedy   H. Coss   'Wink' McReynolds   G. O'Malley   C. Keyes   R. McNichols
   M. Kinney   'Moon' Regan   C. Fisher   'Bo' Culley   ② M. Keller   F. Kellar   L. Miller
C. McNichols   B. Johnson   'Buns' Kerst   G. Bonds   H. Weinman   Wilson   H. Marks   L. Beach
④ ?   D. Miller   Snyder?   R. Reagan   ?   Dawson   ?   ?   K. Segner   J. Padgett   ? F. Spotts

MAIN ST.   TAMPICO, ILL.

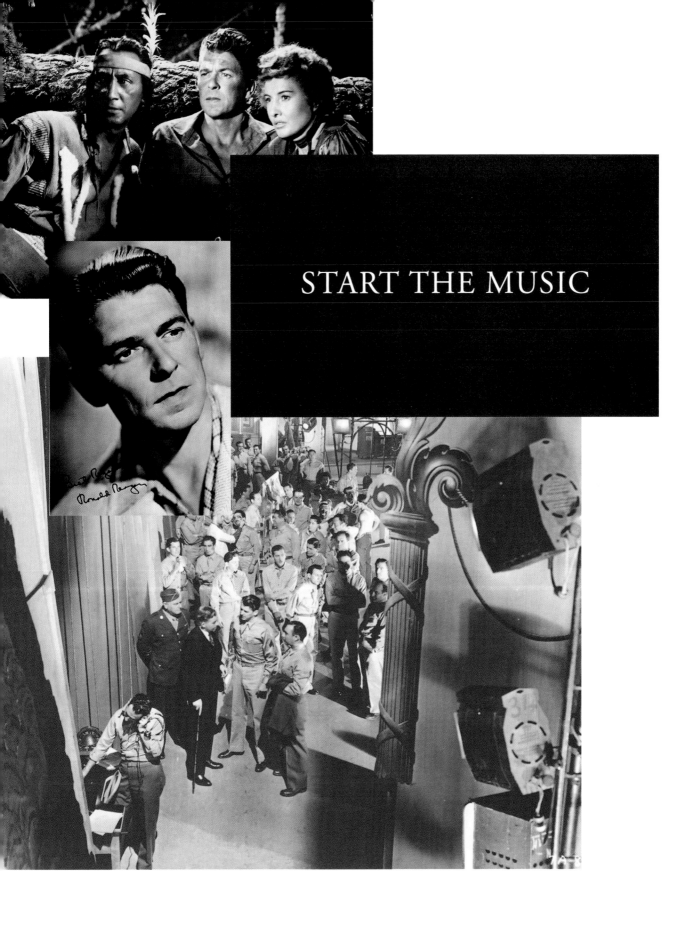

START THE MUSIC

Ronald Wilson Reagan was the second and last child of
John Edward Reagan, the child of Irish immigrants,
and Nelle Wilson Reagan, a gentle, auburn-haired woman of
Scots-Irish descent. His father, called Jack, was a Roman
Catholic. His mother, known for her charitable works, was a
pillar in the Disciples of Christ, then in the forefront of the
temperance movement in Illinois. Ronald Reagan's older
brother, Neil, was baptized in his father's religion, while
Ronald became a member of Nelle's church. Despite a phys-

Birth certificate

ical resemblance to Jack, Ronald took after his mother in outlook and temperament while Neil was more like his father. Ronald Reagan's mother was the great, early influence of his life, as has also been the case with many other American presidents. She was a multifaceted woman—bright, vivacious, and religious—who believed that everything happened according to God's plan. Ronald Reagan would remember her as a "frustrated actress" who encouraged him to perform. On May 6, 1920, the nine-year-old Reagan recited a sentimental tribute, "About Mother," in church. Two years later, according to a newspaper account, mother and son entertained patients at Dixon State Hospital "with a short and enjoyable program" that included a banjo performance by Nelle and two readings by Ronald.

Jack Reagan was a restless traveling shoe salesman, who called his boys by nicknames he had given them at birth—Neil was "Moon" and Ronald was "Dutch." During the first ten years of Ronald Reagan's life his family lived in Tampico, Chicago, Galesburg, and Monmouth before settling in Dixon, in northwestern Illinois. Beginning when he was six, Ronald Reagan attended a different school for each of the next four years. Nancy Reagan, in reflecting on the consequences of her husband's nomadic childhood, believes the continual moving deprived him of close boyhood friendships but also made him self-reliant. He developed solitary pursuits, collecting lead soldiers and butterflies, and enjoyed roaming

Ronald Reagan

Jack, Neil, Ronald (then four), and Nelle

the woods. The Reagans always lived
in rented apartments or houses,
including four in Dixon, and were not
well off. "We didn't live on the wrong
side of the tracks, but we lived so close
to them we could hear the whistle real
loud," Ronald Reagan would later
recall.

Jack Reagan

The greatest difficulty for the
Reagan boys was Jack Reagan's alcoholism. When sober, Jack Reagan was
a witty and charming raconteur. He
was also a principled man who was
mindful of widespread prejudice
against Irish Catholics and taught his
boys that racial and religious intoler-

Tampico, Illinois

ance was wrong. But his drinking bouts left a mark. Ronald Reagan, then eleven, arrived home one snowy night to find his father lying on his back on the front porch, "drunk, dead to the world." More than a half century later, he remembered recoiling at the sight. His father's arms were spread out "as if he were crucified—as indeed he was, his hair soaked with melting snow," Reagan said. "I wanted to let myself in the house and go to bed and pretend he wasn't there." Instead, the young Reagan, who was slight of frame, grabbed his muscular father by his overcoat and wrestled him into the house and to his bed. In an insight advanced for its time, Nelle Reagan told her sons that their father's drinking was not a moral failing but a sickness. Ronald Reagan accepted this maternal counsel but also resolved to follow a temperate course in his own life. As an adult, he limited his drinking to an occasional cocktail or glass of wine. Unlike his father, he exercised regularly and never smoked cigarettes.

Reagan in third grade, Tampico (hand on chin)

With the family settled in Dixon, where his father became a partner in a small shoe store, Ronald Reagan blossomed into a thoughtful teenager who was popular but, as Neil put it, did not "run with crowds." Nearsightedness prevented Ronald from excelling at baseball, his father's best sport; his eyesight was so poor he could barely see a football in flight. But he loved athletic competition and became an underweight lineman on the high school football team, where he won respect for persistence and pluck. Ronald Reagan's best sport was

1923, Dixon

swimming. There was no organized swimming competition in Dixon in those days, but in 1928 he set a record time in an annual round-trip race across a treacherous section of the Rock River where Reagan worked six summers as a lifeguard at Lowell Park. When he applied for the job at the age of sixteen, the park operators were not sure that the slender Ronald could do it, but they hired him after Jack Reagan assured them that his son had taken lifesaving courses at the YMCA.

Soon, young Reagan was demonstrating his prowess by repeatedly rescuing swimmers in distress. The rescues made him a local celebrity; Ronald Reagan made his first appearance on the front page of a newspaper on August 3, 1928, when the *Dixon Daily Telegraph* reported that the seventeen-year-old lifeguard had saved a man from drowning after dark when another rescuer had given up the effort. Reagan, who

Coin set

wore thick, horn-rimmed glasses that
he would throw on the beach before
he plunged into the water, would say
later that he could hardly see the man
he was rescuing. In all, during his six
years as a lifeguard from 1927 through
1932, Reagan rescued seventy-seven
persons. But most of his job was
unglamorous and demanding. As a
lifeguard, he worked twelve-hour days,
seven days a week. Each morning he
picked up food supplies for the park
and a 300-pound block of ice, which
he broke into 100-pound blocks for
three coolers. On very hot days, he
would repeat this process once or

*Rock Creek Park,
Dixon, 1927*

Dixon, Illinois

twice. He ate two of his three meals on duty and cleaned up at the end of the day. For all this work, he received fifteen dollars a week, which was raised to eighteen dollars after five

years. Reagan augmented his salary by teaching swimming lessons to children of well-off parents from Chicago who spent summers at a nearby lodge. He saved every dollar he earned for college.

A teen-age Ronald Reagan

In 1928, Reagan graduated from Northside High School in Dixon, where he had shown interest in dramatics, drawing, and journalism. In youthful writings he displayed his mother's optimism, best expressed in a poem called "Life." A paraphrased line from the poem appears under Reagan's picture in the senior yearbook, of which he was art editor: "Life is just one grand, sweet song, so start the music." That fall Reagan enrolled at Eureka College, near Peoria, a school founded by the Disciples of Christ. In his freshman year, Reagan shot up to his adult height of six feet, and he tried out for the college football team. The coach, Ralph (Mac) McKinzie, called Reagan a "plugger" and made him a starting guard midway through his sophomore season. By his own account, Reagan was at best an average student at Eureka, where he majored in economics under a dean known for lenient grades. But while he sometimes skimped on classwork, Reagan was known at Eureka for his ability to salvage a decent grade. At least one professor and brother Neil attributed this to Ronald Reagan's "photographic mind," which enabled him to

Yearbook

cram for a test and master the course material for final exam-
inations in a single night.

Outside the classroom, Reagan soared. He plunged into
Eureka's highly regarded dramatics program, where he acted
in seven plays, among them *Aria de Capo*, an antiwar play by
Edna St. Vincent Millay. Reagan played a shepherd who is
strangled to death. In his freshman year Reagan took a key
role in a student strike protesting the dropping of classes
that cost some students the credits they needed to graduate.
The strike, Reagan's first political activity, did not accomplish its stated objective but led to the resignation of Eureka's
president. During his four years at Eureka, Reagan also
served as president of the Booster Club
and president of the Student Senate and
was on the staff of the college newspaper
and the yearbook. He worked his way
through college with dishwashing and
food-service jobs and the savings from his
lifeguard's pay. When he became president
of the United States, Reagan would quip
that "hard work never killed anyone, but I
figure, why take the chance?" In fact, he
was never afraid of hard work.

What Reagan had called the sweet
song of life turned bitter as the Depression
settled over the land. When Reagan graduated from Eureka on June 7, 1932, one
in four Americans was out of work. The
jobless included Reagan's father, whose
shoe shop had closed, and his brother,
who worked at a cement plant that had
shut down. To make ends meet Reagan's
mother took work as a seamstress, and the
family sublet most of its rented home, living in a single room and cooking on a
hotplate. Ronald Reagan had decided in
his last year at Eureka that he wanted to

Eureka College, 1929

be a radio announcer, but it seemed a hopeless dream. He hitchhiked to Chicago and made a fruitless round of the studios. Reagan told me many years later that he came back discouraged for one of the few times in his life. But when Lowell Park closed at the end of the summer of 1932 and there were no jobs in Dixon, Reagan borrowed his father's well-worn Oldsmobile and set out on a swing of small radio stations. In Davenport, Iowa, a station manager gave Reagan a tryout as a sports announcer, and Reagan launched into an improvised account of a football game in which he had played at Eureka. (In real life Eureka had lost the game, but in Reagan's recreated version it won a dramatic last-second victory.) The station manager of WOC offered Reagan five

Radio announcer at WHO, circa 1934

dollars and round-trip bus fare from Dixon to broadcast a University of Iowa football game the following Saturday. It was a foot in the door of radio, and Reagan kicked it open. Soon, he moved to a sister station, WHO in Des Moines, where as Dutch Reagan he became the best-known sports announcer of his day in the Midwest. He shared his success with his family, sending money home and successfully encouraging his older brother to resume his studies at Eureka College.

Many years later Reagan would say that he developed a lifelong love affair with radio. He was a natural for the medium, with a remarkable voice that projected warmth, excitement, and earnestness. His voice was his great gift. It was a voice, wrote Roger Rosenblatt, which "recedes at the right moments, turning mellow at points of intensity so as to win you over by intimacy. . . . He likes his voice, treats it like a guest. He makes you part of the hospitality." But Reagan, who paid attention to his shortcomings, recognized that a pleasing voice was not enough. While he was comfortable announcing a football game, or "recreating" Chicago Cubs baseball games from laconic telegraph reports, he knew he was just "plain awful" at reading commercials with the "easy conversational persuasive sell" that sponsors wanted. Reagan found that if he memorized a passage and repeated it out loud before delivering it, the words would sound spontaneous. By this technique, he transformed a weakness into a strength. Reagan's sales pitch, first for products and later for political ideas, was the product of practice and careful preparation.

In Des Moines, Reagan maintained the interest in acting that had been inculcated by his mother in childhood church theatricals and nourished by his drama teachers at Eureka. "I'd rather act than anything else," he wrote in a series for the *Des Moines Register and Tribune* after he went to Hollywood. As was often the case, Reagan helped make his own breaks. In 1937, WHO approved Reagan's request to go to

Catalina Island for the spring training of the Chicago Cubs. On this trip a friend helped him obtain a screen test at Warner Bros. where Reagan was told to read the part of a clean-cut young man from the Middle West (Johnny Case in *Holiday*). Reagan quickly memorized his lines, delivered them flawlessly, and was offered a contract for $200 a week. But Warner Bros. considered the nickname "Dutch" inappropriate for the movies and decided he needed a screen name. As Reagan later recalled, after various possibilities had been tossed around, he volunteered that he had been baptized "Ronald." Casting director Max Arnow, who had the final decision, repeated, "Ronald Reagan, Ronald Reagan,"

Love Is on the Air

and said, "I like it." So Reagan, migrating to an industry where many people lose their identities, was given back the name with which he had been baptized in Tampico twenty-six years earlier.

Reagan debuted in Hollywood as a crusading radio announcer in *Love Is on the Air,* a crime picture that was shot in three weeks and released in October 1937. It was the first of fifty-two full-length feature movies in which he would appear during the next two decades, not counting a made-for-television film that appeared in 1964. This initial role typecast Reagan as a wholesome "good guy," mirroring his behavior in real life. But Reagan knew that his acting skills were raw, and he set out to improve them. The series he wrote for the *Des Moines Register and Tribune* shows a fascination with movie-making and Reagan's close attention to technique: where to stand, what to wear, how to kiss a girl. His diligence won the plaudits of directors. In a business noted for displays of temperament, Reagan was the rare actor who memorized his parts, arrived punctually on location, and never made a fuss. He was so cooperative and professional that he may have spent more time than he should have in Warner's B-film division where, as Reagan put it, "the studio didn't want movies good, it wanted them Thursday." Because these low-budget films were shot quickly, an actor with Reagan's reliable work habits was especially useful.

Reagan broke out of B films in 1940 as the doomed Notre Dame

As George Gipp in Knute Rockne—All American, *1940*

halfback George Gipp in *Knute Rockne—All American.*
Although his role as Gipp is among his best remembered, it
is rarely recognized that the idea for the movie, with Pat
O'Brien in the title role, was also Reagan's. Nonetheless,
Warner Bros. was reluctant to cast Reagan as Gipp because
studio executives said he didn't look like a football player.
Reagan overcame these objections by showing pictures of
himself in football uniform at Eureka and with the help of
O'Brien, who arrived fully made up as Coach Rockne for
the test scene that would determine if Reagan got the part.
This scene, deep into the movie, is vintage Reagan. It is
Gipp's first practice at Notre Dame, and Rockne asks him if
he can carry the ball. With trademark insouciance, Gipp
cocks an eyebrow and asks, "How far?"

*Captain Reagan and Secretary of the Treasury Henry Morgenthau launch
War Loan Drive, January 17, 1944*

The movie played to mixed reviews, but Reagan received critical praise for his portrayal of Gipp. The high point of his performance was a sentimental deathbed scene in which Gipp tells Rockne that "some day when things are tough, maybe you can ask the boys to go in there and win just one for the Gipper." When Reagan ran for president four decades later, the film had a second lease on life and reporters took to calling Reagan "The Gipper."

The year 1940 was also significant in Reagan's private life. He married Jane Wyman, whom he had met during the filming of his ninth movie, *Brother Rat,* in which both of them starred. The next year she gave birth to a daughter, Maureen. A son, Michael, was adopted soon after his birth in 1945. On June 26, 1947, Wyman give birth to a premature baby girl who died the same day. They were divorced in 1948; Wyman said that Reagan had become too absorbed with politics and with his work in the Screen Actors Guild, of which she was also a member of the board.

Buoyed by the critical success of *Knute Rockne—All American,* Reagan landed bigger roles in better pictures, notably the 1942

On the team, circa 1944

Lieutenant Ronald Reagan

film, *Kings Row.* In this movie, based on Henry Bellaman's novel of a small southern town with a darker side than Dixon, Reagan portrayed the rakish Drake McHugh, whose legs are amputated by a sadistic surgeon (Charles Coburn) because McHugh is romancing his daughter. In Reagan's key scene, he awakes and finds that his legs are missing and cries out, "Where's the rest of me?" These words later became the title of Reagan's first autobiography and of a symbolic expression of his desire to do more than act. *Kings Row*, directed by Sam Wood, was praised as "powerful, art-ful cinema" by *Time* magazine reviewer James Agee, and many of Reagan's critical notices were also positive. Based on his work in *Kings Row,* Reagan's agent, Lew Wasserman, was able to triple his salary to more than $3,000 a week.

Law and Order, *1953*

But by the time the movie reached the theaters, Reagan was in uniform, making training films for World War II.

During his Des Moines days, Reagan had joined the U.S. Army Cavalry reserve because he wanted to ride. Four months after Pearl Harbor he was commissioned a second lieutenant, and sent to Fort Dixon, San Francisco, where he was a liaison officer in charge of loading transports. Reagan's nearsightedness kept him out of combat. The Army soon

Santa Fe Trail, *1940*

transferred him to the rapidly expanding Army Air Corps
and sent him to the Hal Roach Studios in Culver City, only
ten miles from the Warner Bros. studio. He spent the rest of
World War II living at home and making training films,
with intermittent leaves that enabled him to participate in
Hollywood's contributions to the war effort. The most
notable of these was an appearance in the movie, *This Is the
Army,* a patriotic 1943 Irving Berlin musical.

Reagan had been on the verge of stardom after *Kings
Row,* but tastes had changed during the war, and new stars
had emerged. Reagan was discharged from the Army as a
captain on December 9, 1945, but his next movie, *Stallion
Road,* about horse ranching, was not released until 1947,

Bedtime for Bonzo, *1951*

when he had been offscreen for four years. Although Reagan
would make another twenty-one films, his congenial relations with Warner's had changed, and he was often at odds
with the studio over the roles in which he was cast. Warner's
valued him in light comedy, while Reagan wanted heftier
roles, and the studio preference prevailed more often than
not. Reagan's memorable postwar movies include *The Voice
of The Turtle* (1947), in which he played opposite the talented Eleanor Parker in a movie version of John Van
Druten's play of the same name; *The Hasty Heart* (1949) in
which he portrayed a malaria-stricken U.S. soldier in Burma
and won critical acclaim in a movie that brought Richard
Todd an Academy Award nomination; and *Bedtime for*

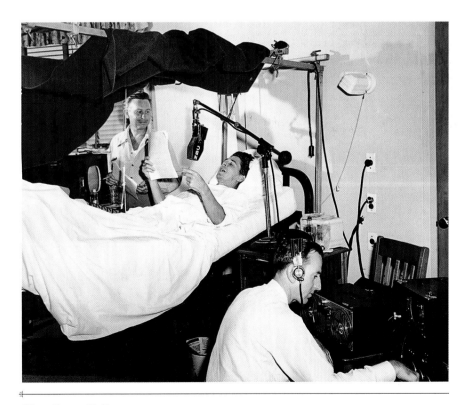

Kings Row, *1942*

Born Anne Frances Robbins in 1921 in a Manhattan hospital, to Edith Luckett, a stage actress, Nancy Reagan overcame a difficult childhood. She was greatly helped by Loyal Davis, a Chicago neurosurgeon who married Luckett when Nancy was seven years old and became her adopted father. Nancy Davis gave up her acting career about the time she married Ronald Reagan on March 4, 1952.

With Nancy Reagan in Hellcats of the Navy, *1957*

Bonzo (1951), a pleasant comedy in which Reagan and the rest of the cast competed with a scene-stealing chimpanzee. One of Reagan's favorite roles was as baseball pitcher Grover Cleveland Alexander in the 1950 film *The Winning Team.* Alexander's drinking bouts masked an epileptic condition he had never revealed to his teammates. Even though Warner's wouldn't permit the taboo word "epilepsy" to be mentioned on-screen, Reagan's acting effectively suggested that Alexander's fainting spells were caused by more than drinking.

As Reagan's film career faded in the 1950s, his personal life took a huge turn for the better after he met a young actress at MGM named Nancy Davis. These were the days of blacklists in Hollywood, and Davis had been receiving unsolicited mail

With Louella Parsons and Doris Day

from left-wing organizations intended for another person
with the same name. She asked a friend, the well-known
director Mervyn LeRoy, what to do about it, and he suggested calling Reagan, then president of the Screen Actors
Guild. Davis asked that he arrange a meeting instead. They
had dinner at LaRue's, a popular restaurant on Sunset Strip,
and both Reagan and Davis were smitten. They were married on March 4, 1952, and Davis, without regrets, abandoned her acting career to become a wife and mother. Their
daughter Patricia was born later that year. In 1958, Mrs.

Wedding Day, March 4, 1952, with Ardis and Bill Holden

Reagan gave birth to a son, Ronald Prescott. Ronald and
Nancy Reagan would become an enduring love story more
compelling than any film romance. They appeared together
in Reagan's last movie, *Hellcats of the Navy,* which premiered
in San Diego on April 11, 1957, and was a hit with the large
naval audience there. In the film Reagan played a naval submarine officer and his wife was a Navy nurse.

   After Reagan went into politics, evaluations of his film
career took on partisan overtones and opponents derided
him as a B-picture actor. Reagan was sensitive about these
attacks—more so than about criticisms of his political views.
In response, he accurately observed that he had received
critical acclaim for many of his roles from such noted
reviewers as Agee and Bosley Crowther of *The New York
Times.* Because he was off the screen for most of the war,
Reagan never quite reached the top rung of movie stardom
that he seemed poised to climb after *Kings Row,* but he had
staying power and was one of the most popular actors at
Warner Bros. He won over audiences, wrote Garry Wills, by
playing "the heartwarming role of himself." Reagan continued in this role after he left Hollywood, which he believed
had prepared him for a larger stage. Near the end of his presidency in 1988, he said to David Brinkley, "There have been
times in this office when I've wondered how you could do
the job if you hadn't been an actor." He was smiling as he
said this, but he meant it.

SOAP BOX DERBY

ELECT
A MAN TO MATCH OUR MOUNTAINS!
REAGAN
REAGAN CITIZENS' TRUST FUND 1011 JAY ST.

25¢ CAR WASH

A TIME FOR CHOOSING

REAGAN FOR GOVERNOR

After he became a candidate, Ronald Reagan called him-self a "citizen-politician" and compared his role to that of Cincinnatus, who left his plow to save the Roman repub-lic and returned to his farm when the crisis was over. But Reagan was interested in public affairs long before his nation faced a crisis. His mother taught him to read when he was still a small child, gave him books and newspapers, and called in neighbors to demonstrate his precocity. At the age of five, Reagan proudly read aloud to his father a newspaper account of the Preparedness Day bombing in San Francisco on July 22, 1916. He read the papers closely most of his life and showed a keen interest in national and world events.

The Reagans were Democrats, and Ronald Reagan, then twenty-one, cast his first vote in 1932 for Franklin D. Roo-

With President Harry Truman

sevelt. FDR revived the nation's sagging confidence at the nadir of the Great Depression, and Ronald Reagan admired him as a political leader. There was a personal dimension to his feelings; FDR's "New Deal for the American people" provided jobs for Reagan's unemployed father and brother, both of whom were hired to distribute public assistance for the Federal Emergency Relief Administration in the Dixon area. Long after his politics changed, Reagan remained grateful to FDR. He also appreciated FDR's mastery of radio technique in the folksy "fireside chats" he used to communicate with the American people. In his own radio speeches, years later, Reagan emulated FDR, especially in using unusual anecdotes to make his points.

With Nancy and Nelle

Reagan remained a loyal Democrat throughout FDR's twelve years in office and well into the Truman years. He was also staunchly pro-union. In 1938, in only his second year in Hollywood, he was invited to become a member of the board of directors of the Screen Actors Guild. He remained on the board for twenty-two years and served six years as president of the Guild, which he led in a successful strike against the major studios. When Reagan was president of the United States four decades later, he told me he considered this experience valuable background for the negotiations on which he was then embarking with Soviet leaders. When I asked the most important lesson he had learned from his labor experience, he replied succinctly: "That the purpose of a negotiation is to get an agreement."

Reagan had a futuristic sensibility. In the 1940s, after World War II, he read science fiction, a genre then preoccupied with themes of nuclear conflict. These became factual concerns throughout the world after the Soviet Union joined the United States as a nuclear power. Reagan had expressed a poignant longing for world peace when he was only twenty years old in a short story written for a class at Eureka College. In 1946, less than a year after U.S. planes dropped atomic bombs on Hiroshima and Nagasaki, Reagan joined the United World Federalists, a utopian organization that advocated one-world government to prevent nuclear war. He remained a member for only a few months, however, dropping out when it became clear that the World Federalists lacked either a practical plan or a widespread following.

But Reagan considered himself a liberal, as well as a Democrat, late into the 1940s. He said subsequently that he was "unusually naïve" during the years after World War II when Hollywood plunged into a cauldron of labor and political strife. During this period Reagan joined two organizations that were dominated or heavily influenced by the Communist Party. He soon quit one of these groups but stayed a year and a half in the Hollywood Independent Citizens Committee of the Arts, Sciences and Professions, leaving, along with other prominent Hollywood figures, after the organization's executive committee in 1947 blocked a resolution offered by James Roosevelt repudiating communism.

These actions and associations should be viewed in the context of the times. The United States and Soviet Union were allies during World War II, when Communists operated openly in Hollywood under relatively moderate leaders. As the Cold War unfolded, however, hard-line Stalinists took over the party in the United States, and Hollywood was shaken by a sensation-seeking investigation by the House Committee on Un-American Activities of alleged Communist influence within the movie industry. Reagan had a low opinion of the committee, and his testimony as president of the Screen Actors Guild during a committee hearing in 1947 did not please it. In what *The New York Times* and *Life*

saw as a swipe at the committee's bullying of witnesses,
Reagan denounced communism but warned about the dan-
gers of using undemocratic measures to contain it. "I detest,
I abhor their philosophy, but I detest more than that their
tactics, which are those of a fifth column, and are dishonest,
but at the same time I never as a citizen want to see our
country become urged, by either fear or resentment of this
group [to] ever compromise with any of our democratic
principles through that fear or resentment," Reagan said. "I
still think democracy can do it."

The committee wanted its witnesses to
identify specific members of the film community as Communists. This Reagan
declined to do. While he acknowledged
under questioning that Communists had on
occasion attempted to be "disruptive"
within the Screen Actors Guild, he refused
to brand anyone a Communist because he
said he had no proof of any Guild member's
party affiliation. By and large, this testimony pleased liberals, who also approved of
Reagan's policy as Guild president of helping actors who were targets of various unof-
ficial vigilante blacklists that sprang up in
the wake of the committee's investigations.
But they were not pleased when Reagan and
the Guild board later went along with a studio blacklist of actors who refused to coop-
erate with the committee. Reagan said the
studios had the right to consider an actor's
outside activities or reputation, since these
could affect public acceptance of a film.

Testifying before the House Committee
on Un-American Activities, October 23, 1947

Reagan emerged from the struggles of
this period as a staunch anticommunist. He never gave
much credence to the committee's overblown accusations of
Communist influence on films, but he blamed the Commu-

nists for exacerbating a series of bitter labor disputes over which union would represent set designers and other craft workers in the movie studios. The Guild twice intervened to settle jurisdictional strikes, but a third such attempt failed, and the Guild and twenty-five other unions crossed the picket lines of another union in which Communists were allegedly influential. Violence flared, and the strike collapsed. Although Reagan did not know it, historical evaluations of this complex labor dispute suggest it may have been provoked less by Communists than by movie producers who took advantage of union rivalry to eliminate jobs and exercise greater control over production.

Reagan was supportive of President Harry Truman for standing up to Soviet expansionism. He summed up his philosophy in a 1947 interview with columnist Hedda Hopper in

Nancy with Patti

which he said, "Our highest aim should be the cultivation of
the freedom of the individual for therein lies the highest dignity of man. Tyranny is tyranny, and whether it comes from
right, left, or center, it is evil." In 1948
Reagan campaigned for Truman and other
Democrats in speeches that emphasized economics more than anticommunism. Typical
of the Reagan approach was a speech he gave
for Truman and Senate candidate Hubert
Humphrey in which he cited a wire-service
report about a craftsman named Smith L.
Carpenter who had retired believing that he
had enough money to last the rest of his life.
"But he didn't figure on this Republican
inflation which ate up all savings," Reagan
said. "The reason this is news is Mr. Carpenter is ninety-one years old."

Reagan, who had been concerned that
left-wing candidate Henry Wallace would
take enough votes from Truman to hand
the election to Republican Thomas Dewey,
was pleased when Truman won an upset
victory. In 1950 he supported liberal Democrat Helen Gahagan Douglas in the U.S.
Senate race in California. She was defeated

Patti, Ron, Nancy, and Ronald

by Republican Richard Nixon after a nasty
campaign in which Douglas was branded "the pink lady."
Reagan was still widely viewed as a liberal Democrat. As late
as 1952, the Los Angeles County Democratic Central Committee declined to endorse Reagan for an open House seat
for which he had been mentioned as a prospective candidate
on grounds he was too liberal.

But Reagan's politics had begun to change. He was now
highly paid on the strength of the contract Wasserman had
negotiated for him after *Kings Row.* In the late 1940s marginal tax rates were at an all-time high and income-tax aver-
aging was not allowed. Reagan thought this unfair to actors,

many of whom have a limited period of high earnings. He once suggested that actors, writers, and others whose income varied radically from year to year be allowed a "human depreciation allowance" similar to the depreciation tax breaks allowed to oil companies.

In 1954, as his film career was fading, Reagan was approached by Taft Schreiber, head of Music Corporation of America's Revue Productions, with a proposal to host a new television series sponsored by General Electric. Reagan jumped at it. The salary of $125,000 a year, soon raised to $150,000, meant economic stability for Reagan's young family and exposure in a then-new medium. But what intrigued Reagan most about the offer was that he would tour the country for ten weeks a year, plugging GE products and giving speeches to company executives and employees. This proposal was the brainchild of Ralph Cordiner, the enlightened president of General Electric, which then had 135 plants in 38 states. Reagan did not know Cordiner but admired what he had read about him. "He was the man who really was the leader of decentralization of industry and business," Reagan said. Cordiner's idea was that Reagan would be a unifying presence for GE, whose plant managers enjoyed considerable autonomy.

This unusual contract turned into a unique political apprenticeship for Reagan. According to Edward Langley, a GE public relations official at the time, the company wanted and got "a Cadillac at Ford prices" in Reagan, who threw himself into the job with his customary discipline. "We drove him to the utmost limits," said Langley. "We saturated him in Middle America." This was fine with Reagan, who had left Dixon without Dixon ever leaving him. By Reagan's account, he gave as many as fourteen speeches a day and spent two of the eight years he was under contract to GE on the road, traveling by train to every one of the company's plants and meeting all of the company's 250,000 employees. All the while he remained in touch with a wider television

audience as host of *General Electric Theater,* which dominated the Sunday-night ratings until *Bonanza* came along in
the 1960s.

No American politician-in-the-making ever had such
training. Reagan had been giving public speeches since his
Des Moines days, but the GE experience enabled him to
develop and polish what ultimately became his standard
political speech without media scrutiny and the other pressures of a campaign. As he had done when new to radio and
films, Reagan worked hard to improve his techniques. He
wrote his own speeches, transcribing them onto cards (first
three-by-five, later four-by-six) in a personal shorthand. As
he traveled around the country, he clipped stories out of
newspapers in the towns he visited to give his speeches a

At a General Electric Plant in Danville, Illinois, October 1955

local flavor. He paid close attention, as always, to his audiences. From questions asked him at the plants he visited, Reagan realized that a growing number of ordinary Americans shared his concern that the federal government was becoming too big and intrusive. This concern became a recurrent theme in his talks, which varied in particulars but evolved into a basic address that would become known as The Speech.

Ronald, Ron, Nancy, and Patti

Reagan's politics also continued to evolve. Along with millions of other Democrats he voted Republican for the first time in 1952 when war hero Dwight D. Eisenhower won in a landslide. Reagan supported Eisenhower again in 1956. In 1960, a decade after he backed Helen Gahagan Douglas in her Senate race against Nixon, Reagan supported Vice President Nixon for the presidency against John F. Kennedy, who won narrowly. Reagan was still a Democrat, but just barely. He reregistered Republican in 1962, when Nixon ran for governor of California and was soundly beaten by incumbent Governor Edmund G. (Pat) Brown.

By now, Reagan was a controversial figure at General Electric, whose executives were nervous about having a Republican conservative as company spokesman with a Democrat in the White House. Reagan had first aroused corporate ire in 1959 when he included the Tennessee Valley

Michael, Ronald, Ron, and Nancy

Authority among his examples of wasteful government, saying that "the annual interest on the TVA deal is five times as great as the flood damage it prevents." TVA was a revered New Deal symbol and a $50-million-a-year customer of GE products. Reagan called Cordiner to see if he was concerned.

Cordiner said he had no intention of censoring Reagan or anyone else, but Reagan volunteered to drop the TVA reference from his speeches. This mollified General Electric for a while, but when Reagan's option came up for renewal in 1962, another GE executive asked him to confine his remarks to selling company products. This Reagan refused to do. "There's no way that I could go out now to an audience that is expecting the type of thing I've been doing for the last eight years and suddenly stand up and start selling them electric toasters," he said. His option was not renewed.

But Reagan, although out of work, was in heavy demand as a public speaker for business groups and conservative causes. In 1964 he campaigned for Arizona Senator Barry Goldwater, a pioneering conservative who set out to wrest the Republican presidential nomination from moderate New York Governor Nelson Rockefeller. Goldwater clinched the nomination with a narrow victory in the crucial California primary. Afterward, Reagan supporters in California urged Goldwater's strategists to use Reagan in the fall election campaign against President Lyndon Johnson. The Goldwater team resisted on the odd grounds that Reagan was too controversial. Reagan was, in fact, less controversial than Goldwater, but the senator's strategists worried that Reagan's presence in the campaign would raise the Social Security issue, which was already hurting their candidate. Social Security was even then the third rail of American politics, and Reagan, in remarks that seem prescient today, questioned the system's long-term solvency. But Goldwater was faltering in the polls, and his campaign was out of money. The argument that Reagan could replenish the party's depleted campaign coffers proved decisive, and Goldwater's advisers reluctantly agreed to put him on national television.

On October 27, 1964, Reagan, then

With Nelson Rockefeller

fifty-three years old, gave the speech he had been rehearsing for years. Called "A Time for Choosing," it celebrated individual freedom, denounced communism, and detailed what Reagan saw as the waste and excesses of government. The emotional peroration borrowed a famous phrase from Reagan's first political idol, Franklin Roosevelt, and another line from Abraham Lincoln. "You and I have a rendezvous with destiny," Reagan said. "We can preserve for our children this, the last best hope of man on earth, or we can sentence them to take the first step into a thousand years of darkness. If we fail, at least let our children and our children's children say of us we justified our brief moment here. We did all that could be done."

Reagan's speech was the bright spot in an otherwise dismal campaign. It brought in $1 million for Republican candidates, more money than had been raised by any political speech until that time. David S. Broder, the nation's leading political columnist, called the Reagan speech "the most successful political debut since Williams Jennings Bryan electrified the 1896 Democratic convention with his 'Cross of Gold' speech." Goldwater was buried in a political landslide the following Tuesday, but in a half hour of television Reagan had transformed himself from a fading celebrity into the nation's most important conservative politician.

After the 1964 election Reagan's star shone even brighter because so few Republican luminaries remained in the political firmament. Republicans at all levels, moderates as well as conservatives, had gone down to defeat with Goldwater. The GOP ranks were so reduced in Congress and state legislatures that the party seemed destined to become a permanent minority; some

Campaigning for Barry Goldwater

columnists even speculated that the Republicans might go the way of the Whigs. But Reagan, optimistic as always, believed that the Goldwater campaign was not an end but a beginning. While he refrained from public criticism of Goldwater or his strategists, he made it known to Nancy Reagan that he believed the problem of the 1964 campaign was less the message than the messenger. Reagan thought he could make Goldwater's case better than Goldwater had done and that voters would be receptive to it.

Reagan's next step was a big one. National conservatives and his financial supporters, most of them self-made millionaires led by Los Angeles automobile dealer Holmes Tuttle, had been promoting Reagan as a candidate for governor of California since Nixon's defeat in 1962. Reagan was unsure at first about seeking state office, in part because most of the issues he raised were federal ones. When his daughter Maureen wrote him from Washington, D.C., in 1962, suggesting that he run for governor, Reagan kiddingly wrote back, using Maureen's family nickname, "Well, if we're talking about what I could do, Mermie, I could be President." But as Reagan surveyed the wreckage of the Republican political landscape after the 1964 election, he increasingly saw the 1966 governor's race as an opportunity for advancing his ideas. California was his home, after all, and the state's voters did not look down on actors. In 1964, even as President Johnson was carrying California by more than a million votes, Reagan's friend, the song-and-dance man George Murphy, had beaten Pierre Salinger and won election to the U.S. Senate.

In light of Murphy's victory it remains a mystery to this day why Reagan was so completely underestimated by the campaign operatives for Governor Pat Brown, who had decided to seek a third four-year-term. Brown bore the inevitable scars of incumbency and knew he faced a tough campaign; he hoped the GOP would nominate Reagan, whom he thought was vulnerable both because of his ideology and his lack of political experience. Reagan was also taken lightly within his own party, where he was opposed for the gubernatorial nomination by moderate George Christopher, a former mayor of San Francisco. Christopher was convinced that if Reagan became the Republican nominee Democrats would demonize him as a "right-wing extremist," as they had done with Goldwater.

Reagan, despite never having spent a day in public office, had political assets that his opponents failed to recognize. Foremost among these was that he was widely known and liked. He had been a familiar figure to the public for nearly thirty years, first as a good-guy movie actor and then as a television host. He was an effective speaker—in person, on radio, and on television—with an intangible quality of identifying with his audiences and reflecting their values. Reagan had firmly held core beliefs that he had shaped into a coherent and accessible speech. As we have seen repeatedly, he was also persistent and competitive. Reagan had no illusion that he understood the ins and outs of politics or government, but he was confident he could learn whatever it took to be a governor.

With Pat Brown

Reagan's biggest obstacle as a candidate in 1966 was neither his inexperience nor the ability of his opponents but the sorry condition of the California Republican Party, which had been torn apart two years earlier by the acrid Goldwater-Rockefeller primary. Grudges from this battle died hard; at the beginning of 1966 most moderates and conservatives weren't speaking to each other, and each faction blamed the other for the Republican debacle of 1964. Reagan, supported by Nancy and the Tuttle-led

businessmen who called themselves the "Friends of Ronald
Reagan," knew they had to unite the party to have any hope
of beating Brown. They began by hiring Spencer-Roberts,
the rising consulting firm that had managed Rockefeller's
1964 campaign in California. Bill Roberts and Stuart K.
Spencer were bright, practical political consultants. They
advised Reagan to sidestep the conflicts of the past by select-
ing local and regional chairmen, most of them quite young,
who had not been involved with either the Goldwater or
Rockefeller factions in 1964. Reagan embraced this advice.
His mantra was the so-called Eleventh Commandment
promulgated by state Republican Chairman Gaylord Parkin-
son: "Thou shall not speak ill of any fellow Republican."

Reagan's willingness to set aside doctrinal differences in
the interests of party unity put him on a winning path. After
he won the Republican primary in June he generously
praised Christopher and solicited his support for the fall
campaign. Unlike some conservatives, Reagan used no

Filing for the governor's race

ideological litmus test and vigorously campaigned for moderate Republicans on the statewide ticket. With the Republicans unified, Reagan reached out to independents and working-class Democrats. The timing was fortuitous because many of these Democrats had become uneasy about the direction of their party and disenchanted by urban disturbances, such as the Watts Riot of 1965, and the escalating Vietnam War. In 1966 violent demonstrations erupted at the Berkeley campus of the University of California, to which the Brown administration responded ineffectually. Reagan took note. As he traveled around the state he was repeatedly asked what he would do about the campus disorders if elected, and Reagan started talking about what he called the "mess at Berkeley" long before it showed up as significant in Spencer-Roberts polls. With a sure-handed feel for his audience, Reagan had correctly gauged the mood of the public. While he upheld the right of peaceful protest, he said that if he were governor, campus demonstrators would be told to "obey the rules or get out."

Pat Brown, an excellent governor and formidable politician who had survived a divisive primary campaign, now found himself on the defensive. He came after Reagan as a right-wing extremist, as Christopher had predicted, but the Reagan smile was less vulnerable than the Goldwater scowl, and the attacks fell flat. So did the anti-actor campaign. Actor Jack Palance walked out of a Democratic telethon that belittled Reagan's acting abilities. "Attack him if you wish for lack of experience, but don't go after him just because he's an actor," Palance said. That didn't deter the Brown campaign from filming a television commercial, *Man vs. Actor,* which showed the governor telling an integrated elementary school class, "I'm running against an actor and you know who shot Lincoln, don'tcha?" Reagan was outraged, but the ad had no discernible effect. On election day, Reagan won by nearly a million votes. He ran slightly behind Nixon's performance four years earlier in moderate Republican precincts in the San Francisco Bay area and well ahead of him nearly everywhere else. Particularly notable were the inroads Reagan

The 1966 campaign

Talking to George Allen, the coach of the (then) Los Angeles Rams

Reagan sworn in as governor of California, January, 1967

made in Democratic, working-class areas in Southern California. These voters would become known as "Reagan Democrats."

Reagan was sworn in as California's thirty-third governor at fourteen minutes after midnight on January 1, 1967, at a ceremony infused with religious and patriotic overtones. He began with a quip, saying to Senator Murphy, "Well, George, here we are back on the late show." But his speech, written entirely by Reagan and delivered without notes, was serious. He promised that he would attempt to follow the "precepts of the Prince of Peace" in his governance and quoted Ben Franklin, saying that anyone who followed the teachings of Christ in public office would revolutionize the world. "I'll try very hard," Reagan said. "I think it's needed in today's world."

Nelle Reagan's son was now the citizen-governor of California, the nation's most populous and trend-setting state.

GOVERNOR REAGAN

S oon after he was elected, a reporter asked Reagan what kind of governor he would be. "I don't know, I've never played a governor," Reagan joked. But he soon learned that it was a most demanding role.

Reagan's first challenge was a fiscal crisis. The California constitution requires the budget to be balanced annually; this had been accomplished in 1966 by an accounting gimmick that averted a tax increase in an election year. Now, Reagan learned, his first budget could not be balanced without a tax increase. This was unwelcome news to a governor who had promised to cut taxes and "squeeze, cut, and trim" state government. Reagan compounded his inherited prob-

Delivering the inaugural address for governor, January 5, 1967

lems by choosing a finance director with scant budget knowledge and fewer political skills. He produced a budget that called for 10 percent across-the-board spending reductions, a plan that would have penalized the most efficient state departments and rewarded departments with padded payrolls and room to cut. Legislators of both parties derided the budget proposal, and Reagan had no choice except to withdraw it. His next proposal called for an additional $440 million in spending and pushed the state budget over $5 billion for the first time.

Reagan's unfortunate choice of a finance director was symptomatic of the early problems that beset his

The Governor's Ball, Sacramento, January 5, 1967

administration. The governor had hoped, he said, to "attract some of the big names in business" to work for him, but few big names were willing to leave lucrative jobs in the private sector to help govern California. So Reagan was forced to rely on the young people who had worked in his political campaign. In the long run this may have been a blessing, for many of the newcomers were able people who improved with time. Initially, however, they knew no more about government than Reagan did. "We were novice amateurs," said Lyn Nofziger, the campaign press secretary who became Reagan's director of communications.

On sensitive issues, amateurism exacted a high political cost. This was a time when the development of tranquilizers and other drugs had made it possible to move mentally ill patients out of the hospital "warehouses" then commonplace in the United States into community treatment. With the patient population of California's mental hospitals rapidly declining, the Reagan administration proposed to close some of them and eliminate 3,700 jobs—one-sixth of the total. Doctors and nurses objected to using patient-staff ratio as the sole guideline; they said that hard-core cases remained in the state hospitals and required a higher proportion of staff. The Reagan plan was leaked to legislative opponents and the press before it was announced, putting the governor and his aides on the defensive for several weeks. Eventually, a compromise was reached that left some of the hospitals open and rescinded roughly one-third of the staff cuts. But Reagan suffered political damage in the process.

Another sensitive situation confronted Reagan at the University of California, where he had been viewed warily since his campaign denunciations of the "mess at Berkeley." In California, the governor is a member of the state university's board of regents, which three weeks after Reagan's inauguration voted to remove university president Clark Kerr, a symbol of "permissiveness" to conservatives. The vote was 14–8, and the regent who made the motion to dismiss

Kerr was an appointee of former Governor Brown, but
Reagan was accused of orchestrating the vote. He denied it.
Reagan told me he would have preferred to defer a decision
on Kerr but had no choice once the motion was made
because "you can't turn around and give a man a vote of
confidence in January and then fire him five months later."
After the Kerr incident, Reagan faced another firestorm, this
one of his own making. Carrying out a campaign promise,
Reagan proposed that all students at the university pay
tuition, which then was levied only on out-of-state students.
This was a touchstone issue. The university establishment
stood firm behind a long-standing policy of "free tuition,"
something of a misnomer for it had been maintained only
through steep increases in student fees. Reagan stuck to his
guns. After the regents voted down tuition, Reagan won
approval (on August 31, 1967) of a compromise for a $200-
a-semester "charge" for students. "If it walks like a duck and
quacks like a duck, it must be a duck," said Nofziger, and
the "charge" was indeed tuition by another name. This was
fine with Reagan, who was more than willing to give the
regents a face-saving phrase. And he wound up giving much
more than that to higher education. During his eight years
as governor spending for the university and state colleges
increased 136 percent compared to a 100 percent increase in
overall state spending.

Campus demonstrators proved less tractable than the
regents. Reagan tried for two years to clamp down on violence
through university procedures. But on February 4, 1969, students trying to enter the Berkeley campus through Sather
Gate were mauled by pickets from the Third World Liberation Front. This was too much for Reagan. He held a press
conference to denounce the beatings of students and disrup-
tion of classes, proclaimed a state of emergency, and called out
the California Highway Patrol to protect the university from
"criminal anarchists" and "off-campus revolutionaries." In
May, radicals and street people occupied university-owned

land in Berkeley that they called "People's Park" and stoned police who tried to eject them. The police sought help from the California Highway Patrol and the Alameda County sheriff's department. On May 15, a protest march turned into a riot, with marchers hurling back tear-gas canisters into police ranks. The deputies resorted to firearms. A twenty-five-year-old San Jose man was killed by a shotgun blast fired by deputies, scores were injured, and hundreds arrested. At the request of Alameda County authorities, Reagan called out the National Guard, which stayed on duty for seventeen days in Berkeley. Reagan said that maintaining public order was paramount. Polls showed that a large majority of Californians agreed with him.

The Berkeley situation had been predictable but neither Reagan nor others in Sacramento foresaw the other emotional issue that would take center stage early in his governorship. In 1967 the national debate on abortion was just beginning; the Supreme Court would not issue its landmark ruling in *Roe v. Wade* until 1973. But California often rides the wave of the future; campus demonstrations against the Vietnam War that swept the nation in 1968 began three years earlier in California, which was also a forerunner on the abortion issue. Early in 1967 a soft-spoken Democratic state senator from Beverly Hills named Anthony Beilenson introduced the Therapeutic Abortion Act in an effort to reduce what he called the "barbarous" practice of back-room abortions. The legislation received a boost after nine doctors

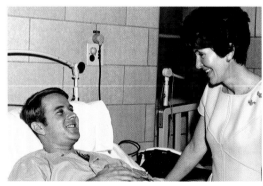

Visiting the wounded from Vietnam

in the San Francisco Bay area were charged with performing illegal abortions on women who had contracted German measles, a disease that can cause birth defects. Thousands of women signed a petition asking that the doctors be spared from punishment and urging that the law be changed. State legislators were sympathetic. The battle was drawn on religious rather than partisan lines with most Catholics opposing the Beilenson bill and almost everyone else supporting it. A large majority of Republicans favored the legislation. Reagan insisted on amendments he was told would restrict the scope of abortions. Beilenson accepted them, and the Legislature sent the bill to Reagan's desk. Reagan did not know what to do. His staff was divided (also largely on religious lines), and he was lobbied heavily from both sides. "Those were awful weeks," he told me later. But Reagan made a determined effort to sift through the arguments. He met with Cardinal Francis McIntyre, who presented the Roman Catholic Church's case against abortion. He discussed the issue with his father-in-law, Loyal Davis, a prominent surgeon who favored the bill. After several days of indecision, Reagan reluctantly signed the Therapeutic Abortion Act. He did not anticipate that some two million abortions would be performed as a result, most of them because of a provision in the bill allowing abortions to protect the mental health of the mother. Reagan later pointed out that he had been governor for less than four months when the bill came to him and said he would not have signed it had he been more experienced. After he recognized its consequences, he became an opponent of abortions, except to save the life of the mother or in cases of rape or incest.

Reagan's lack of experience in government was sometimes beneficial. During the 1966 campaign he had claimed that his inexperience would enable him to take a fresh look at state government, which he sometimes did. Steve Merksamer, then a young aide who later became chief of staff to Governor George Deukmejian, recalls an early briefing of Reagan on the state prison system. The meeting concluded with a rundown on the activities of the state's Catholic and Protestant chaplains. Reagan asked about the activities of the Jewish chaplains. We don't have many Jewish inmates, he was told. Reagan persisted. Were there any Jewish inmates? A few, was the reply. If they requested it, a rabbi could be brought from outside. This wasn't good enough, said Reagan, who on the spot directed that the system be changed to provide Jewish inmates with chaplains of their faith.

A similar common-sense approach animated many of Reagan's other decisions relating to the penal system. He approved, for the first time in California, a program of conjugal visits (called "family visitations") for inmates after being told by his director of corrections that this would reduce homosexual rape in prisons. And while Reagan talked tough about cracking down on crime in his speeches and favored capital punishment, he tended to be reasonable and even compassionate when dealing with people instead of abstractions.

Because of a Supreme Court decision suspending imposition of the death penalty, Reagan faced only two requests for clemency from condemned men during his eight years as governor. Denial of clemency in the first case was a foregone conclusion—the victim was a Sacramento police officer, and his killer previously had been denied clemency by Governor Brown, who had commuted many death sentences. The appeal came to Reagan again on a technicality, and he affirmed the sentence. But to the dismay of prosecutors, Reagan unexpectedly granted clemency in the second case, to a man who had been sentenced to death after he firebombed his girlfriend's home and killed a baby. Reagan acted on the basis of a defense contention that the killer had brain damage, a claim that had not impressed the jury or the sentencing judge.

As time went by, Reagan mastered the job of governor, which he now recognized was much more than a role. While

the learning curve was steeper in Sacramento than it had
been in Des Moines or Hollywood, Reagan's behavior pattern was similar. As always, he paid close attention to what
was said about him and to what he should do when things
went wrong. What went especially wrong during Reagan's
first year in office was his chief of staff, who took too much
power into his own hands, but was forced to resign after
becoming the center of an alleged "homosexual scandal."
The allegations, although never proved, shocked Reagan.
He responded by installing a corporate management system
in which capable chiefs of staff (William Clark and after
him Edwin Meese) used the cabinet as a central forum for
decisionmaking. Every major decision came to Reagan summarized on what Clark called mini-memos with arguments
for each course of action neatly summarized. This suited

Addressing the California assembly

Reagan's style. He was decisive when presented with an objective list of options, and he saw himself as a chairman of the board. Students of government have compared the Reagan system to the one used by Dwight Eisenhower when he was president.

With his new management team in place, Reagan focused on rallying public support for his policies and cultivating legislative support. Reagan liked people, and he found opposition legislators more reasonable than he had expected. Legislators in turn liked Reagan, who swapped stories with them and treated them with respect. What they most appreciated about Reagan was that he kept his word. It was a reputation that would serve him well in Washington, where the Democrats also controlled the lower house of Congress.

Seen in the light of his subsequent career, Sacramento was a valuable training ground for Reagan in his battles with such Washington titans as House Speaker Thomas P. (Tip) O'Neill. The State Assembly, controlled by Democrats for all but two of Reagan's eight years in Sacramento, was led by Jesse M. (Big Daddy) Unruh, then California's most powerful Democrat and a nationally renowned legislator. Unruh wanted to be governor and tested Reagan at every opportunity. The State Senate, where Democrats were also in control, was less partisan but many of its members were skeptical of Reagan. He surprised these skeptics by being far more practical than they had expected. Reagan intuitively understood that politics is the art of the possible. While he held his ground on matters of principle, he was open to compromises that led in the direction he

Jesse Unruh presiding over the California Assembly

wanted to go. When an ultra-conservative state senator accused him of abandoning the conservative cause, Reagan dismissed him as "a guy who jumps off the cliff with all flags flying." In contrast, said Reagan, "I'm willing to take what I can get."

Two actions early in his first term, one involving policy and the other personnel, attest to the success of Reagan's on-the-job political training. The first was his prompt recognition in 1967 that it was impossible to balance the budget without raising taxes. Reagan reasonably blamed the tax increase on the economic situation he had inherited, but he went beyond what was necessary to make up for the shortfall that had been bequeathed to him. In large measure, he accepted a tax bill crafted by Unruh, who wanted simultaneously to make up for the budget shortfall and provide property tax relief for homeowners. Unruh proposed increasing income and sales taxes and also boosting taxes on liquor, tobacco, insurance companies, banks, and corporations. The overall thrust of the legislation changed the state's revenue-raising system from a regressive one that took little account of ability to pay to a more progressive structure. If later minor adjustments are included, corporation taxes nearly doubled during Reagan's governorship, from 5.5 to 9 percent, while the tax on banks rose from 9.5 to 13 percent. Some conservatives grumbled at the billion-dollar size of the 1967 tax bill, by far the highest in state history, and a handful of right-wing Republicans voted against it. But Reagan was confident he had put the state on a sound financial footing for years to come, and the judgment of history supports this view.

For his part, Unruh was jubilant. He favored the tax increase on its merits, and he also believed he had scored a political coup after Reagan adopted the tax bill as his own. Unruh, who was planning to run against Reagan in 1970, knew that California governors who raise taxes usually pay for it at the next election. But in this instance the supposedly naïve governor had surer political instincts than the savvy and experienced Assembly speaker. When I asked Reagan in 1968 if the tax bill would hurt him, he noted dryly that the legislation had been passed in the first year of his term and that he would never have to raise taxes again. Without saying so directly, Reagan made it clear that he understood that the tax increase would be ancient history by the time he ran for reelection.

Soon after the tax bill took effect, Reagan made a personnel decision that also demonstrated his growing knowledge of the way things worked in Sacramento. Thirteen months into his governorship Reagan accepted the resignation of his finance director and replaced him with Caspar W. Weinberger, a Harvard-educated lawyer who was well informed on state finance. Weinberger was a former legislator, a former state Republican chairman, and a newspaper columnist. He had been on the short list for the job originally but was vetoed by members of Reagan's "kitchen cabinet" because he had favored Rockefeller over Goldwater in the 1964 primary. By 1968 this litmus test seemed irrelevant to Reagan, who knew he needed a capable finance director. Weinberger filled the bill. Reagan soon took to calling him "my Disraeli," after the astute nineteenth-century British prime minister. When Weinberger later left to join the Nixon administration in Washington, Reagan replaced him with his deputy Verne Orr, also a capable professional.

With the fiscal crisis resolved, Reagan made a foray into presidential politics with the help of F. Clifton White, a New Yorker who had played a leading role in securing the 1964 nomination for Goldwater. Unlike Goldwater, however, Reagan was circumspect about his presidential ambitions, in part because he wanted to deflect criticism that he was using the governorship as a stepping stone to the presidency. So without declaring his candidacy, Reagan traveled around the country giving speeches, concentrating on states in the South and the Mountain West that were citadels of conservatism. When Reagan's undeclared candidacy was launched in 1967 the leading candidates for the Republican presidential nomination were Rockefeller and George Romney of Michigan, neither of them conservatives. But Romney withdrew after verbal mishaps, and Richard Nixon emerged as the frontrunner. He had impressive conservative support, including Goldwater, who urged Reagan not to run. Reagan demurred. He and his strategists thought of Nixon as a loser, as he had been in 1960 and 1962. If Nixon faltered again, Reagan wanted to be around to pick up the pieces. He saw himself, as he later said, as a contingency candidate.

But the contingency did not arise in 1968. Nixon won a string of primaries and his supporters in the South locked up additional commitments in states that chose delegates by the convention process. Reagan had rank-and-file support in several of these states, but their entire delegations were bound to Nixon on the first ballot under the party's rules. Too late, Reagan became a declared candidate at the Republican National Convention in Miami Beach, where Nixon was easily nominated. Reagan took the outcome in his customary fatalistic stride. Later that summer he told his aide, Mike Deaver: "I wasn't ready to be president."

Reagan was, however, ready for a second term as governor. In 1970, as expected, he faced off against Unruh, who had won the Democratic nomination by defeating

With Richard and Pat Nixon

Los Angeles Mayor Sam Yorty. Reagan, by now a polished
candidate, ran a forward-looking campaign in which he
promised to clean up "the welfare mess" as he had once
inveighed against "the mess at Berkeley." Neither Reagan nor
the Legislature had addressed the issue during his first four
years in office, and welfare rolls were soaring as California
suffered through an economic slump. "Welfare is the greatest domestic problem facing the nation today and the reason
for the high cost of government," Reagan said repeatedly.

In his campaign Unruh portrayed Reagan as a tool of
big business and his wealthy kitchen cabinet. But Unruh
blundered early in his campaign, and Reagan mostly ignored
his attacks. The nation was in recession, however, and
Reagan's strategists worried that economic conditions might
prompt Democrats who had crossed party lines in 1966 to
return to the party fold. Enough of them did so to reduce

On the campaign trail

Reagan's margin of victory to half of what it had been against Pat Brown. Still, Reagan won 52.9 percent of the vote to Unruh's 45.1 percent, with the rest going to minor candidates. This was a strong showing in a good Democratic year. In California, Democrat John Tunney defeated Reagan's old friend George Murphy in the Senate race. Nationally, the GOP lost eleven statehouses, and nine seats in the House. Except for Reagan's victory and Governor Rockefeller's election to an unprecedented fourth term in New York state, Republicans had little to cheer about in 1970.

With Los Angeles Times *reporter Paul Beck (left) and San Francisco reporter Jack McDowell (wearing glasses, right)*

When Reagan began his second term, he was no longer a novice-amateur who believed that government was an automatic enemy of the people. His low opinion of politicians also had undergone a subtle change, as demonstrated by a campaign exchange in working-class South Gate, where a member of the crowd called out to the governor, "When are you going to clean up politics?" In 1966, Reagan might well have agreed. In 1970, he replied, "Politics is far more honest than you may think."

Reagan's respect for the political system he had once decried helped him make good on his campaign promise to reform welfare. He was unexpectedly joined in this effort by Bob Moretti, a young and energetic Los Angeles Democrat who was now the Assembly speaker. Moretti knew that the Legislature had accomplished very little in the final two years of Reagan's first term, as the governor and Unruh had maneuvered for position in the 1970 campaign. Reagan's aides suspected that Moretti wanted to build a record on which to run for governor. That didn't bother them, for Reagan had long ago ruled out running for a third term. For their part, Moretti and his strategists believed that Reagan wanted to build a record on which to run for president.

Political ambitions aside, a more immediate reason for cooperation was that both Reagan and Moretti had grown tired of unproductive partisan rhetoric and realized that they would have to work together to accomplish anything. Welfare, which threatened to bust the budget, was a logical issue on which to start. Aid to Families with Dependent Children (AFDC), a program that was federally mandated but with benefits set by the state, had 375,000 California recipients in 1963. It had doubled to 769,000 recipients by the time Reagan took office in 1967 and more than doubled again, to 1,566,000 recipients, when his second term began in 1971. Caseload was increasing by 40,000 recipients a month, imposing an enormous financial burden on taxpayers. In an interview with *California Journal,* Reagan raised the prospect that the state would have to cut back on parks and other programs "to feed this welfare monster."

Although Reagan didn't mention it in this interview, the "monster" wasn't doing well in feeding its recipients. AFDC grants had not been raised a penny during the eight years of Pat Brown's administration or during Reagan's first four years as governor. A state study showed that minimum subsistence income for a family of three in San Francisco in 1971 was $271 a month; the maximum that could be paid such a family under the benefit level at the time was only $172.

Conservatives in the Legislature and county district attorneys throughout the state thought that one answer to rising caseloads was to crack down with vigorous prosecution of welfare cheaters. The Reagan administration agreed that welfare fraud was serious but rejected a piecemeal approach. Instead, Reagan drew upon the recommendations of a task force he had appointed before the election and issued a report to the Legislature early in 1971 calling for seventy specific changes in welfare laws, including a boost in grants for "the truly needy who have nowhere else to turn to meet their basic needs."

Democrats in the Legislature disputed Reagan's premises about the caseload increase, which they blamed largely on the

recession. Welfare rolls always increase during recessions, but the Democratic argument
did not explain why AFDC rolls had been
rising unimpeded for a decade and a half.
Moretti realized that unemployment was not
the whole story of the caseload increase. He
took Reagan's proposal seriously and decided
to negotiate face to face with the governor, if
Reagan was willing. Reagan, who trusted his
negotiating skills, was eager to meet with
Moretti. With encouragement from top subordinates (notably Meese on the governor's
side and Moretti's top aide William Hauck
for the speaker) Reagan and Moretti rolled
up their sleeves and pounded out a bill. In
the process, as Moretti later put it, he and
Reagan developed "a grudging respect" for
each other.

The Reagans lived at this home in Sacramento because the old Victorian-era governor's mansion was deemed unsafe

The final version of the California Welfare Reform Act of 1971, as it was known, was a complex measure that tightened regulations to reduce welfare fraud while boosting grants for the poorest recipients. Welfare rolls began to decline almost immediately. Within three years the AFDC caseload dropped from a peak of 1,608,000 to 1,330,000. Democrats attributed this to an improvement in the national economy, which certainly was a factor. But a thoughtful study by Frank Levy of the Urban Institute, who was no member of Reagan's fan club, found that the rolls had declined by 6 percent more than they would have without the Reagan reforms. Three decades later, the California Welfare Reform Act has stood the test of time. It was in every respect more generous and balanced than the sweeping federal welfare measure passed by a Republican Congress in 1996 and signed into law by President Bill Clinton. Beyond doubt, it was the premier legislative achievement of Reagan's governorship.

Other benefits flowed from the welfare bill. It strengthened Reagan's hand in dealing with the Nixon administration, which wanted to federalize the welfare system with a program called the Family Assistance Plan. Reagan's opposition to this plan helped sink it in Congress. Ironically, Reagan had by now become a defender of the very welfare system he had criticized. He contended that the only serious problem with the system was that the federal government did not give states sufficient flexibility to require able-bodied recipients to work. Because of Reagan's prodding, California eventually received a waiver allowing the state to experiment with a limited "workfare" plan. Only 9,600 persons were assigned to jobs under the program before it was discontinued by a subsequent governor, but it became a model for Wisconsin's statewide workfare plan a generation later, provisions of which found their way into the 1996 federal bill.

The cooperation between Reagan and Moretti on the welfare bill also became a model for other cooperative efforts—and for concessions on both sides. In 1971, as part of a budget package that gave him most of what he wanted, Reagan abandoned his resistance to state-income tax withholding, which he had long opposed on the grounds that it would be easier for future legislatures to raise income taxes if the money was taken out of weekly paychecks rather than paid in a lump sum. Reagan had said his feet were "in concrete" on this issue. When he conceded, he good-naturedly quipped, "the sound you hear is the concrete breaking around my feet."

In 1972, Reagan and Moretti were at it again, negotiating another compromise that combined federal revenue-sharing funds, a one-cent sales tax increase, and a budget surplus into a package providing a billion dollars for property-tax relief and financing of local schools. During Reagan's eight years as governor spending for elementary and secondary schools increased by 89 percent compared to 71 percent during his predecessor's eight years. Reagan also backed a program for early childhood education and a master plan for education put forth by Wilson Riles, a progressive Democrat who was the state superintendent of public instruction. "We did not go backward [on education] under Reagan's regime," Riles said. "We went forward."

California also advanced on the environmental front during the Reagan years, which was surprising to many considering Reagan's attitude during his 1966 campaign, when he told a timber group, "A tree's a tree. How many more do you need to look at?" But Reagan appointed Norman (Ike) Livermore, a lumberman who was also a member of the Sierra Club and a nature lover, as his director of resources, and he followed most of his recommendations. Livermore was regarded by all sides in environmental disputes as an honest broker; although he was nearly as inexperienced in government as Reagan, he also had a gift for compromise. The most important of these compromises produced a 53,000-acre National Redwood Park, which Reagan had originally opposed, created by Congress by combining federal land, two state parks, and other acreage purchased from lumber companies. Meanwhile, Reagan vastly expanded the state park system. This, too, was a byproduct of a wise appointment, in this case William Penn Mott as state director of parks and recreation. Mott had a national reputation as an empire-builder who found innovative ways to sequester parklands. He had no trouble convincing Reagan that such land would become ever more expensive in California, and that the state should buy as much as it could before the price became prohibitive.

On other environmental issues Reagan needed no convincing. He advocated and saw into law legislation that required environmental impact statements on state public-works projects. He signed tough water-quality and smog-control measures, although some of his appointments to smog-control boards were criticized for being too pro-business. He took the unheard-of action of turning down federal funds and siding with Livermore and Clark against the state's powerful water establishment and the Army Corps of Engineers, which wanted to build a high dam on the middle fork of the Eel River and flood a scenic valley on California's picturesque north coast. In rejecting the high dam Reagan said it would flood sacred Indian sites and noted that the government had too often violated treaties made with Indian tribes. In another preservationist action Reagan helped block a long-sought federal highway through the Minarets region of the high Sierra that would have intersected the John Muir trail. He was critical of the State Highway Commission "for its tendency to go by the rule of the shortest distance between two points, regardless of what scenic wonder must be destroyed."

Reagan's record on the issue that mattered most to him—holding the line on the costs of government—is more elusive. On fiscal matters, as a onetime legislative aide put it, Reagan was less an underachiever than "an overcommitter." He really wanted to cut the state budget and failed to appreciate the difficulty of achieving this dream. As Tom Goff of the *Los Angeles Times* wrote in a 1974 evaluation of Reagan's governorship, "The entire thrust of the Reagan administration has been to reduce or at least contain the role of government in the lives of Californians, as measured by the taxes it collects."

If numbers alone are the guide, Reagan did not meet his goals, for the state budget more than doubled to $10.2 billion during his governorship. But as Goff observed, the raw budget numbers do not tell the full story. Inflation was sky-high during most of Reagan's years in Sacramento, and many of the state's most costly programs were mandated by federal law. In matters over which Reagan had more control, he posted a record of achievement, notably in holding state employment at a near constant level for eight years. He also persistently used his line-item veto to keep the budget within reasonable bounds. The threat of his veto and Reagan's constant exhortations to economize raised the consciousness of constituents and legislators about the costs of an ever-expanding government.

Reagan set a tone that continued after he left Sacramento. Before Reagan, under progressive Republicans like Earl Warren and unabashed New Deal Democrats like Pat Brown, Californians looked to government as the principal agent of social and economic change. Nearly everyone assumed that state government would be perpetually expansive no matter which party was in power. Reagan changed these assumptions. He was succeeded by a Democrat, Pat Brown's son, Jerry, who differed on many issues but shared Reagan's belief in budget discipline; indeed, Brown was more miserly than Reagan in funding higher education and mental hospitals. Brown was succeeded by two Republican governors, both of whom followed Reagan's fiscal lead. When a Democrat became governor in 1998, he ran as a centrist who promised to economize.

Reagan left a strong historical imprint in Sacramento. His lasting legacy as governor is that he changed the terms of the California political debate.

A NEW BEGINNING

Ronald Reagan left office in January 1975 as a popular governor at a time when his party was still reeling from the Watergate scandal. On August 9, 1974, President Richard Nixon had resigned to avoid impeachment and was replaced by Vice President Gerald Ford. A month later Ford gave Nixon an unconditional pardon and his poll ratings plummeted, never fully to recover. The 1974 elections were a disaster for the GOP, which lost forty-six House seats plus the governorships of California, New York, and every major state except Michigan and Ohio. In the wake of Watergate, observed political demographer Michael Barone, the country was "more Democratic than in the presidential landslide years of 1936 or 1964, more Democratic than in the recession years of 1948 and 1958, more Democratic (for the moment) than when it was led by its paladins Franklin Roosevelt and John Kennedy."

Back home in Pacific Palisades, Reagan discussed his options with Nancy Reagan and their friends. He had earlier rejected the entreaties of his kitchen cabinet to run for the Senate, in which he had no interest, but planned to run for president again in 1976 at the end of Nixon's second term. Nixon's resignation had changed the equation. Now, Reagan had the choice of waiting until 1980, when he would be sixty-nine, or challenging Ford for the nomination. Neither alternative looked promising. By 1980, he might be considered too old to mount a presidential candidacy. But running against Ford in 1976 could split the Republican Party. Republicans had rallied around Ford; polls taken early in 1975 indicated that Reagan would have no chance against him.

Reagan was by nature a loyalist. While no admirer of Nixon, he had stuck with him as his troubles mounted during the Watergate inquiries. On May 1, 1973, he said that the Watergate conspirators "are not criminals at heart." Early in 1974, he was incredulous when John Sears, a talented lawyer who had worked for Nixon and was now advising

Reagan, predicted that Nixon would not finish out his presidency. When the prediction proved accurate, it convinced Reagan that Sears was the best man to run his presidential campaign. But he was not yet persuaded that he should take on a sitting president of his own party.

Reagan later told me that he could not pinpoint the precise moment when he swallowed his doubts and decided to run. To Sears and others who wanted him to run, he seemed reluctant. But as the months went by, Reagan became increasingly critical of Ford's leadership. He was also bothered, as were many conservatives, by Ford's choice of Nelson Rockefeller as his vice president. Reagan worried that if a Ford-Rockefeller ticket prevailed in 1976, the New Yorker would inherit the Republican nomination four years later. Eventually, Ford recognized the depth of anti-Rockefeller sentiment among conservatives and dropped him from the ticket. But by that time, Reagan had already decided to run.

As in 1968, Reagan began his pursuit of the presidency as an undeclared candidate. This enabled him to give his weekly radio speeches, which were aired on more than 230 stations, and which under Federal Communications Commission regulations had to be discontinued once he became a declared candidate. Reagan also wrote a weekly column that appeared in 174 newspapers, and he was in high demand as a speaker. Operating through an advertising agency established by former aides Mike Deaver and Peter Hannaford, which also sold the column and the radio speeches, Reagan made eight to ten speeches a month at an average fee of $5,000 a speech.

While this activity kept Reagan's name before the public, Sears in July formed an

Ron, Maureen, Michael, and Patti

"exploratory" committee chaired by Senator Paul Laxalt, a
Reagan friend who had been governor of neighboring
Nevada during Reagan's first term as governor. Not until
November 20, 1975, did Reagan announce his candidacy.
While he was now gaining in the polls, his candidacy was
dismissed in many quarters, especially in the East. On the
morning he announced, James Reston wrote in *The New
York Times:* "The astonishing thing is that this amusing but
frivolous Reagan fantasy is taken so seriously by the news
media and particularly by the President. It makes a lot of
news, but it doesn't make much sense."

Reagan, however, was on his way to New Hampshire
and its famous first primary where his strategists hoped to
score a decisive victory and knock Ford out of the race.
This had happened before in New Hampshire to Democratic presidents. In 1952, Harry Truman
had decided against seeking a second term
after suffering a stinging defeat in New
Hampshire. Lyndon Johnson had made an
identical decision after running below
expectations in 1968. Ford recognized the
danger, but also saw New Hampshire as an
opportunity. If Reagan could be defeated in
this bastion of conservatism, he might find
it impossible to sustain his candidacy.

Ford's biggest advantage in New
Hampshire was a rumpled political consultant named Stuart K. Spencer, who had
masterminded Reagan's campaign for governor in 1966. Unlike others on the Ford
team, Spencer never doubted that Reagan
would run. Spencer was convinced that a
Republican contest for the nomination
would hand the White House to the
Democrats, and he jumped at the chance to
stop Reagan in New Hampshire before his
campaign could gather steam. He soon

Senator Paul Laxalt

found an opening. On September 26, Reagan had addressed the Executive Club in Chicago. Reagan wrote many of his own speeches, but this one had been crafted by a conservative activist who thought Reagan's basic speech too timid. The activist wanted Reagan to make news and succeeded beyond his wildest expectations. In Chicago, Reagan promised "a systematic transfer of authority and resources to the states" from the federal government, which he said would reduce federal spending by $90 billion.

This figure was pulled out of the air, as Reagan himself realized once the speech became an issue. But he was stuck with what he had said, and Spencer exploited it. Since it was unclear if the $90 billion would pay for all the new responsibilities assumed by the states, the Ford team contended that Reagan's plan would require additional state taxes. This was a potent argument in New Hampshire, which has no state income tax. Reagan spent the primary on the defensive, trying to explain that there was no magic either to the $90 billion figure or his plan. Eventually, the "$90 billion speech" faded as an issue, but on February 24 it cost Reagan New Hampshire. He lost the primary by the extremely narrow margin of 1,317 votes.

New Hampshire had a domino effect. Ford followed it up by winning uncontested primaries in Massachusetts and Vermont and then capturing Florida, where Reagan had waged a strong campaign. On March 16 Ford won the primary in Reagan's home state of Illinois by a 20 percent margin. On the ropes and out of money, Reagan was urged by other Republicans to withdraw in the interest of party unity. Even within his own camp hope was fading. But Reagan, his back against the wall, refused to quit. Instead, he made a last stand in North Carolina.

Had Reagan not been so resolute when all appeared lost he would never have become president. As often in his life's endeavors, Reagan started slowly but learned as he went along. In the North Carolina primary campaign he became a defiant candidate who rebuffed continual questions about

when he would withdraw and focused on foreign policy.
Reagan thought that the Ford administration was not doing
enough to match the Soviet military buildup. He also
denounced the "giveaway" of the Panama Canal, which the
Ford administration was negotiating to return to Panama.
"We bought it, we paid for it, it's ours, and we're going to
keep it," Reagan said to increasingly enthusiastic crowds.
Surveys by Reagan's pollster Richard Wirthlin showed that
the Panama Canal issue resonated with conservatives who
felt the nation had been humiliated by withdrawing from
Vietnam. The Panama Canal "giveaway" became to Reagan's
1976 campaign the equivalent of what the "mess at Berkeley" had been to his campaign for governor in 1966.

Against all expectations, even his own, Reagan won
North Carolina. His victory startled Ford, who had coasted
during the primary because he believed Reagan was finished.
Instead, the contest was just beginning. As the primaries
moved south and west into Reagan country, Reagan swept
Texas and won primaries in Georgia, Indiana, Nebraska,
Arkansas, Idaho, Nevada, and South Dakota. Ford also won
several primaries, but the race was now almost even and
Reagan was able to raise money again. Ford went on the
attack. In the California primary Spencer commissioned a
television commercial based on Reagan's stray comment that
he would send a token force of U.S. troops as part of a
United Nations command if Rhodesia requested them to
fight guerrillas. The punch line of the commercial, intoned
above a hand reaching for the nuclear hotline telephone,
said: "When you vote Tuesday, remember: Governor Ronald
Reagan couldn't start a war; President Ronald Reagan
could." Unimpressed by these scare tactics, California
Republicans gave Reagan a 2–1 victory in the primary.

In the end, though, the power of the presidency and
Reagan's slow start proved just enough for Ford. When the
primaries were over, Sears made a determined effort to corral
uncommitted delegates before the Republican National
Convention in Kansas City. But James Baker III, Ford's chief

delegate counter, went him one better by inviting these delegates to the White House for private meetings with the president. Because many of the uncommitted delegates were Pennsylvanians, Sears persuaded Reagan to announce that he would pick the state's moderate Republican senator, Richard Schweiker, as his running mate. It was a bold move, but Schweiker could not persuade his fellow Pennsylvanians to support Reagan. Ford won the nomination with 1,187 delegates to 1,070 for Reagan.

Reagan, although weary from the long battle, was strangely elated. He responded to his defeat as if it were a victory, which in some respects it was. By refusing to give up when all seemed lost, Reagan had cemented the loyalty of conservatives and gained the respect of moderates as well. The morning after Ford's nomination Reagan consoled weeping supporters in the ballroom of a Kansas City hotel. "Don't get cynical," Reagan urged his followers, then quoted to them from an English ballad he had memorized in childhood: "Lay me down and bleed a while. Though I am wounded, I am not slain. I shall rise and fight again."

That November, former Georgia governor Jimmy Carter was elected president. As Reagan had done in the primaries, Ford rallied from behind and came up short. He had no doubt that Reagan, who grudgingly gave him minimal support, had played a spoiler's role. For their part, Reagan's supporters believed that their man might well have beaten Carter. It cannot be proven, either way. Carter was a fresh face then, and strong in the South, which Reagan would have needed to win.

But Reagan did not waste time exploring the might-have-beens of 1976. Even before the election he sent what Wirthlin considered "distinct signals" that he would run again. The clearest signal came when Reagan took $1 million in leftover campaign funds that he was legally entitled

FOLLOWING TWO PAGES: *Radio address titled "Two Worlds"*

The ideological struggle dividing the world is between communism and our own belief in freedom to the greatest extent possible consistent with an orderly society.   I'll be right back

I was going through a ~~collection~~ bundle of quotations I've collected over the years looking for something appropriate for ~~an speech~~ upcoming speech. I keep them on cards & they aren't indexed or catalogued so I literally have to shuffle through the whole stack.

While doing that ~~on~~ a thought came to me apropos of the present world situation where we continue to believe we can maintain a detente with the Soviet U. and that ~~they must~~ their leaders down underneath must be pretty much like us. ~~That the~~ I was shuffling through statements of great Americans & mixed in with them were quotes by the past & present greats of the Soviet U.

There was that poetry ~~inscribed~~ from whence comes the inscription on ~~the~~ statue of liberty: "Her name – Mother of Exiles. From her beacon hand glows world wide welcome; her mild eyes command the air bridged harbor that twin cities frame. Keep your ancient lands, your storied pomp! cries she with silent lips. Give me your tired, your poor, your huddled masses yearning to breathe free, the wretched refuse of your teeming shore. Send these, the homeless, tempest-~~tossed~~ TOST to me. I lift my lamp beside the golden door."

How that contrasts with these words of the Soviet U's founding father – Nicolai Lenin: "It would not matter if $\frac{3}{4}$ of the human race perished; the important thing is that the remaining $\frac{1}{4}$ be communist." And his invitation; "The Communist party ENTERS into bourgois institutions not to do constructive work but in order to direct the masses to destroy from within the whole bourgois state machine & the parliament itself."

John Winthrop on the deck of the tiny Arbella in 1630

off the coast of Mass. said to the little band of pilgrims; "We shall be as a city upon a hill. The eyes of all people are upon us, so that if we shall deal falsely with our God in this work we have undertaken & so cause him to withdraw his present help from us, we shall be made a story & a by word through out the world."

The oath of the Communist Party U.S.A. written in 1930 says nothing of a city upon a hill. ~~It says~~: "I pledge myself to rally the masses to defend the Soviet U. the land of victorious socialism. I pledge myself to remain at all times a vigilant & firm defender of the Leninist line of the party, the <u>only</u> line that insures the triumph of Soviet power in the U.S."

Thomas Jefferson said, "The policy of the Am. govt. is to leave their citizens free, neither restraining nor aiding them in their pursuits." And he added, "The God who gave us life gave us liberty — can the liberties of a Nat. be secure when we have removed a conviction that these liberties are the gift of God."

Prawda responds with these inspiring words; "The world wide nature of our communist program is not mere talk but all embracing & all blood soaked reality."

There were dozens more and from our Founding Fathers to present day leaders the plea was for social justice, decency & adherence to the highest standards man has evolved in his climb from the swamp to the stars. From the Soviet leaders came calls for treachery, deceit, destruction & bloodshed

Détente — isn't that what a farmer has with his turkey — until thanksgiving day?

This is R R Thanks for listening.

to pocket and formed a political action committee headed by Lyn Nofziger. Throughout 1977, letters from this committee stoked conservative fires with periodic attacks on the Panama Canal treaty, the Soviet Union, Cuba, and the supposed duplicity of the Carter administration. Without directly attacking Carter, Reagan did his own stoking in the weekly radio speeches and newspaper columns he resumed soon after the election. Reagan wrote these speeches himself, with material drawn from newspaper clippings, books, and congressional testimony. Many of the speeches, along with other Reagan writings, have since been collected in a book by Kiron Skinner, Martin Anderson, and Annelise Anderson, called *Reagan In His Own Hand.*

Reagan formally announced his third presidential candidacy on November 13, 1979, in the ballroom of the New York Hilton. His announcement speech was tame by Reagan standards, and reporters sensed that he was running a cautious front-running campaign against a crowded field. Too cautious, as it turned out. While Reagan flew across the country giving speeches, George Bush was spending his time on the ground in Iowa, which held its precinct caucuses the week before the New Hampshire primary. Bush won the Iowa caucuses and replaced Reagan as the Republican front-runner.

In New Hampshire, as in North Carolina four years earlier, Reagan showed that he was at his best as an underdog. Abandoning his above-the-battle approach, Reagan waged a fierce ground-level campaign. His opponents were now pointedly suggesting that he was too old to be president; Reagan defused the issue by celebrating his sixty-ninth birthday, which he referred to at a series of parties with a line borrowed from his friend, the late Jack Benny, as "the thirtieth anniversary of my thirty-ninth birthday." More substantively, he resolved the doubts he had raised in Iowa by holding his own in a February 20 debate in Manchester with the five other Republican presidential candidates. The turning point came three days later when he went head-to-head with

Bush in Nashua, in a debate from which Bush had tried to
exclude the other candidates. At Sears's invitation the
excluded candidates showed up anyway, and Reagan insisted
they be allowed to participate. The moderator, *Nashua Telegraph* editor Jon Breen, ordered that Reagan's microphone be
turned off. "I paid for this microphone, Mr. Green," Reagan
said with controlled fury, mangling the moderator's name
but making his point with a line borrowed from Spencer
Tracy in the 1948 film, *State of the Union*. It was the beginning of the end for Bush. Reagan demolished him in the
debate and went on to win the primary handily.

Once Reagan had demonstrated his competence there
was never any doubt he would win the nomination. Reagan
was by 1980 a known quantity in the Republican Party. He

Campaigning in 1980

had been a presence on the political scene since 1964, and he articulated values in which most Republicans believed. Furthermore, he had served capably as governor of the nation's most populous state and demonstrated that he could work effectively with Democrats. He had never been touched by a hint of personal scandal. The only question about Reagan in 1980, for those who stood with him on the issues, was whether he had the vitality and energy to be president. Once he answered this question affirmatively in New Hampshire, the nomination was his for the taking.

And take it Reagan did. Three of his opponents—Howard Baker, Bob Dole, and Phil Crane—dropped out soon after New Hampshire. So did John Connally, who had not competed in New Hampshire but was soundly beaten by Reagan in South Carolina. John Anderson lasted a while longer and continued to run as an independent candidate. But the GOP field was reduced to two, and Reagan won twenty-nine of the thirty-three primaries in which he and Bush faced each other. What distinguished Bush in this one-sided competition was his version of the true grit that Reagan had displayed in 1976. His doggedness was rewarded when Reagan selected him as his running mate at the Republican National Convention in Detroit.

So now it was Reagan against President Carter, who had beaten back a primary challenge from Senator Edward M. Kennedy but was nonetheless a troubled candidate. Carter's political decline began in January 1979 when the shah of Iran, whom Carter had visited and toasted a year earlier, fled for his life as Iranian militants rioted in the streets. On February 1, the Ayatollah Ruhollah Khomeini returned from exile to establish his fundamentalist rule. Even before he arrived, the riots had disrupted Iranian oil exports. Oil prices soared, abetted by the Organization of Petroleum Exporting Countries (OPEC), which exploited the crisis by reducing production. Long lines formed at gasoline stations in the United States, accompanied by runaway inflation. Michael

The Reagans traveled to Iran in June of 1978

Barone's calculations show an inverse relationship between the inflation rate and Carter's popularity. In September 1978, when the inflation rate was 8.3 percent, Carter's approval rating in the Gallup poll was 56 percent. By June of 1979, with inflation at nearly 11 percent, his rating had dipped to 29 percent.

Then on November 4, Iranian "students" backed by the Khomeini regime seized fifty-two Americans at the U.S. embassy in Tehran as hostages. Americans rally around their president in times of crisis, and they stood with Carter as he patiently tried to free the hostages through diplomacy. By December his approval rating reached the 60-percent mark and helped wreck Kennedy's challenge to Carter, who won

Republican National Convention, July 17, 1980

decisively in the Iowa caucuses and New Hampshire primary. But foreign policy crises continued to dog Carter. On Christmas day Soviet troops conducted a bloody invasion of Afghanistan. Carter, who had decried "inordinate fear of communism" and in June 1979 embraced and kissed Soviet leader Leonid Brezhnev at a summit meeting, was nonplussed. In a comment that Reagan found startling, Carter said "the action of the Soviets made a more dramatic change in my opinion of what the Soviets' ultimate goals are than anything they've done in the previous time I've been in office."

By the time Reagan and Carter faced each other after securing their nominations both candidates had experienced ups and downs. The hostage crisis that had once helped Carter had become a political albatross around the neck of the president, who on April 24 abruptly abandoned diplomacy and tried to free the hostages by force of arms. The effort failed disastrously. Meanwhile, interest rates reached record levels as the Federal Reserve Board under Paul Volcker tried to maintain fiscal discipline. The nation slipped into recession in the second quarter of 1980.

Throughout the summer and early fall, polls showed that a majority of Americans had given up on Carter, but had not decided if Reagan should replace him. Reagan was strong in the West and cutting into Carter's base in the South, but independent voters, especially in the East, still harbored doubts. Reagan contributed to these doubts with a stumbling start to his general election campaign. On August 3, en route to New York and a speech to the Urban League, he stopped off at the Neshoba County Fair in Philadelphia, Mississippi, where three civil rights workers had been slain with police complicity in 1964. Reagan told a shirt-sleeved crowd that he "believed in states' rights" and as president would do all he could to "restore to states and local governments the powers that properly belonged to them." Then, speaking to the Veterans of Foreign Wars

convention in Chicago on August 18, Reagan tromped on
his message that Carter had made a "shambles" of national
defense by referring to the Vietnam War as a "noble cause."
These and other blunders after the formal campaign began
on Labor Day shook Reagan's self-confidence and persuaded the vigilant Nancy Reagan that her husband was in
trouble. As always in such circumstances, she was willing to put aside past grievances and do whatever
would help Ronald Reagan. On this occasion
she called Stuart Spencer in California and
summoned him to campaign headquarters in
Virginia.

It was an inspired decision. Reagan and
Spencer liked and understood each other, and
Spencer soon became his chief strategist again.
Never one to hold grudges, Reagan was uncon-
cerned that Spencer had been an architect of his 1976
defeat at the hands of President Ford. The Reagans knew he
could be trusted, and Spencer believed that a confident
Reagan would be unbeatable. He modestly described his
mission as helping Reagan get "over the bumps."

Reagan soon did. By mid-September his sunny
nature had reasserted itself, providing a beneficial
contrast to his opponent's dour demeanor. In a
nationally televised speech on July 15, 1979,
Carter had said that Americans suffered from "a
crisis of confidence . . . that strikes at the very
heart and soul and spirit of our national will."
Reagan took issue with this pessimistic premise.
"I find no national malaise," he said. "I find
nothing wrong with the American people."

Reagan would later say that his greatest
achievement was restoring the faith of Americans in
their own capacities. His model was the iconic Franklin
Roosevelt, the "happy warrior" who had inspired
Reagan as a young man. Stylistically, at least, FDR was
inside of Reagan. When Reagan asked audiences, "Are

Campaign memorabilia

you better off now than you were four years ago?" he was slightly paraphrasing words that FDR had used in a 1934 radio fireside chat. Carter, meanwhile, was cast in the role of the unfortunate Herbert Hoover, also overwhelmed by economic conditions he could not control. Reagan knew that the Great Depression was a living memory to members of his generation and had a mythic impact on younger Americans. Over the objections of his literal-minded economic advisers Reagan called the Carter recession a "depression" in a speech to a Teamsters group in Ohio. Carter said that Reagan was wrong, but hard-pressed Americans were not interested in technical definitions. They were more attuned to Reagan's response: "If he wants a definition, I'll give him one. Recession is when your neighbor loses his job. Depression is when you lose yours. And recovery—recovery is when Jimmy Carter loses his!" Reagan's crowds became so fond of this refrain that they would call out for him to deliver it and say the punch line aloud with him.

After making no headway on economic issues Carter campaigned against Reagan as a warmonger. On September 23, before the California AFL-CIO, Carter said the election would determine "whether we have peace or war." Even Carter's press secretary, Jody Powell, acknowledged this was an "overstatement." Reagan was steaming. He told an airport rally in Pensacola, Florida, that it was "beneath decency" for Carter to suggest that he would lead the nation into war. "I have two sons," Reagan said. "I have a grandson. I have known four wars in my lifetime and I think like all of you that world peace has to be the principal theme of this nation."

This did not deter Carter. He had little choice, for even Democrats disapproved of his record. With the economy sour and the hostages still in captivity, Carter knew that his only hope for reelection was to persuade voters that Reagan was an unacceptable risk. Carter began by assailing Reagan's old proposal to transfer federal programs to state and local government. When this approach elicited little response, he suggested that Reagan would wreck Social Security and was a "very dangerous" warmonger. At a fundraising dinner in Chicago the president became strident and said that it would be a "catastrophe" to put Reagan in the White House. Carried away by the cheers of a partisan audience, Carter added: "You'll determine whether or not this America will be unified, or if I lose this election, whether Americans might be separated, black from white, Jew from Christian, North from South, rural from urban." Reagan, campaigning in Pennsylvania, said he was "saddened" by these remarks.

From late September though mid-October, Reagan maintained a steady lead of a few percentage points in published polls. But private surveys by Wirthlin for the Reagan team painted a more complex picture. They showed that Carter had damaged his own reputation, especially among independents, with his repeated negative campaigning. At the same time, however, he had deepened the doubts about Reagan. The issue on which Reagan appeared to be most vulnerable was on whether his repeated call for a military buildup would increase the risk of confrontation with the Soviet Union. Wirthlin believed that Carter's gain was not worth his loss, for the president had forfeited the moral high ground that had been his strong point. Still, the race was too fluid to suit the Reagan side. And there was a wild card—the fate of the hostages held captive in Iran. Both Carter and Reagan had tiptoed around this issue, knowing that any attempt to exploit the plight of the hostages could backfire. But the Reagan camp anticipated that Carter would spring an "October surprise," probably involving the hostages, in an effort to turn the tide. This concern, more than any other, led the Reagan team to drop its opposition to debating Carter one on one. (Reagan had previously insisted that independent candidate John Anderson should be included; instead, he debated Anderson separately.) Reagan's advisers were divided on the merits of debating Carter, but the candidate himself was fatalistic about it. "I think I'm going to have to debate him," he told Spencer.

In 1980, nationally televised debates between presidential nominees were not the political fixtures they have since become. The first such debates, between Richard Nixon and John F. Kennedy in 1960, had contributed to JFK's narrow victory and sounded a cautionary note for future candidates. No incumbent president had ever debated his opponent on television. Lyndon Johnson had ducked a debate in 1964 and Nixon did the same in 1972 in campaigns in which they held big leads. Conventional political wisdom held that a challenger automatically became "presidential" by the very act of occupying the same stage as the president. Carter couldn't worry about such theories; he knew he was trailing and needed a knockout blow to win. The Carter camp saw Reagan as a showman whose deficiencies might be exposed in a face-to-face encounter with a knowledgeable president. Reagan was accustomed to such condescension. Being an actor meant always being underestimated, as Reagan had learned when he sought the governorship of California.

In fact, Reagan had reason for confidence. The night before he agreed to debate he had shared the stage with Carter at the Alfred E. Smith dinner at the Waldorf-Astoria Hotel in New York. At this tradition-laden event speakers are supposed to blend humor with homage to Smith, a legendary governor of New York and Democratic nominee for president in 1928. Carter used a heavy hand. After an opening joke, he called attention to Reagan's support by Christian fundamentalists, then launched into a recitation of his own efforts to make peace between Israel and Egypt at Camp David. Reagan stuck to the customary format and won the plaudits of the audience with a graceful, self-deprecating speech in which he said there wasn't any truth to the rumor that he looked younger "because I keep riding older and older horses."

The positive reviews Reagan received for this performance put him in a good mood for his debate with Carter at the Cleveland Music Hall on October 28. At the outset he walked over and shook the president's hand, which appeared to startle Carter. Soon both candidates had reverted to their usual themes, with Carter raising questions about Reagan's positions on issues of war and peace. Reagan, for his part, mentioned "peace" so often that it sounded as if he had invented the word.

Joint appearances such as this one—not debates in a genuine sense, since most of the questions are initiated by journalists—are matters of style as well as substance. On substance the two candidates were more evenly matched than Carter had expected. On style, Reagan was the clear winner. Near the end of the debate Carter drew attention to Reagan's long-ago opposition to Medicare. "There you go again," Reagan said, drawing laughter from even some of Carter's supporters. It was the debate's most effective line.

The only other passage of the debate that resonated with audiences came from Carter and was no help to him. In his closing remarks, against the advice of aides, Carter said: "I think to close out this discussion, it would [be] better to put in perspective what we're talking about. I had a discussion with my daughter Amy the other day before I came here to ask her what the most important issue was. She said she thought nuclear weaponry and the control of nuclear arms." The audience groaned. Amy was twelve years old, and Carter's closing statement seemed a ludicrous and round-about way of reasserting that Reagan would be a dangerous president. In the final week of the campaign "Amy" became a staple for columnists and comedians. "Ask Amy" signs pro-liferated at Republican rallies.

The debate clinched the election. Reagan might have won—in all probability would have won—without it, but his assured performance in Cleveland had destroyed Carter's last hope for victory. A CBS poll contained a telling statistic: the percentage of people who thought that Reagan would "lead the country into war" declined from 43 to 35 after the debate. Reagan was too superstitious to claim victory, but a feeling of exhilaration and good humor pervaded his campaign plane. When photographer Michael Evans jokingly warned Reagan about the number of pictures he would have to autograph after he became president, the candidate replied, "You know, after you've canceled Social Security and started the war, what else is there for you to do?"

Reagan won the election with a plurality of 8,417,992 votes. He received 50.7 percent of the vote, compared to 41 percent for Carter and 6.6 percent for Anderson. Carter's percentage was the lowest of any incumbent president seeking reelection in the twentieth century except for Hoover in 1932. And Carter did worse than Hoover in the electoral college, in part because Anderson had siphoned off enough votes in the Northeast to enable Reagan to carry even such liberal bastions as Massachusetts. Reagan had 489 electoral votes to 44 for Carter, who carried his home state of Georgia plus Hawaii, Maryland, Minnesota, Rhode Island, West Virginia, and the District of Columbia. Republicans gained twelve Senate seats, taking Senate control for the first time since 1952 and only the third time since Hoover's defeat. Republicans also gained thirty-three House seats. Many of the congressional newcomers attributed their victories to Reagan, which would help him in the years to come.

On election day Reagan acted like a man who had been happily surprised by unexpected good fortune. As Nancy Reagan recalls it, he was taking a shower and she was in the bath when a television network report projected that he had won the election. Wrapped in towels and bathrobes, they watched the report, which was interrupted by a phone call. It was President Carter calling to concede.

Later that evening Reagan went to the top-floor suite of the Century Plaza Hotel to watch the extended election coverage. His brother Neil wandered by to congratulate him, and they talked about the old days.

"I bet there's a hot time in Dixon tonight," Neil said.

"I'd like to be there off in a corner just listening," said Ronald Reagan, the small-town boy who had just been elected the fortieth president of the United States.

TRIUMPH AND TRAGEDY

Ronald Reagan believed in portents, and he was pleased that January 20, 1981, dawned warm for a winter's day in Washington. It had been cold and icy throughout the month, reminding Reagan of boyhood winters in Illinois, but a warm front had moved in during the night, raising the temperature by twenty degrees into the mid-fifties. At Blair House, across from the White House, Nancy Reagan sent Michael Deaver in to rouse her husband and have him dress for the inauguration.

"It's time to get up, governor," Deaver said.

"Why do I have to get up? " Reagan said, and both men laughed.

That was Reagan's way. Jocular by nature, he had learned long ago to lighten tension with a quip. His aides expected it of him. But on this big day Reagan was not excited at all, which he thought strange. He had discussed it

A good-luck kiss on inaugural day, January 20, 1981

with Nancy, who was also calm. Ever since election day, he told me later, they had expected "a moment when all of a sudden it hits us but things kept happening . . . and you still did not have the thing that you thought would happen, that moment of awesomeness."

Perhaps the opening inaugural cere-monies the night before had drained the Reagans of emotion. As fireworks streaked the sky against the gleaming background of the Lincoln Memorial, a crowd of well-wishers shouted, "We want Ronnie." Reagan kept his silence but stepped forward to acknowledge the cheers. As the Mormon Tabernacle Choir sang "God Bless Amer-ica," Reagan felt a sudden surge of patriot-ism. "It was cold, but it was so moving I was crying frozen tears," he told speech-writer Ken Khachigian.

On this almost balmy day in Washing-ton, there were tears of joy throughout the land at the news that the fifty-two Ameri-cans held hostage for 444 days in Iran were finally coming home. Their release was the product of intense diplomatic negotiations during a transition in which both the out-going and incoming administrations spoke with a single voice to tell Iran's rulers: Don't expect a better deal from Ronald Reagan. With the election over, Reagan

Driving to the Capitol with President Jimmy Carter

sympathized with Carter for his unrelenting efforts to free the hostages. He wanted them released on Carter's watch so he could thank him during his inaugural speech. But it was not to be. After Chief Justice Warren Burger had adminis-tered the oath of office, the new president glanced at Carter, who motioned that the release was not completed. Although arrangements had been made to fly the hostages to West

Germany, both Carter and Reagan knew it was risky to
make an announcement until the planes had cleared Iranian
air space, as they did soon after the swearing-in ceremony.
Instead of thanking him before the nation, Reagan showed
his appreciation by sending Carter to greet the freed Americans in Germany.

Reagan's inauguration was the first on the restored west
front of the Capitol, from which he enjoyed a panoramic
view. To his left, beyond the Potomac, rose the Jefferson
Memorial and the hills of Arlington Cemetery. Before him,
across the mall and the reflecting pool, stretched the spired
elegance of the Washington Monument and, beyond, the
Lincoln Memorial. "Standing here, we face a magnificent
vista, opening up this city's special beauty and history,"

The swearing-in ceremony, January 20, 1981

Reagan said. "At the end of this open mall are those shrines to the giants on whose shoulders we stand."

Reagan's inaugural address that day celebrated not only these "giants." A few weeks earlier, as he read Khachigian's evocative speech draft, Reagan thought that it needed a story providing a dramatic link to the past. He found what he was looking for when a California rancher told him about a soldier named Martin Treptow, killed by artillery fire during World War I. Treptow had left behind a diary in which he had written "My Pledge" on the flyleaf and beneath it the words: "America must win this war. Therefore I will work, I will save, I will sacrifice, I will endure, I will fight cheerfully and do my utmost as if the issue of the whole struggle depended on me alone." Reagan added this story to his speech. He said that America's present crisis did not require the ultimate sacrifice made by Treptow and thousands of other ordinary soldiers but did require "our best effort and our willingness to believe in ourselves, and to believe in our capacity to perform great deeds." Reagan believed that every American could be a hero. "Let us renew our determination, our courage, and our strength," he said. "And let us renew our faith and hope. We have every right to dream heroic dreams."

In the weeks ahead, Reagan showed he was more than a dreamer. Despite his lack of Washington experience, his administration was quick off the mark. Determined to avoid the chaos that had beset the early months of the Carter administration, Reagan named a transition team headed by Edwin Meese even before he was elected and gave it authority to sift through policy positions and potential appointments. The result, according to a scholarly study, was that "the Reagan transition was the most carefully planned and effective in American history."

FOLLOWING THREE PAGES: *A selection from the hand-written draft of Reagan's first inaugural address and inaugural memorabilia*

3

It is made up of men & women who raise our food, patrol our streets, man our mines & factories, teach our children, keep our homes and heal us when we're sick. They are professionals, industrialists, shop keepers, clerks, cabbies & truck drivers. They are in short — "We the people".

Our objective must be a healthy, vigorous, growing economy that provides equal opportunities for all Americans with no barriers born of discrimination. Putting America back to work means putting all Americans back to work. Ending inflation means freeing all Americans from the terror of runaway living costs. All must share in the productive work of this "new beginning" & all must share in the bounty of a revived economy. With the idealism & fairplay which is the core of our strength we can have a strong, prosperous America at peace with itself & the world,

In this new beginning let us first take inventory. We are a nation that has a government — not the other way around. And this makes us special among the nations of the earth. Our govt. has no power except that granted it by the people, It is time to check & reverse the growth of govt. which shows signs of having grown beyond the consent of the governed.

It will be my intention to curb the size & influence of the Fed. establishment and to demand recognition of the distinction between the powers granted to the Fed. govt. and those reserved to the states or to the people, All of us need to be reminded that the Fed. govt. did not create the states — the states created the Fed. govt,

So there will be no misunderstanding; it is not my intention to do away with govt. It is rather to

4

make it work. Work with us not over us; to stand by our side not ride on our backs. Govt. can & must provide opportunity not smother it; foster productivity not stifle it.

If we look for the answer as to why ~~it~~ for so many years we acheived so much, prospered as no other people on earth, it was because here in this land we unleashed the energy and individual genius of man to a greater extent than had ever been done before. ~~Liberty, freedom~~. Freedom & the dignity of the individual have been more available and assured here than in any other place on earth. The price for this [freedom] has at times been high — but we have never been unwilling to pay that price.

It is no coincidence that our present troubles parallel the intervention ~~by govt~~. and ~~the~~ intrusion in our lives that have resulted from ~~the~~ unnecessary & excessive growth of govt.

We are ~~too~~ great a nation to limit ourselves to small dreams. ~~This is~~ We are not, as some would have us believe, doomed to an inevitable decline. I do not believe in a fate that will fall on us no matter what we do — I do believe in a fate that will fall on us if we do nothing.

So, with all the creative energy at our command, let us begin a new era of national renewal. Let us renew our determination, our courage, our strength, our faith & our hope. ~~We have every right to~~ dream heroic dreams. Those who say we are in a time when there are no heros ~~some~~ ~~say~~ Just ~~dont~~ don't know where to look. You can see ~~heros~~ every day going in & out of factory gates. Others, a handfull in number, producing food enough to feed all

9

in 1917 to go to France with the famed Rainbow
Division. There on the Western front he was killed
trying to carry a message between battalions under
heavy artillery fire.

On his body was found a diary. Written on the
flyleaf under the heading "My Pledge", were these
words: "America must win this war. Therefore I will
work, I will save, I will sacrifice, I will endure,
I will fight cheerfully and do my utmost, as if the
issue of the whole struggle depended on me alone."

The crisis we are facing today does not require
the kind of sacrifice that Martin Treptow & so
many thousands of others ~~made~~ were called upon to
make. It does however require our best effort, our
work and our willingness to ~~sacrifice~~ believe ~~in~~ ourselves
~~Our problems can be solved. They can be solved~~
~~because we have the ability to perform great deeds~~
~~& we have great deeds to do. But do them we will.~~
~~After all —, we are Americans~~

and in our capacity to perform great
deeds; ~~together~~ that together and with
God's help we can & will resolve the problems
~~with~~ which confront us.

Why shouldn't we believe that? After all — we
are Americans.

Reagan and his advisers knew that the economy was in
such dismal straits that it had to be their most urgent priority. The timely release of the hostages contributed to this
strategy, for it enabled the administration to shove foreign
policy to the back burner. On Reagan's first day in office he
ordered a federal hiring freeze. And in what would become a
pattern of his presidency, he immediately took his case for
change to the country. In a February 5 nationally televised
address that he largely wrote himself, Reagan said the United
States was in its "worst economic mess since the Depression"
and promised that his remedies would not be timid. "It is
time to recognize that we have come to a turning point,"
Reagan said. "We are threatened with an economic calamity
of tremendous proportions and the old business-as-usual
treatment can't save it."

Reagan was helped in these early days by the clarity of
his agenda. While his goals were controversial, they were not
obscure. During the campaign Reagan had promised to
reduce taxes, boost military spending, and cut domestic programs except for Social Security. That is what he tried to do.
When his opponents argued that his proposed budget cuts
went too far too fast, he amended them by barring substantial reductions in five programs that were called the "social
safety net": Medicare, veterans' benefits, school lunches,
Head Start, and summer youth jobs. Everything else was on
the table.

Another reason for Reagan's fast start was his willingness
and ability to draw on the experience of past administrations. While Reagan held strong views on the direction in
which he wanted to lead the country, he was also an
immensely practical politician. All presidents bring with
them into the White House a cadre of home-state loyalists,
as John Kennedy had done from Massachusetts, Lyndon
Johnson from Texas, and Carter from Georgia. Reagan was
no exception, but he blended his California outsiders with
old Washington hands. One of his key appointments,
encouraged by Nancy Reagan, was the selection of James

Baker, a veteran of the Nixon and Ford administrations, as his White House chief of staff. Never before had a president picked an opponent's campaign manager for this crucial job. Baker had run George Bush's campaign in 1980, and helped Ford block Reagan's presidential bid in 1976. That didn't matter to Reagan, who valued Baker's experience and organizational skills. According to Stuart Spencer, the only question Reagan asked when Baker's name was broached for the job was, "Do you think he'd do it?"

Because of Reagan's practical approach, his cabinet, and even more his White House staff, resembled a coalition government. His top aides, soon dubbed "the troika," were Baker,

Inaugural memorabilia

Deaver, and Meese, who had hoped to become chief of staff but was instead named counsellor. On legislative strategy, Baker relied on Richard Darman, a Harvard liberal. Economist Martin Anderson, a veteran of the Nixon administration and a libertarian conservative, was named chief domestic policy adviser. David Stockman, a Harvard-trained Michigan congressman who was an intellectual leader among House Republicans, was appointed to head the Office of Management and Budget, a particularly crucial post.

The cabinet was similarly eclectic. General Alexander Haig, the new secretary of state and former NATO commander, had kept a steady hand on the White House tiller during Nixon's shaky final days as president. Caspar Weinberger, secretary of defense, had saved Reagan from budgetary catastrophe in Sacramento before serving in the Nixon administration. Donald Regan, the Treasury secretary, was a successful Wall Street broker. Richard Schweiker, secretary of Health and Human Services, was a moderate Republican senator from Pennsylvania who in 1976 had been Reagan's choice for vice president. William French Smith, the new attorney general, was the only Reagan confidant in the cabinet. He was a member of the California kitchen cabinet and had once been Reagan's lawyer.

Reagan needed his fast start, for he and his team faced a daunting economic challenge. Inflation was out of control, and the budget deficit was increasing daily. The new president pinned his hopes on his proposed tax cuts, in percentage terms roughly the size of the cuts President Kennedy had advocated in 1961 to "get the country moving again." Reagan had faith that these "supply-side" tax cuts would prove a powerful stimulus to economic recovery; he predicted during the campaign that the federal budget would be balanced by 1984. That goal seemed improbable, even to many Republicans. In the primaries, Bush had derisively described Reagan's tax proposals as "voodoo economics," a phrase picked up by the Democrats. The media coined another word, "Reaganomics," which stuck.

Reaganomics made its debut in a February 18 economic message that proposed cutting $41 billion from the Carter budget. Reagan's budget made mild to fatal cuts in eighty-three federal programs and sought a $28 billion hike in military spending, the largest in peacetime history. Treasury Secretary Regan predicted that this budget would cause business investment to rise 11 percent a year for the next five years—a level the U.S. economy had never achieved. Despite the skepticism of economists, a poll taken by *The Washington Post* and ABC News showed the public favored Reagan's plan by a 2–1 margin. The president then broadened his support by incorporating into the budget some additional economies suggested by conservative Democrats.

With Tip O'Neill

These Democrats, known as Boll Weevils, and largely from the South, were the swing votes in a protracted battle over tax and budget legislation waged during Reagan's early months in office between the administration and House Speaker Thomas P. (Tip) O'Neill of Massachusetts, a popular Irish-American from Boston who was then the most powerful Democrat in Washington. With the White House and the Senate in Republican hands, O'Neill had become the faithful keeper of the flickering New Deal flame. He and Reagan disagreed and competed on many issues but respected each other's political skills and in time developed a friendship across party lines.

FACING PAGE: *Maintaining the relationship with the speaker*

_144._

THE WHITE HOUSE

WASHINGTON

RECOMMENDED TELEPHONE CALL

TO: House Speaker Thomas P. "Tip" O'Neill, Jr. (D-Mass.)

DATE: Tuesday, or Wednesday, March 3, 4, 1981

RECOMMENDED BY: Max L. Friedersdorf _M.G._

PURPOSE: To placate the Speaker who is upset about reports
                             that the President is using a story involving
                             George Busby of Georgia and the Speaker.

BACKGROUND: A story was going around that Governor Busby
                             told the Speaker he would not be Speaker after
                             the next election if he didn't support the
                             President's program. The Speaker then bit off
                             the end of his cigar, the story goes. Speaker
                             O'Neill vehemently denies the exchange with Busby
                             ever took place. The Speaker has picked up a
                             report that the President has been repeating the
                             story, and Gary Hymel, top aide to the Speaker,
                             has contacted me to complain and request that
                             the President phone the speaker. I told Gary
                             I was unaware of the President repeating any
                             story, and the President has nothing but the
                             highest regard and respect for the Speaker, and
                             considers their relationship a good one.

TOPICS OF DISCUSSION: 1. Tell the Speaker you had heard the story
                             about Busby because it was repeated to you
                             during the group of Governor's visit, but
                             you have no control over what people tell you.

                         2. Tell the Speaker you don't care to be involved
                             in conversations between the Governors and
                             the Speaker, and hope this incident doesn't
                             injure the fine relationship between you and
                             the Speaker.

                         3. Ask the Speaker if there is anything you can
                             do for him today and wish him well.

ACTION   _Mission accomplished_

O'Neill tested Reagan even before he became president. When they met during the transition he told Reagan that Sacramento was equivalent to baseball's minor leagues and that he was now in the "big leagues" of Washington. Some of Reagan's aides were annoyed by this put-down. Reagan, however, was amused and said nothing, once again recognizing the benefit of being underestimated. After Reagan became president, O'Neill said to him that the Republican leaders in the House were friends "after six o'clock" and on weekends. Reagan liked this formulation and adopted it as his own. When he felt a need to talk to O'Neill, he would call the speaker's office at any time of day and ask him if it was after six o'clock. "Absolutely, Mr. President," O'Neill would invariably respond.

When the budget and tax fights were joined in 1981, the outcomes were too close to call. The Democrats held a fifty-one-vote majority in the House, which meant that Reagan needed the votes of every Republican and at least twenty-six Democrats to pass his bills. O'Neill could win easily if he held his party together, but he knew that the Boll Weevils were on shaky ground. Most of them represented districts that Reagan had carried in 1980; voting against a popular president could cost them their seats in 1982. To encourage the Boll Weevils to cross party lines, Reagan accepted a suggestion by James Baker and promised that he would not campaign in 1982 against any Democratic members of Congress who voted for both his tax and budget bills. Republican politicians in the South, especially Texas, grumbled that the Boll Weevil districts were high on the GOP target list for 1982. But Reagan dismissed their complaints, since he viewed his economic program as more important than a handful of House seats. And passage was far from assured. Even with several pledges of support from conservative Democrats, the fate of the economic program still hung in the balance late in March.

. . .

February 11, 1981
LINCOLN MEMORIAL SERVICE, February 12, 1981

Of the millions who come to this city each year there is always a stop to be made here at the base of the reflecting pool and a statue to be seen of a backwoodsman who became a lawyer, a Congressman, and a President.

It is said that by standing to one side of this statue there can be seen a profile of a man of wisdom. And by standing to the other side: a profile of a man of compassion.

Those two views of Lincoln symbolize our own memory of him today—Lincoln, the national leader who in time of crisis called his countrymen to greatness. And Lincoln the man, whose grace, compassion, and earnest commitment are remembered in countless biographies, folktales, and poetry.

Yet there is more left to us of Lincoln than a ceremony, a moment, or even a memory of his greatness as a leader and a man. There are his words, words that speak to our time, to any time — words from a mind that sought wisdom and a heart that loved justice.

Today, do our national leaders agonize over the dilemma between doing what is practical and what is right?

"Let us have faith that right makes might," Lincoln wrote, "and in that faith let us to the end do our duty as we understand it."

Or do we fear failure in defense of principle?

"I am not bound to win," Lincoln said, "but I am bound to be true. I am not bound to succeed but I am bound to live up to what light I have."

Do we sometimes question the commitment upon which this Nation was founded—a belief in the uncommon wisdom of the common people, a belief in their right to render a final verdict on the Nation's course?

"I appeal to you constantly," Lincoln said on his way to assume the presidency, "bear in mind that not with the politicians, not with the president, not with the office-seekers but with you is the question "Shall the liberties of this country be preserved to the latest generation?"

In Lincoln's life there is ample testimony to the depth of his mind, to the compassion of his heart, to the breadth of his virtue—and, above all, to the value of putting country over self-interest.

But for today, I will say of him only what he said so well of those who had fallen at Gettysburg: that the memory of his life and death is greater than any written or spoken tribute could ever be.

The memory of Lincoln belongs to us, but never *only to us. For, as it was said at the hour of his death, "now he belongs to the ages."*

Notes for an address at the Lincoln Memorial Service, February 12, 1981, show Reagan's ability to use the briefest of notes and deliver a polished speech

On the morning of March 30, 1981, Reagan dressed in a brand-new blue suit. For reasons he never knew, he decided against wearing his best wristwatch, and put on an old one he often wore when doing chores at his California ranch. After breakfast he gave a pep talk to sub-cabinet members in the East Room, emphasizing the need for economic reform and concluding with a favorite quotation from Tom Paine, "We have it in our power to begin the world over again." Late in the morning he went to the Washington Hilton Hotel and gave a luncheon speech to 3,500 union representatives from the building trades. Many of them had reservations about Reagan's economic plan, but they received him with polite applause. He left the hotel through a side entrance, passing through a line of cameras. After pausing momentarily at a reporter's shouted question, Reagan waved and moved on. He had almost reached his limousine when he heard the popping of what sounded like firecrackers to his left.

"What the hell's that?" Reagan asked.

As he uttered these words, Jerry Paar, the head of the president's Secret Service detail, grabbed

The assassination attempt, March 30, 1981

Reagan around the waist and flung him into the limousine. He landed atop the armrest in the backseat with Paar on top of him. Reagan felt a flash of excruciating pain and told Paar he had broken a rib. "The White House," Paar said to the driver. Then as Reagan straightened up he coughed hard and noticed that the hand he put to his mouth was red with blood. Parr saw the bubbles in the frothy blood and told the driver to head for George Washington Hospital instead.

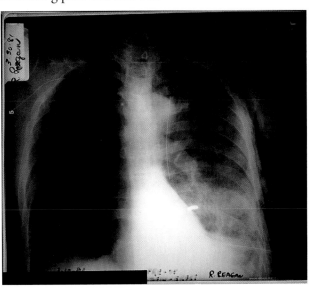

An X-ray of Ronald Reagan's chest shows where the bullet was lodged

This split-second decision may have saved the life of the president, who had been shot and was rapidly losing blood. At the hospital Reagan walked the fifteen yards to the emergency room under his own power with a Secret Service agent on each side of him. Once inside, he collapsed. He had been hit by a "Devastator" bullet that contains a small aluminum canister designed to fly apart inside the body of its target. The bullet had lodged within an inch of Reagan's heart, narrowly missing the vital aorta. Ignoring first reports that her husband had not been hurt, Nancy Reagan rushed to the hospital. "Honey, I forgot to duck," Reagan told her, borrowing fighter Jack Dempsey's line to his wife the night he lost the heavyweight championship to Gene Tunney in 1926. Later, while being wheeled into the operating room for surgery, Reagan told a doctor that he hoped he was a Republican.

"Today, Mr. President, we're all Republicans," the doctor replied.

·   ·   ·

The man who shot Reagan was John W. Hinckley Jr., a mentally disturbed twenty-five-year-old drifter who claimed he was trying to impress actress Jodie Foster. Hinckley squeezed off six shots within two seconds before he was tackled by Secret Service agents, and four of the bullets hit members of the presidential party. Injured with Reagan were Press Secretary James Brady, Secret Service Agent Timothy McCarthy, and Washington police officer Thomas Delehanty. Brady, the most seriously wounded with a bullet in the brain, was near death.

The shooting shocked the nation, and Reagan's gallantry in the face of danger inspired it. Any lingering suspicions that he was a cardboard man whose aspirations and emotions were as synthetic as a celluloid screen were dispelled forever. During the first sixty-nine days of his presidency Reagan had shown an abundance of charm. "When he displayed that same wit and grace in the hours after his own life was threatened, he elevated those appealing human qualities to the level of legend," wrote columnist David Broder of *The Washington Post.*

The assassination

The cabinet conferring after the assassination attempt and Al Haig addressing reporters

attempt had a deep and lasting impact on Reagan's presidency. Nancy Reagan, always protective, insisted that every possible measure be taken to protect her husband's safety. Reagan had waded into crowds during his political campaigns; he would rarely do so again. Of necessity, in the weeks after the shooting, Reagan also delegated more work to his subordinates. He was an effective delegator—on balance, it was a strength of his presidency—and his staff was competent, but there were those who thought that Reagan delegated too much.

For the president's economic program, the trauma of the assassination attempt and its aftermath was a political boon. Congressional Republicans united behind him, and Democrats became receptive, too. On April 28, less than a month after he was shot, a gaunt but smiling Reagan was greeted with prolonged cheers and applause when he gave a nationally televised speech on the economic program to a joint session of Congress. His audience roared with laughter when Reagan read a letter from a second-grader, "I hope you get well quick or you might have to make a speech in your pajamas." But members of the media noticed that Democrats, some of them for the first time, joined Republicans in applauding Reagan's renewed call for a tax cut.

Reagan's physical recovery from the shooting was remarkable. His health habits were excellent—he exercised regularly, watched his weight, limited his alcoholic intake to an occasional cocktail or glass of wine, seldom drank coffee or other stimulants, and had not used tobacco since his pipe-smoking days as a sportscaster in Iowa. Every evening before dinner he worked out in a little room in the White House residence that had been converted into a gym. To strengthen himself after the shooting, Reagan added a vigorous weight-lifting routine to his workout. Even though he was the nation's oldest president, he projected an image of youthful vigor in his public appearances.

But the shooting's most significant impact on Reagan

was probably spiritual. Although Reagan didn't wear religion on his sleeve, he shared his mother's faith that everything in the world happens according to God's plan and believed he had survived for a purpose. "Whatever happens now I owe my life to God and will try to serve him in every way I can," he wrote in his diary after he had returned to the White House from the hospital. Although Reagan had known from the beginning what he wanted to accomplish, he became an even more focused president after he was shot.

This inner consequence of the assassination attempt wasn't evident at the time. Reagan's diary was private, and he rarely talked about the shooting in public. But it was during his recovery from his wounds that Reagan took his first steps toward what in time would be his greatest achievement by reaching out toward the Soviet Union. On April 24, against the recommendation of Secretary of State Haig, Reagan lifted the grain embargo that President Carter had imposed against the Soviets after the invasion of Afghanistan. On the same day, also against Haig's strenuous objections, Reagan sent a handwritten letter to Soviet leader Leonid Brezhnev suggesting that the lifting of the embargo could lead to a "meaningful and constructive dialogue which will assist us in fulfilling our joint obligation to find lasting peace." Nothing came of this overture, and Reagan's letter was not made public, but he would reach out to the Soviets for the rest of his presidency until he found someone on the other side who shared his interest in a dialogue.

Reagan's brush with death also heightened his appreciation of the perils of leadership. On June 5, 1981, he did what his predecessor had refused to do and gave Ethel Kennedy a special congressional medal that honored her husband, who had been assassinated thirteen years ago that day. Reagan had taken a different political course than

FOLLOWING FOUR PAGES: *Reagan's letter to Brezhnev*

SYSTEM II
90204

April 24, 1981

THE WHITE HOUSE

WASHINGTON

My Dear Mr. President

In writing the attached letter I am reminded of our meeting in San Clemente a decade or so ago. I was Governor of California at the time and you were concluding a series of meetings with President Nixon. Those meetings had captured the imagination of all the world. Never had peace and good will among men seemed closer at hand.

When we met I asked if you were aware that the hopes and aspirations of millions and millions of people throughout the world were dependent on the decisions that would be reached in your meetings.

You took my hand in both of yours and assured me that you were aware of that and that you were dedicated with all your heart and mind to fulfilling those hopes and dreams.

The people of the world still share that hope. Indeed the peoples of the world, despite differences in racial and ethnic origin, have very much in common. They want the dignity of having some control over their individual destiny. They want to work at the craft or trade of their

DECLASSIFIED
Authority: N. Menan, NSC 10/11/91
By: DSD, NARA Date: 10/16/91

own choosing and to be fairly rewarded.
They want to raise their families in peace
without harming anyone or suffering harm
themselves. Government exists for their
convenience, not the other way around.

If they are incapable, as some would
have us believe, of self government, then
where among them do we find any who
are capable of governing others?

Is it possible that we have permitted
ideology, political and economic philosophies,
and governmental policies to keep us from
considering the very real, everyday problems
of our peoples? Will the average Soviet
family be better off or even aware that
the Soviet Union has imposed a government
of it's own choice on the people of Afghanistan?
Is life better for the people of Cuba because
the Cuban military dictate who shall
govern the people of Angola?

It is often implied that such things have
been made necessary because of territorial
ambitions of the United States; that we
have imperialistic designs and thus constitute
a threat to your own security and that of
the newly emerging nations. There not only
is no evidence to support such a charge,
there is solid evidence that the United States,
when it could have dominated the world
with no risk to itself, made no effort

whatsoever to do so.

When World War II ended, the United States had the only undamaged industrial power in the world. Our military might was at it's peak — and we alone had the ultimate weapon, the nuclear weapon, with the unquestioned ability to deliver it anywhere in the world. If we had sought world domination then, who could have opposed us?

But the United States followed a different course — one unique in all the history of mankind. We used our power and wealth to rebuild the war-ravaged economies of the world, including those nations who had been our enemies. May I say there is absolutely no substance to charges that the United States is guilty of imperialism or attempts to impose it's will on other countries by use of force.

Mr. President, should we not be concerned with eliminating the obstacles which prevent our people — those we represent — from achieving their most cherished goals? And isn't it possible some of those obstacles are born of govt. objectives which have little to do with the real needs and desires of our people?

It is in this spirit, in the spirit of helping the people of both our nations, that I have lifted the grains embargo. Perhaps this decision will contribute to creating the circumstances which will lead to the meaningful and constructive dialogue which will assist us in fulfilling our joint obligation to find lasting peace.

Sincerely

Ronald Reagan

Robert Kennedy, but he understood what Kennedy had
done. "He aroused the comfortable," said Reagan. "He
exposed the corrupt, remembered the forgotten, inspired his
countrymen, and renewed and enriched the American conscience."

Reagan had also inspired his countrymen and, unlike
Robert Kennedy, or John F. Kennedy, had somehow survived. He was not a martyr, nor did he want to be, but seven
weeks into his presidency he was a legend. The man who
urged his fellow Americans to dream heroic dreams had
been transformed by fate and events into an American hero.

A full recovery

RONALD REAGAN

Want budget resolution

Need to stick together

Don't like deficits

I'll veto spending bills

I'll push balanced budget constitutional amendment

Update from Bob, Del & Trent

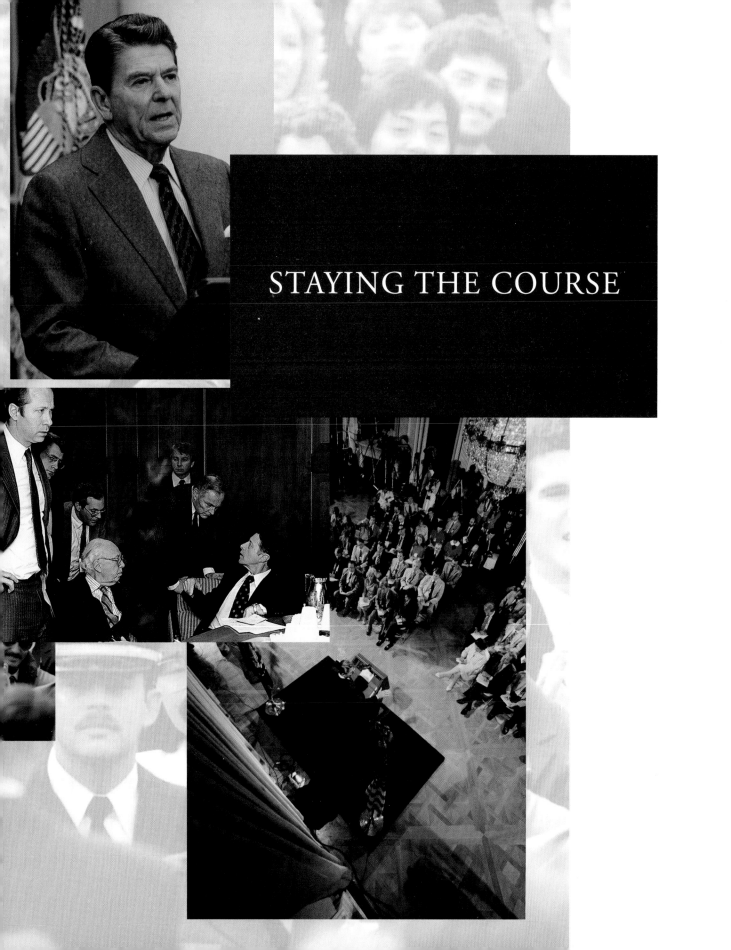

STAYING THE COURSE

President Reagan's goal of balancing the federal budget by 1984 depended on a complex set of assumptions that needed to work in tandem for his plan to succeed. The most crucial of these assumptions was that his proposed 30 percent income tax reduction, to be delivered in 10 percent increments over three years, would powerfully stimulate business investment and economic growth. Based on this expectation, the first Reagan budget confidently projected a growth rate of 5.2 percent for fiscal 1982.

Reagan also had faith that he would be able to slow the rate of federal spending. This was a dubious assumption because much of the budget was effectively off limits. As late as the mid-1960s, the president and Congress controlled three-fourths of the budget. But beginning with the Great Society programs of President Johnson in 1965 and continuing through the Nixon and Carter administrations, Congress passed numerous "entitlements" that automatically mandated payments to millions of Americans based on formulas that had been written into law. These included Medicare in 1965, big benefit increases in the early 1970s, and the automatic indexing of Social Security in 1972. Because of these actions, as well as long-term federal contracts and interest on the national debt, more than 70 percent of federal spending was virtually uncontrollable when Reagan took office in 1981. Of the spending that was controllable, half involved national defense, which Reagan had promised to increase. In addition, the monetary restraint that the Federal Reserve Board was exercising to restrain inflation tended to increase federal spending across the board. As the Fed tightened credit by raising interest rates, unemployment increased. This in turn boosted federal outlays for unemployment insurance, food stamps, and various welfare programs.

The obstacles to reducing federal spending were no mystery to Reagan's budget director, David Stockman. He was an economics whiz who had made his reputation with a searing indictment of the "social pork barrel" of federal spending pushed ever higher by collaboration among congressional, bureaucratic, and business interests. Stockman was later faulted and his authority diminished for sharing his acerbic criticisms of Congress—and of Reaganomics itself—with William Greider of *The Washington Post* for a story in *The Atlantic Monthly* that embarrassed the administration. But in the early months of the Reagan presidency, Stockman struggled valiantly to make as many budget cuts as possible before the deficit spiraled out of control. The budget director realized that the administration, although winning budget battles, was losing the economic war. In the spring and summer of 1981 Congress narrowly approved two rounds of spending cuts that were hailed as Reagan victories but fell far short of the administration's budget targets. This was the fault of Republicans as well as Democrats. As Stockman knew from his House experience, most members of

Visiting the Mormon Welfare Cannery in Ogden, Utah

Congress, regardless of political philosophy, resist cutting programs that benefit their districts. And even if the Reagan budget cuts had been approved in their entirety, they would not have been sufficient to offset the built-in budget increases of the entitlement programs.

Frustrated because the Reagan budget was seriously unbalanced, Stockman tried a risky political gambit. With the backing of Richard Schweiker, the secretary of Health and Human Services, the budget director persuaded Reagan to endorse a proposal that would have eliminated the Social Security minimum benefit and reduced disability payments. Its most controversial feature was a sharp reduction in Social Security benefits for workers who retired before reaching the age of sixty-five. The plan was a blunder—all the more so

Meeting with David Stockman

because Stockman had earlier convinced Reagan to pass up a far less controversial bipartisan Senate proposal that would have slowed the rate of growth in Social Security cost-of-living increases and accomplished most of Stockman's budgetary goals without the political risk. House Speaker Tip O'Neill denounced the Stockman plan as "despicable," the Republican-controlled Senate voted unanimously against it, and Reagan withdrew it in a nationally televised speech in which he attacked the Democrats for "demagoguery." To cover his retreat, Reagan dusted off a campaign proposal calling for an independent commission to study Social Security. He named Alan Greenspan to chair this bipartisan group.

Reagan fared better with his tax cuts than his budget reductions, although he again was forced to accept congressional changes that increased the deficit. Supporters of the tax bill did as much damage to it as its adversaries; business lobbyists helped trim the Reagan income tax cut from 30 percent to 25 percent while insisting on an 18 percent business depreciation allowance that reduced federal revenues. Nor was that the end of the largesse. House Ways and Means Committee Chairman Dan Rostenkowski added tax breaks sought by various lobbyists, especially the savings-and-loan and oil industries, who treated the tax bill as a Christmas tree under which they could place expensive presents for themselves. There wasn't much that either Reagan or Stockman could do to keep the tax bill under control. Facing a close vote, the president reluctantly accepted the revival of a protectionist sugar-import quota that Congress had abolished two years earlier. This won support from Democrat John Breaux, then a House member (and later senator) from Louisiana. When Breaux was asked if his vote on the tax bill was for sale, he famously replied, "No, but it is available for rent."

Congress passed the tax cut in July. On August 3, 1981,

FOLLOWING TWO PAGES: *Talking points on the budget*

(3 x 5 CARDS)

SUGGESTED TALKING POINTS FOR THE PRESIDENT

- As heads of agencies, you are very important to the success of
  our economic recovery program. Some agencies have budgets larger
  than ~~Cabinet~~ SOME Departments.

  Wanted to be sure we have a good understanding of the situation.

  We face a tough job as we work with Congress on the 1982 budget at the
  same time ~~as~~ we prepare ~~by~~ the 1983 budget.

- We set our course last February when I outlined our program for
  economic recovery and ~~we cannot~~ we're not going to deviate from it.

- We succeeded in getting tax relief. We've been partially successful in getting budget cuts. But, high interest rates and higher
  costs from automatic spending programs have threatened us with
  higher deficits than I will accept or the nation can stand.

- On September 24th, I outlined the new measures:

  1. cut 12% from the budget requests proposed last March.

  2. tight outlay targets for 1983 and 1984 for all government
     agencies.

  3. reduce government employment by 75,000 jobs by 1984.

- These actions place a great burden on all of you as you go
  to the Congress to defend these reductions and as you prepare
  your 1983 budget proposals that you are sending to OMB. I wish
  ~~that~~ these tough actions were not necessary. But, we must begin
  now. We have only a short time to achieve a major redirection
  in the size, role and cost of government.

- I appreciate all that you have done already in defending my budget proposals. I know you sometimes face hostile Congressional committees and hostile special interest groups.

- Ed Meese and Dave Stockman will continue the briefing on the economic situation and the actions we must take to keep on track, reduce deficits and move toward a balanced budget.

- To help meet these goals I formed a Budget Review Board. I also want you to understand that those tough new budget and employment ceilings you have been receiving from Dave are not just OMB targets. The 1983 and 1984 ceilings have been reviewed by my Budget Review Board (Ed Meese, Jim Baker and Dave Stockman) and I have approved them.

- So, thanks for all the help, hard work, dedication and support, so far. ~~And know that~~ We continue to count on your support and assistance.

- What I said to the Cabinet certainly applies here ---
  If not now, when?
  If not us, who?

Reagan faced another test of leadership when 13,000 members of the Professional Air Traffic Controllers Organization (PATCO) walked off their jobs. At the urging of PATCO president Robert E. Poli, the union had backed Reagan in 1980 when labor support for Republicans was rare and prized. But Reagan firmly, if unhappily, took the view that his responsibility to public safety exceeded any debt of gratitude to the union. "I'm sorry, and I'm sorry for them," he said as he fired controllers who had not returned to work within forty-eight hours after their walkout. "I certainly take no joy out of this." Reagan's decisive action sent an anti-inflationary message that resonated throughout the remainder of his presidency and contributed to wage restraint.

Reagan fires striking air traffic controllers, August 3, 1981

Reagan's show of leadership could not save the nation from recession in the summer of 1981. The economy had surged briefly early in the year, then sputtered under the weight of continuing inflation and high interest rates as the Federal Reserve Board maintained a stranglehold on the money supply. A few days after Reagan fired the air traffic controllers, he received a stack of July economic indicators signaling that a recession was under way.

The next eighteen months were hard for Reagan and the nation. The president's optimism made him resistant to warnings from Stockman and White House chief of staff James Baker that the recession could be deep and prolonged. Reagan did not publicly concede the existence of a recession until October, when he described it as "slight" and said he hoped it would be "short." In November, however, unemployment figures reached a six-year high, and Reagan stopped predicting either a short recession or a balanced budget. The economy was now in full retreat, with no signs of the magic stimulus that tax reduction was supposed to provide. Instead of growing 5.2 percent, as Reagan's budget projected, the economy contracted by 1.5 percent during the fiscal year.

Worse was to come. By 1982, the interest-sensitive housing industry had slowed to its lowest pace since 1946. Automobile sales fell to a twenty-year low, and manufacturers and farmers cried out for relief. On April 21, CBS aired *People Like Us,* a documentary narrated by Bill Moyers that emotionally presented harrowing accounts of hardship and destitution and pointed a damning finger at the Reagan administration. "These are people who slipped through the safety net and are falling away," Moyers said. "In the great outcry about spending, some helpless people are getting hurt." Reagan thought the documentary unfairly blamed the administration for hardships that were not its fault, but Democrats picked up the theme of "unfairness" and hammered away at it. At political fundraisers Reagan was greeted

UNPUBLISHED
January 12, 1982
5:00 pm

THE WHITE HOUSE

WASHINGTON

THE PRESIDENT'S SCHEDULE
Wesnesday, January 13, 1982

9:00 am (30 min)	Staff Time (Baker, Meese, Deaver)	Oval Office
9:30 am (15 min)	National Security Briefing (William P. Clark)	Oval Office
9:45 am (15 min)	Senior Staff Time	Oval Office
10:00 am (60 min)	Personal Staff Time	Oval Office
11:00 am (15 min)	Meeting with the President's Foreign Intelligence Advisory Board (Edwin Meese) (Tab A)	Cabinet Room (draft remarks attached)
11:15 am (10 min)	Presentation by Representatives of the Association of American Editorial Cartoonists (Larry Speakes) (Tab B)	Oval Office
11:30 am (25 min)	Presentation of Diplomatic Credentials by the Ambassadors-designate of Sierra Leone, Austria and Cameroon (William P. Clark) (Tab C)	Oval Office
12:00 m	To the Residence for remainder of the day	Residence

Non defense bund, encreases

'82 - 364 Bil
'83 - 391 "
'84 - 417 "
'85 - 446 "
'86 - 472 "
        2,090 "

Phil. Fed Reserve Banks - Business Review" - article by Stephen Meyer Sr, economist - Fed. Research dept. + Robt. Rossana asst. Prof. Ec's. Penn St. —

Our 3 yrs. tax cut is not cut. Bracket creep & inflation see security taxes will find people paying higher tax in real $ than they did in 1980.

by demonstrators who bore banners proclaiming, "Welcome President Hoover."

In times of crisis, however, Reagan's role model was never Hoover but always his successor, Franklin D. Roosevelt. As FDR had done during the Great Depression, Reagan turned a happy face to the cameras and proclaimed his faith in the people and the resilience of the American economic system. Ignoring an accumulation of bad economic news and a steep decline in his approval ratings, Reagan remained steadfastly optimistic that his program would lead to prosperity and (also like FDR) blamed the "failed policies of the past" for the nation's plight. His optimism was not a pose. Away from the cameras, Reagan tried to cheer up downcast aides. On one occasion, when Stockman and Richard Darman showed him a set of particularly gloomy charts, the president took note of a tiny scrap of data that pointed to an eventual upturn. "What about that?" he asked.

Reagan was persistent as well as optimistic. At the depth of the recession he had the courage to defy a growing clamor from leading Republicans as well as Democrats for the political scalp of Paul Volcker, the embattled chairman of the Federal Reserve Board. Reagan owed nothing to Volcker, a Wall Street banker and Democrat whom President Carter had named chairman of the Fed. But Reagan met with Volcker, who convinced him that high interest rates were necessary to wring inflation out of the economy. The president and the Fed chairman shared, in Stockman's words, a "purgatory view of inflation," that made Reagan more steadfast in support of Volcker than Carter had ever been. "Our administration is cleanup crew for those who went on a non-stop binge and left the tab for us to pick up," Reagan

FACING PAGE: *A day at the Oval Office*

said in a New York speech. "The recession hurts. It causes pain. But we'll work our way out of it."

The recovery moved too slowly for western and southern Republicans, who adored Reagan but abhorred the tight-money policies of the Fed. With an eye to the midterm congressional elections of 1982, Senator Howard Baker of Tennessee told Republican congressional strategists, "Volcker's got his foot on our neck, and we've got to make him take it off." White House chief of staff James Baker agreed, but neither of the Bakers could dissuade the president from his stubborn support of Volcker. On occasion, Reagan sounded even more determined than the Fed chairman to hold the line until inflation subsided. His only public criticism of Volcker during the entire recession—and a very mild

With Paul Volcker

one at that—came early in 1982 when he suspected that the Fed might ease up on interest rates too early. In 1983, Reagan reappointed Volcker as chairman of the Fed over opposition from Treasury Secretary Donald Regan and several Republican senators.

Republicans paid a price in the 1982 midterm elections for the Fed's tight-money policies, but less so than most political analysts had predicted. By then, Reagan was urging "stay the course" in all his speeches, and the Republican Congressional Committee adopted the slogan as its own. The Democrats picked up twenty-six seats in the House, running especially strong in Midwestern industrial districts where the recession had taken a heavy toll. But the party that holds the White House usually loses House seats in midterm, and the Democratic gains in 1982 were less than the historic average. Democrats were also helped by reapportionments conducted by friendly legislatures after the 1980 census; an analysis by Michael Barone showed this accounted for fifteen of the twenty-six Democratic gains. In the Senate, where redistricting does not apply, Republicans won every close race and held onto their 54–46 majority.

Reagan was relieved by the election, but he was still not out of the woods. The economy remained mired in recession, and his approval rating continued to drop—to a low of 35 percent in January 1983. At the time less than 20 percent of Americans thought the economy was improving, but Reagan already saw signs of recovery. On February 5, in his weekly Saturday radio speech, the president claimed his program was working and referred to it as "Reaganomics," even while joking that it was not the name he would have chosen. ("It sounds like a fad diet or an aerobic exercise," he said.) By April 29, with the recovery in full bloom, he had fashioned the one-liner he would use throughout his presidency: "They aren't calling it Reaganomics anymore."

Whatever the nomenclature, the recession was over. It was followed by a prolonged prosperity that lasted through the remaining six years of the Reagan presidency and halfway through the Bush administration. Eighteen million new jobs were created, and inflation melted away. It was "morning again in America," as Reagan's political strategists proclaimed in 1984 when he was reelected in a monumental landslide in which he won every electoral vote except those of Minnesota and the District of Columbia. But to those who saw Reagan at close quarters, his great achievement as president came not when he was running loose in the lead in 1984 but when his administration seemed down and out during the dark days of 1982. At a time when even ardent supporters were discouraged, Reagan scoffed at his critics, brushed aside the fears of fellow Republicans, and defied the polls. He showed that he was temperamentally suited for the presidency. In domestic crisis, Reagan truly stayed the course.

The balance sheet on Reaganomics, however, is mixed. Its biggest debit was the accumulation of record budget deficits. Reagan was able to joke about it—he said at one point that he didn't worry about the deficit "because it was big enough to take care of itself"—but he also described it as the greatest disappointment of his presidency. The national debt more than quadrupled on Reagan's watch, from $700 billion to nearly $3 trillion. The trade deficit also more than quadrupled, to $137.3 billion. The budget imbalances—the exact opposite of Reagan's goal—were partly the result of the military buildup and partly because neither the administration nor Congress made any significant reductions in domestic spending. But the largest single reason for the mounting deficits was that the vaunted "supply-side" tax cuts failed to deliver their promised economic growth. In the six years of the Reagan presidency after the recession ended, the nation's private wealth grew by 8 percent. In contrast, in the five years between 1975 and 1980, a period often described by Reagan as unproductive, private wealth increased 31 percent.

There is another side to the deficit story, however, that was not apparent while Reagan was in office. Industrial

A presidential pastime

nations typically run deficits during wartime, and the United States throughout the Reagan years was engaged in the expensive confrontation with the Soviet Union known as the Cold War. Conservative analyst David Frum has described the Reagan deficits as "wartime deficits" caused largely by intensified military spending. If one believes that Reagan's policies hastened the demise of the Soviet Union and shortened the duration of the Cold War, then the deficits were a small price to pay. The decline in the percentage of the budget devoted to military spending created a context in which a Democratic president and a Republican Congress were able to agree on budgets that in the 1990s turned deficits into surpluses.

Meanwhile, the Reagan tax cuts, despite failing to ignite supercharged economic growth, had profound consequences. Congress modified some of the 1981 cuts in later budgets, then in 1986 passed a substantial tax reform that eliminated many special preferences. The cumulative impact of these measures largely accomplished Reagan's purposes. When Reagan took office, the marginal tax rate (the rate at which the last dollar of income is taxed) was 70 percent. When he left, the marginal rate had been slashed by more than half, to 33 percent. These tax cuts rippled across the world's industrialized economies. "You just can't have tax rates differing substantially across advanced countries because you would have a flight of both capital and brains," observed economist William Niskanen, a member of the Council of Economic Advisers during Reagan's first term.

Beyond doubt, the most politically stabilizing economic accomplishment of the Reagan years was the long-term reduction of inflation. The annual inflation rate, 12.5 percent in the last year of the Carter presidency, was 4.4 percent in 1988. Moreover, the unemployment rate fell from 7.1 percent to 5.5 percent and the prime interest rate by nearly six points to 9.3 percent. These numbers reflected a fundamental change made possible by the Federal Reserve Board's harsh strictures to control inflation and Reagan's support of them. Under Reagan, Volcker's policy of treating inflation as Public Enemy No. 1 became national doctrine. When Volcker's term expired in 1987, Reagan replaced him with Alan Greenspan, who continued the anti-inflation strategy with a defter hand. Greenspan served as chairman of the Fed under three subsequent presidents, developing a consensus for the monetary policies that began in the Reagan years.

Before he became chairman of the Fed, Greenspan helped Reagan avert a Social Security crisis. When the Stockman plan for a Social Security quick fix collapsed in 1981, Reagan appointed Greenspan to head a National Commission on Social Security Reform, to which other members were named by House Speaker Tip O'Neill and Senate Majority leader Howard Baker. After the 1982

With Alan Greenspan, left, and Paul Volcker

elections Greenspan engineered a delicate compromise that
increased payroll taxes for employers and employees in two
stages, gradually raised the retirement age from sixty-five to
sixty-seven by 2027, and taxed the benefits of high-income
Social Security recipients for the first time. These changes
did not resolve the long-term structural problems of Social
Security, but they bought time for future presidents.
Approved overwhelmingly by Congress in 1983, the changes
proposed by the commission and backed by Reagan were
the only substantive Social Security reform of the century.

Other aspects of the Reagan economic legacy are more
problematic. During the Reagan years the United States
became a debtor nation for the first time since 1914 as foreign investors financed the trade deficit with loans and purchases of U.S. stocks, bonds, land, and factories. Economists
disagree on the impact of this development. While it certainly made the United States more dependent on foreign
capital and hence more vulnerable, it also marked the beginning of a new and interdependent global economy.

Reagan himself had no fear of the global future. He was
an internationalist throughout his adult life and a free-trader
who began his 1980 campaign with a call for a "North
American accord" among the United States, Canada, and
Mexico. As president, Reagan sought and eventually (in
1988) achieved a Canada-U.S. Free Trade agreement. He
took the next logical step toward a North American common market by approving a "framework agreement" with
Mexico that was the predecessor of the North American Free
Trade Agreement negotiated by his successors. Reagan
believed in the power of freedom, and he was freedom's
advocate. After staying the course in domestic crisis, he confidently turned his attention to the world.

FOLLOWING THREE PAGES: *Talking points on school prayer*

TALKING POINTS

FOR

MEETING WITH PRO-SCHOOL PRAYER LEADERS
July 12, 1983

-- Welcome to the White House and first let me say thank
you for all ~~the~~ your help ~~you have given our~~ in the fight to restore
voluntary school prayer.

-- I think we are ~~very~~ close to victory ~~now~~ if we all pull
together.

-- ~~The status of our Voluntary Prayer Amendment is this.~~
On Thursday, the full Senate Judiciary Committee has
scheduled a mark-up session ON THE VOL. PRAYER AMENDMENT. The vote will ~~surely be~~
UNDOUBTEDLY BE very close.

-- I KNOW YOU ARE AWARE ~~realize~~ that Senator Orrin Hatch, who supports my
amendment, has also put forth, as a possible alternative,
a silent prayer amendment. Frankly, I don't believe
we have been fighting this ~~prayer~~ battle for the right
to remain silent. ~~My friend~~ MY FRIEND & YOURS, Senator Hatch, does have
a valid point, though, about the need to change the
original wording of our amendment.

-- The Senate hearings and the communications I have
received from many leaders have convinced me that
we can unite all supporters of school prayer only if
we can end the fears that government officials will
be drafting prayers for school children. Therefore,
I have asked the Chairman of the Senate Judiciary Committee,
Senator Thurmond, Senator Hatch and other supporters of

voluntary school prayer to revise the amendment
they have submitted at my request for the past two
years.

-- T~~he chan~~ge I am requesting i~~s this__~~ **THAT** at the end of the
second sentence, **WE** add these words -- "nor shall the
United States or any state compose the words of any
prayer to be said in public schools."

-- This w~~ording~~ **WOULD** solve**s** the sticky problem of state-drafted
prayers without endangering currently acceptable and
praiseworthy practices such as inviting clergy to
offer invocations at high school graduations.

-- As revised, our amendment will assure the constitutionality
of voluntary student religious groups, children voluntarily
saying grace before meals, voluntary devotional periods
and silent prayer periods.

-- This is still a local option Amendment. Each state and
local jurisdiction would still have the right to permit
spoken prayer, silent prayer, or no periods for prayer
at all. The Federal courts would have to stay out
of regulating local decisions except to make sure that
no one could be required to participate in prayer and
that the government could not draft prayer for use in
public schools.

-- I need your help to pass this badly needed amendment.
If things go as I hope, we can convince a majority of
the Senate Judiciary Committee to pass our revised

3

Amendment this week. Then we could aim for full
Senate passage in the Fall and getting a vote in
the House of Representatives early next year.

--   The first step, though, is winning in the Senate
Judiciary Committee this week. I know you can
help there.

Page 4

Now, this is not to say the Soviet Union is planning to make war on us. Nor do I believe a war is inevitable — quite the contrary. But what must be recognized is that our security is based on being prepared to meet any contingency.

There was a time when we depended on coastal forts and artillery batteries because with the weaponry of that day any attack would have to come by sea. This is a different world and our defenses must be based on recognition and awareness of the weaponry possessed by all nations.

We can't afford to believe we will never be threatened. There have been two world wars in my life time. We didn't start them and indeed did everything we could to avoid being drawn into them. We were ill-prepared for both.

For 20 years the Soviet Union has been accumulating enormous military might. They didn't stop when their forces exceeded all requirements of a legitimate defensive capability. And they haven't stopped now.

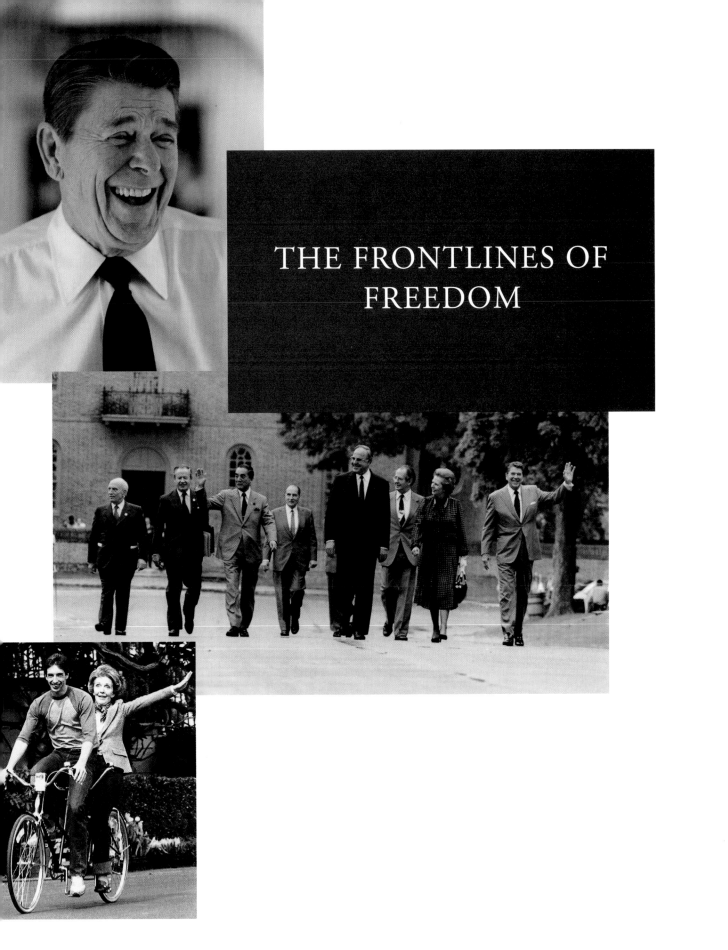

THE FRONTLINES OF FREEDOM

Ronald Reagan believed that freedom was indivisible. As an FDR Democrat in the 1930s, he sided with the internationalists, who decried the rise of fascism and Nazi Germany against the isolationists who argued that Europe's quarrels were not our own. After World War II he became convinced that communism, backed by the military power of the Soviet Union, menaced democracy. He supported President Truman's actions to block the spread of communism in Iran and Greece and then Korea. Reagan remained an internationalist after he became a Republican and defended U.S. intervention in Vietnam. And when he became president of the United States in 1981, he committed the nation to a defense buildup he believed was necessary to match Soviet military spending and counter communist expansionism throughout the world.

Reagan's internationalism was orthodox in many respects. Following the lead of every American president since the North Atlantic Treaty Organization was formed in 1949, he regarded NATO as the bedrock of collective security in Europe. Reagan believed that the Anglo-American relationship was special, and he found a kindred spirit in Margaret Thatcher, whom he had met and immediately liked in 1975 after she was elected leader of the Conservative Party. Thatcher became prime minister of Britain in 1979, a year before Reagan was elected president. She visited Washington a month after the inauguration and soon became the president's friend as well as his ally. Less sure-handed in foreign affairs than domestic matters early in his presidency, Reagan regarded it as a blessing, as he put it, to have "Maggie on my side." Thatcher in turn recognized that Reagan had the greater gift for communicating their shared commitment to freedom.

In their close relationship, which was critical in the East-West struggle of the 1980s, Thatcher was the practical partner and Reagan the idealist. The president was less experienced than the prime minister in diplomacy; he was also bolder and

Margaret Thatcher's visit in 1981

looked upon the protracted conflict between the West and the
Soviet Union as a competition of ideas as well as weapons. To
his critics, Reagan's forceful denunciations of Soviet actions
seemed naïve at best and provocative at worst, but Reagan had
a realistic understanding of the economic deterioration that
was occurring within the Soviet Union. At a visit to *The
Washington Post* on June 18, 1980, when he was campaigning
for president, an editor suggested to Reagan that the defense
buildup he advocated would intensify the arms race. His
answer was sanguine. "I think there's every indication and
every reason to believe that the Soviet Union cannot increase
its production of arms," Reagan said. "Right now we're hearing of strikes and labor disputes because people aren't getting
enough to eat. They've diverted so much to military [spend-
ing] that they can't provide for the consumer needs." Reagan
believed that if the United States and its Western allies wielded
sufficient military power the Soviet Union would have no
choice except to negotiate. For Reagan, the arms race was
always a means to this end.

Because Reagan believed that the ideological battlefield
was crucial, he saw it as his mission to make an eloquent
case for the cause of freedom and believed he would be
heard within the Soviet Union. Reagan had a visionary
understanding of the power and reach of global communica-
tion and was convinced that neither the Iron Curtain nor
the Berlin Wall was an effective barrier to freedom's message.
In a prophetic address to British members of Parliament at
the Palace of Westminster on June 8, 1982, Reagan said that
the Soviet Union was gripped by a "great revolutionary crisis" and that Poland, then under martial law, was "magnifi-
cently unreconciled to repression" and would win its
freedom. Indeed, developments in Poland were part of a
"global campaign for freedom" that would ultimately prevail.
"It is the Soviet Union that runs against the tide of human
history by denying human freedom and human dignity to
its citizens," Reagan said. "It is also in deep economic difficulty." He then detailed the "astounding" dimensions of the

Soviet economic failure. "The constant shrinkage of economic growth combined with the growth of military production is putting a heavy strain on the Soviet people," he
said. "What we see here is a political structure that no longer
corresponds to its economic base, a society where productive
forces are hampered by political ones."

The Westminster speech was Reagan's most cogent
expression of his view that freedom would triumph over
communism. Some of its passages forecast events that would
transpire after his presidency—he envisioned, for instance,
"repeated explosions against repression" in Eastern Europe
from which the Soviet Union itself would not be immune.
In a paraphrase of a famous Marxist line, Reagan said, "the
march of freedom and democracy . . . will leave Marxism-
Leninism on the ash-heap of history as it has left other
tyrannies which stifle the freedom and muzzle the self-
expression of the people." Reagan called upon the West to
encourage the development of democratic institutions
behind the Iron Curtain such as a free press, labor unions,
political parties, and universities. He concluded by saying,
"Let us now begin a major effort to secure the best—a cru-
sade for freedom that will engage the faith and fortitude of
the next generation. For the sake of peace and justice, let us
move toward a world in which all people are at last free to
determine their own destiny."

Reagan's speech, described by Thatcher as a "triumph,"
struck a patriotic chord in Britain, which was embroiled in
the Falklands War. In the United States, the address was
largely dismissed as wishful thinking. Typical of the commentary was an editorial in *The New York Times* that
scorned Reagan's appeal for "flower power" and added,
"curiously missing from his plan was any formula for using
Western economic strength to promote political accommo-
dation." The omission was purposeful, for Reagan could

FOLLOWING TWO PAGES: *An excerpt from the Westminster speech, June 8, 1982*

(RR)
May 24, 1982
Noon

SP629

ADDRESS TO THE PARLIAMENT, WESTMINSTER, LONDON, ENGLAND
TUESDAY, JUNE 8, 1982

My Lord Chancellor, Mr. Speaker:

Speaking for all Americans, I want to say how deeply you
have honored us by your invitation for me to speak here. I feel
at home in your house. Every American would, because this is one
of democracy's shrines. Here the rights of free people and the
processes of representation have been debated and refined.

And I cannot allow this moment to pass without recalling the
generous words of the member for Bristol, Mr. Burke, concerning
conciliation with the rebellious colonists in North America.

It has been said that an institution is the lengthening
shadow of a man. This institution is the lengthening shadow of
all the men and women who have sat here, and all those who have
voted to send representatives here. Here is the preeminent
symbol of government with a friendly face.

This is my second visit to Great Britain as President of the
United States.

My first opportunity to stand on British soil occurred
almost a year and a half ago when your Prime Minister graciously
hosted a diplomatic dinner at the British Embassy in Washington.
Mrs. Thatcher said then she hoped that I was not distressed to
find staring down at me from the grand staircase the portrait of
His Royal Majesty George III. She suggested it was best to let
bygones be bygones and -- in view of our two countries'
remarkable friendship in succeeding years -- she added that most

Union might contribute. Public involvement in the peace movement would grow as it has in the West -- the enormous Soviet military budget -- nearly 15 percent of the gross national product would suddenly be subjected to public scrutiny. The problem of verification -- one of the central difficulties in negotiating arms control agreements -- could be dramatically eased. We could, in fact, introduce an "open land" policy to complete the tacit "open skies" policy. This would permit much more thorough verification and possibly lead to the abolition of whole categories of arms such as chemical weapons. Above all, the suspicion and distrust which is endemic to closed political systems, and which so poisons the pursuit of peace, would be greatly alleviated.

Yet, even if this process does not take place soon, I believe the renewed strength of the democratic movement complemented by a global campaign for freedom would strengthen the prospects for arms control.

I have discussed on other occasions including in my address May 9th the elements of Western Policies toward the Soviet U. to safeguard our interests & protect the peace. What I am describing now is a policy and a hope for the long term — the march of freedom & democracy which will leave Marxism-Leninism on the ash-heap of history as it has left other totalitarian ideologies which stifle the freedom and muzzle the self expression of citizens.

~~Such a campaign would make clear that we in the West do not intend to continue the mistakes of prior generations and other governments who failed to take seriously the stated intention of their adversaries, who engaged in the self-delusions that in 1939 led to the invasion of Poland or in 1980 the invasion of Afghanistan.~~

That is why we must continue our efforts to strengthen NATO even as we move forward with our zero option initiative and our proposal for two-thirds reductions in strategic weapons.

not persuade his allies, even Thatcher, to oppose a pending Soviet natural gas pipeline. But Reagan thought the Westminster speech was one of his best. To Reagan, the reluctance of other Western leaders to challenge the Soviet Union resembled the familiar story in which no one except an honest child would say that the emperor had no clothes. Years later Reagan said that everyone knew in the early 1980s that "Marxist-Leninist thought [was] an empty cupboard" but no one had wanted to offend the Soviets.

Over time, Reagan's perception coalesced into a policy of opposing Marxist regimes and Soviet-backed "wars of liberation" in many corners of the globe. The Reagan administration supplied weapons and moral support to "freedom fighters" in Afghanistan, Africa, and Central America. Reagan never gave this policy a name, but columnist Charles Krauthammer called it the "Reagan Doctrine" after the Truman Doctrine that opposed Soviet expansionism in Europe after World War II. In an April 1, 1985, essay in Time magazine, Krauthammer defined the Reagan Doctrine as a policy of "democratic militance" that "proclaims overt and unashamed American support for anti-Communist revolution" on grounds of "justice, necessity, and democratic tradition."

This analysis was perceptive, but Reagan's foreign policy did not always fit neatly into the box of anticommunist doctrine. In Mozambique, on the east coast of Africa, the administration provided financial aid to a Marxist dictatorship that was under pressure from murderous right-wing guerrillas. Across Africa on the west coast, the administration gave covert military aid to anti-Marxist rebels, led by Jonas Savimbi, who were attempting to overthrow a leftist Angola regime maintained in power by thousands of Cuban troops. The conflict in Angola ended not on the battlefield but through the constructive diplomacy of U.S. Assistant Secretary of State Chester Crocker, who in the final year of the Reagan administration brokered a settlement providing for gradual withdrawal of Cuban troops from Angola and the independence of neighboring Namibia.

Meanwhile, in Cambodia, the Reagan administration made common cause with Communist China and other nations that made no pretense of being democracies to end Vietnamese occupation even though this stance risked a return to power of the genocidal Khmer Rouge. This was a more difficult brokerage; it was finally accomplished under United Nations auspices without restoration of the Khmer Rouge a year after Reagan left office.

In Mozambique and Cambodia, Reagan relied on the counsel of foreign policy professionals and submerged his anticommunism to the practical needs of international power politics. And even in Afghanistan, where Reagan's sympathies were entirely with the *mujahadeen* in their brave resistance to Soviet invasion, he was slow to provide military assistance. During his first term Reagan often expressed revulsion at the brutal destruction of Afghan villages and such Soviet practices as the scattering of mines disguised as toys that killed and maimed Afghan children. But Reagan, on the advice of Pentagon officials, was reluctant to give the *mujahadeen* what they most needed—U.S. Stinger missiles that could be used against the Soviet helicopter gunships that were the most devastating weapon of the war. The Pentagon argued that Stinger missiles sent to Afghanistan would inevitably fall into Soviet hands. But as the conflict continued and the civilian death toll mounted, Undersecretary of Defense Fred Ikle, a staunch conservative, teamed up with William J. Casey, the director of central intelligence, and a bipartisan coalition in Congress to persuade Reagan to send the Stingers and turn the tide of the Afghan war.

On Afghanistan, Reagan and Congress moved slowly but together. This was rarely the case in Central America, where the administration and Congress clashed repeatedly over covert military assistance to the "contras" (from an abbreviation of the Spanish word for "counterrevolutionaries"), a band of rebels that opposed the Sandinista

government of Nicaragua. This avowedly Marxist government was barely on Reagan's radar screen during his first
year in office; his only action of significance in Central
America was to increase military assistance to an El Salvadoran government that was engaged in bloody suppression of a
leftist insurrection. Despite qualms about Salvadoran death
squads, Congress went along with what was essentially a
continuation of a policy pursued by President Carter. But
the contras were not part of the Carter package. They were
the brainchild of CIA Director Casey and William Enders,
the assistant secretary of state for Latin America, who envisioned a force that would (as Enders put it) "harass the government" and make the Sandinistas receptive to free
elections. Few of Reagan's top policy advisers liked the idea.
Defense Secretary Caspar Weinberger went along because he
had been worried for months about Secretary of State Haig's
expressed willingness to "go to the source" in Cuba and
thought that a limited covert action was preferable to the
risk of war with Cuba. Haig, who had a low opinion of the
military potential of the contras, supported Casey for the
opposite reason. Since
Reagan was dead set against
using U.S. troops in Central
America, Haig thought that
covert aid was preferable to
doing nothing. White
House chief of staff James
Baker had his own con-
cerns; he was preoccupied
with getting Reagan's economic program through
Congress and knew that any
overt U.S. military action in
Central America would be
politically diverting. At the
same time Baker under-

With Al Haig (center) and Richard Allen

stood that southwestern conservatives were concerned that the Sandinistas were the cutting edge of Marxist expansion in Central America. In this context, the contras seemed the lesser of two evils. It is hard to imagine a more negative consensus, but that is how the U.S. policy of aiding the contras was born. On December 1, 1981, Reagan signed a presidential order approving covert aid to the Nicaraguan rebels.

Reagan's attention, like Baker's, was focused on his economic program and the developing recession; he had no inkling that he had made one of the high-stakes decisions of his presidency. But Reagan did have a sense, best expressed in the Westminster speech, that the winds of change were blowing throughout the world. What united the disparate conflicts in Africa, Asia, Europe, and the western hemisphere was a cry for self-determination and freedom from authoritarian rule, whether of right or left. Argentina turned to democracy after a military regime collapsed in the wake of the Falklands War. The white apartheid rulers of South Africa had their backs to the wall. In the Philippines the people rose up against the corrupt rule of Ferdinand Marcos.

The Reagan administration stood on the sidelines in some of these struggles and was heavily involved in others. In the Falklands War, Reagan quietly rooted for the British and his ally, Margaret Thatcher. In South Africa, Reagan was slow to see the potential of democratic change but heeded the counsel of Republican leaders in the Senate and reluctantly went along with congressionally imposed sanctions

With George Shultz

aimed at ending white-minority rule. In the Philippines,
Reagan accepted the advice of State Department profession-
als and the Joint Chiefs of Staff and used his influence with
Marcos to encourage a peaceful transition of power.

Reagan had known and liked Marcos since 1969, when
he visited the Philippines on a mission for President Nixon.
But as Marcos resisted mounting demands for reform, the
United States turned against him. On February 7, 1986,
Marcos was defeated at the polls by Corazon Aquino, but
stole the election. U.S. officials urged him to step aside and
avoid a revolution. Marcos vowed to stay unless Reagan personally urged him to quit. Reagan then issued a public statement calling upon Marcos to resign. When Marcos still
clung to power, Reagan's closest congressional ally, Senator
Paul Laxalt, called him from the White House. "I think you
should cut and cut cleanly," Laxalt said. "I think the time
has come." Marcos realized that Laxalt's call was a message
from the president. He fled to Hawaii.

Such direct action in behalf of overseas democracy was
not yet contemplated by Reagan in 1983, when the United
States emerged from recession and the president turned his
attention to the world. His international priority was the
Soviet Union, which had responded to the Westminster
speech with militant denunciations and continued deployment of intermediate-range nuclear missiles in Eastern
Europe. These missiles were targeted on NATO allies in
Europe and were meant to discourage the United States
from deploying its own medium-range missiles in Europe, a
decision already made by President Carter. Reagan was
determined to go forward with the deployment.

In dealing with the Soviet Union at this time Reagan
faced formidable problems at home and abroad. Strategic
differences existed within the administration over the best
methods of confronting the Soviets. Congress had become
skeptical about crucial aspects of the defense buildup, especially the MX missile. A nuclear freeze movement, also active

in the United States, pressured governments in Western Europe to reject deployment of U.S. missiles. In Eastern Europe, as Reagan had observed at Westminster, cracks were showing in the façade of the Soviet empire, most notably in Poland, and living conditions became grimmer day by day.

Hidebound Soviet leaders, their outlook rooted in the past, were startled by Reagan's blunt challenge to their legitimacy. Their first response, observed Moscow correspondent Dusko Doder, was to ignore the challenge, "as if it could be wished away." But when it became clear that Reagan had no intention of backing down, the Soviets launched a propaganda counterattack. In a speech to Soviet generals and Defense Ministry officials on October 28, 1982, Soviet leader Leonid Brezhnev accused the United States of pursuing a policy of "adventurism, rudeness, and undisguised egoism" that threatened "to push the world into the flames of nuclear war."

It was Brezhnev's last major speech. He died on November 10, 1982, and was replaced by Yuri Andropov, a more creative leader but also in ill health. Andropov died on February 9, 1984, and was succeeded by Konstantin Chernenko, a caretaker for the Soviet old guard, who died on March 10, 1985. Later in his presidency, when he was engaged in serious discussions with Chernenko's successor, Mikhail Gorbachev, Reagan often said he would have negotiated sooner than he did except that Soviet leaders "kept dying on me." It was an odd way to put it—a White House aide told me tongue in cheek that Communists would stop at nothing to frustrate Reagan—but it was the right point. In the first half of the 1980s, the questions of Soviet leadership were too unsettled to permit negotiation with any American president.

Nor was everything settled within the Reagan administration. Reagan had a difficult time finding the right national security adviser; he went through six of them during his presidency. His biggest instability was at the State

18/
1.

BENJAMIN SPOCK, M.D.
BOX N, ROGERS, ARKANSAS 72756

SECRETARY (501) 636-6044
RESIDENCE (501) 925-2775

April 6, 1982

President Ronald Reagan
The White House
Washington, D.C.   20500

Dear Mr. President:

    We should have a nuclear freeze now, not wait for years until we have
spent hundreds of more billions, which will be matched by the Soviet Union
as usual. To continue the futile arms race will risk annihilation, prolong
inflation and surely augment the debt.

    Many arms experts, including generals and admirals, believe we have
parity now.

Ben Spock

BS/rg

Suggested ans.
RR

Dear Dr. Spock

    I'm afraid the experts you mention are not all
that expert. We do not have # Strategic parity. In throw
weight—meaning destructive power the Soviets are far
superior. They also are technologically superior in a
number of other features.

    We are going to engage them in negotiations to
reduce nuclear weapons. This will be the 20th attempt
by the U.S. to get such a reduction since W.W.II. Always the
Soviets refuse. I believe our intention to build the M X might
offer an incentive to them to think of a mutual reduction in
                     nuclear weapons.

Department. Reagan had begun his presidency with confidence in Al Haig, who had served with distinction as head of NATO. But Haig was prickly and territorial; as Reagan put it in his memoirs, he regarded foreign policy as "his turf" and "wanted to formulate it and carry it out himself." Haig clashed repeatedly with the White House staff and then lost Reagan's confidence by assuring him and the world that Israel's 1982 invasion of Lebanon was limited to securing a safe zone in the southern section of the country. When the Israeli army instead proceeded on to Beirut, Haig's days were numbered. "This has been a heavy load," Reagan wrote in his diary on June 25, 1982, after he accepted Haig's resignation. His replacement was George P. Shultz, a distinguished economist and former Marine who shared with Haig the distinction of surviving the Nixon administration with his record of integrity intact. But Shultz was more tractable than his predecessor and also more supportive of U.S.-Soviet negotiation. He was a stabilizing presence as secretary of state throughout the remainder of the Reagan presidency.

While the Shultz appointment brought a temporary lull to the administration's foreign policy infighting, Reagan soon became embroiled with Congress in a battle over deployment of the MX intercontinental ballistic missile (ICBM), a gigantic weapon armed with ten nuclear warheads. The MX had been a Pentagon priority since 1977, when President Carter was informed that the Soviets had developed an accurate guidance system for its mammoth ICBMs that would enable it to destroy the entire arsenal of 1,000 U.S. Minutemen land-based nuclear missiles in a single surprise attack. Carter wanted to deploy the MX on moving rail tracks in the desert, where they would presumably be harder to hit. His plan was blocked by an unusual coalition of environmentalists, the Church of Jesus Christ of

FACING PAGE: *Child-rearing expert Dr. Benjamin Spock weighs in with some advice on nuclear disarmament*

Latter-day Saints, and Republicans from Utah and Nevada including Reagan's ally, Senator Laxalt. The Reagan administration then came up with its own exotic MX basing plans, none of which passed muster with Congress. On December 8, 1982, the House handed the Reagan administration its first major defense policy defeat by voting 245–176 to delete funds for MX production from the budget.

This vote paved the way for the most creative and controversial proposal of the Reagan presidency—the Strategic Defense Initiative (SDI). Ever since the Soviet Union acquired the hydrogen bomb in the early 1950s, nuclear war had been averted through a policy of deterrence that depended on the presumed rationality of both U.S. and Soviet leaders. The premise of deterrence, sometimes known as "mutual assured destruction" or MAD, was that the prospect of mutual annihilation would discourage either side from launching a nuclear strike. Deterrence required a nuclear balance of power so that neither superpower would be tempted to launch a surprise attack that would destroy the other's missiles before they could be launched. U.S. deterrence in the 1980s depended on a triad of missiles that could be launched from land, sea, or air. But the bomber fleet was old, and the accuracy of submarine-launched missiles uncertain. From the Pentagon's perspective, rejection of the MX undermined deterrence and created a "window of vulnerability" to Soviet attack.

Reagan shared the Pentagon's concern but had a more fundamental objection to deterrence. He was appalled by the moral implications of a policy in which the only available response to nuclear attack was a counterstrike that would incinerate millions of innocent civilians. Early in his administration he saw the film *War Games,* in which a teenage computer whiz accidentally accesses the computers of the North American Aerospace Defense Command (NORAD) and almost starts World War III. This was a movie, to be sure, but when Reagan asked experts about it, he was told that the notion of accidental war was not far-fetched. In fact, although no one wanted to talk about it, both sides knew of incidents where miscalculations had brought the world perilously close to a nuclear exchange. Reagan concluded that if the United States and Soviet Union stayed on hair-trigger missile alert into perpetuity, the possibility of an accidental war was not at all remote.

Reagan also had read widely about Armageddon, the biblical account of the end of the world. He thought this might be a prophecy of nuclear war, but his response to this story was not fatalistic—if the world was threatened by a nuclear holocaust, it was his duty to avert it. Reagan had been shaken in 1979 when he toured NORAD headquarters at Cheyenne Mountain, Colorado, and was told by the commanding general that America was defenseless from incoming missiles. This was supposedly the moment when Reagan began to question the doctrine of deterrence, but he had begun raising questions about alternatives as early as 1967, when he was briefed by noted nuclear physicist Edward Teller. By the time Reagan ran against President Ford in 1976, he was using an analogy he repeated to me in an interview soon after he left office: "It's like you and me sitting here in a discussion where we were each pointing a loaded gun at each other and if you say anything wrong or I say anything wrong, we're going to pull the trigger. And I just thought this was ridiculous . . . it really was a mad policy."

Others shared Reagan's skepticism. Almost unnoticed, the platform of the 1980 Republican Party convention that nominated Reagan opposed MAD as "a Hobson's choice between mutual suicide and surrender." In 1981, an informal group of White House conservatives discussed missile-defense issues with military advisers and scientists, including Teller, but nothing came of it. After the House rejected the MX, however, missile defense was suddenly a hot topic among Reagan's national security aides and the

Joint Chiefs of Staff. Reagan appointed a commission of outside experts headed by Brent Scowcroft in an effort to find an MX basing mode that Congress would accept; while this group did its work, deputy national security adviser Robert C. (Bud) McFarlane considered defense alternatives. Unrestrained by public opinion or a parliament, the Soviets were building ever more powerful ICBMs and attaching multiple warheads to them. McFarlane believed that a U.S. ballistic missile defense had the potential of forcing the Soviets to compete with American technology in developing highly sophisticated computers and complex software that could distinguish between real missile warheads and decoys. The costs of such a system would be staggering, but the United States would have a clear edge in the technological competition. McFarlane found an ally on the Joint Chiefs in Admiral James D. Watkins, the chief of naval operations, who was interested in the technological possibilities of missile defense and shared Reagan's view that the policy of mutual assured destruction was "morally distasteful." At a February 11, 1983, meeting between Reagan and the Joint Chiefs, Watkins and McFarlane made the case for missile defense. They were supported by John Vessey, the chairman of the Joint Chiefs and a highly respected Army general. Vessey said that sole reliance on deterrence was immoral and illogical.

Reagan often sat through high-level meetings without committing himself, but he made no secret of his excitement at what he was hearing. He had always hoped for an alternative to MAD; now his top military men were telling him that missile defense was worthy of exploration. McFarlane wanted Reagan to wait for the report of the Scowcroft Commission before he said anything, but the president couldn't wait. Reagan believed in the unlimited capacity of American inventiveness; if scientists could imagine something, they would find a way to build it. William Clark, who had been Reagan's chief of staff in Sacramento and was now his

national security adviser, realized immediately that Reagan
would never back down on missile defense and wanted to
announce his plan. He did so on March 23, in a surprise
ending to a nationally televised speech in which he made the
case for his defense budget. Reagan said that depending on
the threat of mutual nuclear annihilation to keep the peace
was "a sad commentary on the human condition":

> Wouldn't it be better to save lives than to avenge
> them? Are we not capable of demonstrating our peace-
> ful intentions by applying all our abilities and our
> ingenuity to achieving a truly lasting stability? I think
> we are. Indeed we must.
>
> After careful consultation with my advisers,
> including the Joint Chiefs of Staff, I believe there is a
> way. Let me share with you a vision of the future
> which offers hope. It is that we embark on a program
> to counter the awesome Soviet missile threat with
> measures that are defensive. Let us turn to the very
> strengths in technology that spawned our great indus-
> trial base and that have given us the quality of life we
> enjoy today.

And so was born the Strategic Defense Initiative, which
dominated the strategic arms debate for the rest of the 1980s
and cost $60 billion over the next two decades. SDI was
derided by the Democrats, who dubbed it "Star Wars" after
the popular movie, and scientists questioned its feasibility. It
is often forgotten that Reagan acknowledged he was proposing a "formidable technical task" that "may not be accomplished before the end of the century." In fact, Reagan was
doing more than that. His speech was a challenge to the scientific community "who gave us nuclear weapons, to turn

FOLLOWING FIVE PAGES: *The Star Wars speech*

:ached became known as the
r Wars Speech.

ught this should be in
idential files -- this is his
ting.

jh   3/23/83

Draft
3/22/83 - 0930

S E N S I T I V E

A CALL FOR A BOLD DEFENSE

Thus far tonight I have shared with you my thoughts on the
problems of national security we must face together. My predecessors
in the Oval Office have appeared before you on other occasions to
describe the threat posed by Soviet power. ~~They~~ and have proposed steps
to address that threat. But since the advent of nuclear weapons,
those steps have been directed toward deterrence of aggression through
the threat of retaliation -- the notion that no rational nation would
launch an attack that would inevitably result in unacceptable losses
to themselves. And it is true that this approach to stability
through offensive threat has worked. We and our allies have been
fortunate enough to live for nearly four decades in a period of
relative security within our borders.

And yet, ~~as I have shouldered this awesome responsibility over
the past two years~~, I have become more and more deeply convinced
that the human spirit must be capable of rising above dealing with
other nations and human beings by ~~menacing~~ threatening their ~~very~~ existence.
~~As my conviction deepened~~ Feeling this way, I have ~~sought to investigate~~ explored other
approaches. ~~surely~~ One of them is ~~to try harder at~~ of course to lowering the
level of all arms, ~~but~~ and particularly nuclear arms. ~~We simply must
never in negotiations with the Soviet U. to bring about a mutual reduction
succeed in this endeavor, and~~ We are engaged right
I will make public to you a week from
tomorrow some new ideas on that score. ~~of all weapons.~~ But let me first say I
am totally committed to this course.

S E N S I T I V E

If the Soviet Union will join with us in our effort to achieve
major arms reduction -- ~~an effort to which I am firmly committ~~ed --
we will have succeeded in stabilizing the nuclear balance. *Nevertheless we* ~~but we~~
will still continue to rely upon the strategy of retaliation of
mutual threat, and that is a sad commentary on the human condition.

Would it not be better to embark upon a path that will eventually
let us and our allies use _defensive_ measures -- not the threat of
retaliation -- to deter aggression against the free world:

~~Would it not be better~~ to give our children and our children's
children a more uplifting example of human values than that? Are
we not capable of demonstrating our preference for peace by applying
all *(abilities + our)* our ingenuity to achieving a truly lasting stability? I think we
are -- indeed, we must!

After careful consultation with my advisors, including the
Joint Chiefs of Staff, I believe there is a way. *Let me* ~~and I would like~~
~~to~~ share with you ~~what I believe is~~ a vision of the future which
offers hope. *It is that we* ~~We can and must~~ embark *on* ~~upon~~ a program ~~dedicated~~ to
counter~~ing~~ the awesome Soviet threat with measures that are defensive.
Let us turn to ~~We can accomplish this through innovative use of~~ the very strengths
in technology that spawned our great industrial base and that have
given us the quality of life we enjoy today.

~~Our ultimate goal and, I caution you, one that will not be rapidly or easily obtained, must be to diminish the threat of enemy ballistic missiles from striking our own soil or that of our allies.~~

~~As I have said,~~ Up until now we have based our strategic posture upon ~~possessing~~ the threat of retaliation to deter Soviet aggression. But ~~how much better it would be~~ what if free people could live secure in the knowledge that they no longer relied upon the threat of U. S. retaliation to deter a Soviet attack but rather that a Soviet attack that nuclear missiles could never strike ~~on our own soil or that of our allies~~ simply could not succeed; ~~In short, how much better it would be if we could begin to shift from a strategy of deterrence with offensive weapons to a strategy of forward strategic defense.~~

Recently, the Joint Chiefs and my other advisors have reviewed the current status and future prospects for defensive technologies. H~~ere~~, I am talking about systems that would intercept and destroy ballistic missiles before they could reach their targets. ~~My advisors~~ I know ~~tell me that~~ this will be a formidable technical task, one that may not be accomplished before the end of this century. Yet, current technology has attained a level of sophistication where it is reasonable for us to begin this effort. ~~Let me emphasize again, such defense is no near-term panacea.~~ It ~~will~~ may take years, ~~indeed~~ even decades, of effort on many fronts. There will be failures and setbacks just as there will be successes and breakthroughs. But is it not worth every investment necessary to free the world from the threat of a nuclear war? We know ~~Of course~~ it is!

~~But,~~ In the meantime, we ~~must aggressively~~ _will continue to_ pursue real

reductions in nuclear arms, negotiating from a position of strength

that can be ensured _only_ ~~by~~ modernizing our strategic forces. At the

same time, we must take steps to reduce the risk of a conventional

military conflict escalating to nuclear war. America does possess --

now -- the technologies to attain revolutionary improvements in the

effectiveness of our conventional, non-nuclear forces. Proceeding

boldly with ~~the innovative application of~~ these new technologies,

we can significantly reduce any incentive that the Soviet Union may

have to threaten attack against the United States or its allies.

_I call upon the scientific community who gave us nuclear weapons to
turn their great talent to the cause of mankind & world peace; to give
us the means of rendering these weapons impotent & obsolete._

~~I call upon the Nation -- our men and women in uniform, our
scientists and engineers, our entrepreneurs and industrial leaders,
and all our citizens -- to join with me in taking a bold new step
forward in defense to ensure a more peaceful and stable world of the
future.~~

Tonight, I am directing the development of a comprehensive

and intensive effort to define a long-term research and development

program that will ~~let us forge ahead~~

OPTIONS:

(1) to a position of defense. If successful, this will

    ultimately conclude the era of exclusive reliance upon

    offensive nuclear weapons. This

S E N S I T I V E

(2)   to a position of defense. If successful, this

(3)   over time to end the era of exclusive reliance upon
      offensive nuclear weapons. This

will move us a long step toward our ultimate goal of eliminating
not only the threat posed by nuclear offensive weapons, but the
weapons themselves.

My fellow Americans, tonight we are launching a truly new
beginning which holds the promise of changing the course of human
history. There will be risks, and results will take time. But with
your support, I believe we can do it. As we cross this threshold,
I ask for your support.

Good night and God bless you!

their great talents now to the cause of mankind and world peace, to give us the means of rendering these nuclear weapons impotent and obsolete." This, he said, could change the course of human history.

The defensive system that Reagan called "my dream" was a nightmare to Soviet leaders. Reagan had offered in his speech to share the fruits of any defensive technology with the Soviets, but they did not believe him. Two weeks earlier, in a March 8 speech to the National Association of Evangelicals in Orlando, Reagan had offended the Soviet Union by describing it as "the focus of evil in the modern world." This was also the speech in which Reagan called the Soviet Union "an evil empire," a phrase that Secretary of State Shultz, among others, thought too blunt. Soviet leader Andropov responded in kind. He accused Reagan of "attempting to disarm the Soviet Union in the face of the U.S. nuclear threat" and said his strategic proposals were "irresponsible" and "insane." And the tense U.S.-Soviet relationship soon went beyond words. On September 1, 1983, a Korean Air Lines jumbo jet with 269 people aboard, including 61 Americans, wandered into Soviet airspace and was shot down by a Soviet fighter. Reagan denounced the act as a "crime against humanity." A war scare developed in Europe, where French President François Mitterrand warned that the situation was comparable to the Cuban missile crisis of 1962. This was not an overstatement. Although the people of the United States and the Soviet Union were not told what was happening, as they had been in 1962, their nations were closer to war than at any time since the Cuban missile crisis.

Tension reached its peak in November when the United States and its NATO allies conducted Exercise Able Archer, which tested communications and command procedures for using nuclear weapons in case of war. This exercise, routinely carried out for many years, had been planned as a more extensive undertaking in 1983 but was scaled back because of Soviet concerns. Even so, it frightened the Soviets. A report from Oleg Gordievsky, the Soviet intelligence chief in London who was secretly working for British intelligence, said that some KGB units were inaccurately telling Moscow that NATO troops were on the move in preparation for an attack against the Soviet Union. Later, the CIA came up with a similar report from its agents in Eastern Europe. The president read this report somberly. "I don't see how they could believe that—but it's something to think about," he told McFarlane. Adding to the tension was the political situation in Europe where, on November 22, the West German Bundestag approved the deployment of U.S. Pershing II and cruise missiles. The following day the Soviets broke off missile talks in Geneva amidst denunciations on both sides aimed at European public opinion. By then the Soviet press was comparing Reagan to Adolf Hitler.

While Reagan was determined to continue campaigning for freedom, he realized that the bristling rhetoric had reached a danger point. In separate year-end interviews with *Time* and *Newsweek,* he said he would no longer use the phrase "focus of evil" to describe the Soviet Union. *Time* chose Reagan and Andropov as their "men of the year," featuring them on the magazine cover standing back to back. But Reagan already was looking ahead to a day when he would be face to face with a Soviet leader. Although the world didn't know it, Reagan had made a conciliatory decision after the downing of KAL 007, which occurred while he was at his California ranch. When he returned he met with advisers in the Situation Room where Clark, CIA Director Casey, and Defense Secretary Weinberger urged Reagan to take a hard line against the Soviets. Shultz argued that it was important not to overreact. Reagan agreed. "The world will react to this," he said. "It's important that we not do anything that jeopardizes the long-term relationship with the Soviet Union." Later that month, Shultz arranged for Soviet Foreign Minister Andrei Gromyko, who was in the

United States to address the United Nations, to meet with Reagan for three and a half hours at the White House.

In the weeks ahead Reagan would speak out on the twin themes of peace and freedom. On November 11 he addressed the Japanese Diet in the first speech ever given by an American president to the Japanese parliament. He was interrupted by applause twenty-five times, the loudest when he declared: "I believe there can be only one policy for preserving our precious civilization in this modern age: a nuclear war can never be won and must never be fought. The only value in possessing nuclear weapons is to make sure they can't be used—ever. I know I speak for people everywhere when I say our dream is to see the day when

Memorial for those killed in the downing of KAL 007

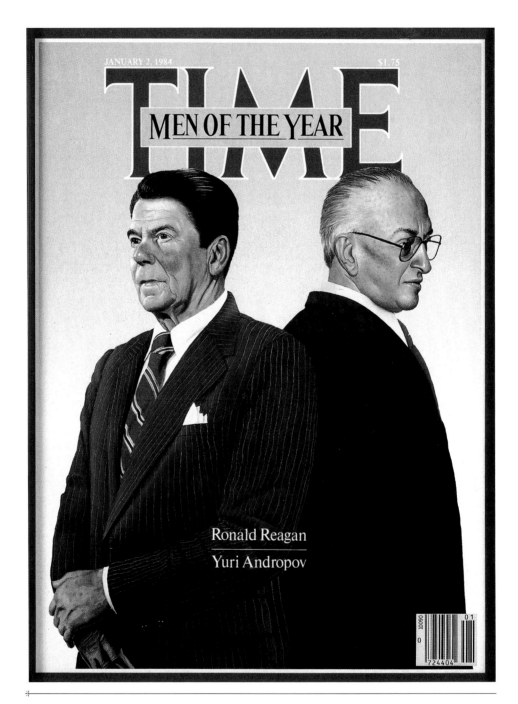

Time *magazine*

nuclear weapons will be banished from the face of the earth."

Reagan saw no contradiction between standing firmly for peace while continuing to draw a contrast between democratic and communist systems. He went from Japan to Korea, where in a speech overlooking the Korean Demilitarized Zone he thanked American solders for their service on "the frontlines of freedom." Reagan's speech was calculated to appeal to men who had the lonely duty of patrolling the windswept dividing line between the two Koreas. He told them that they stood "between the free world and the armed forces of a system that is hostile to everything we believe in as Americans."

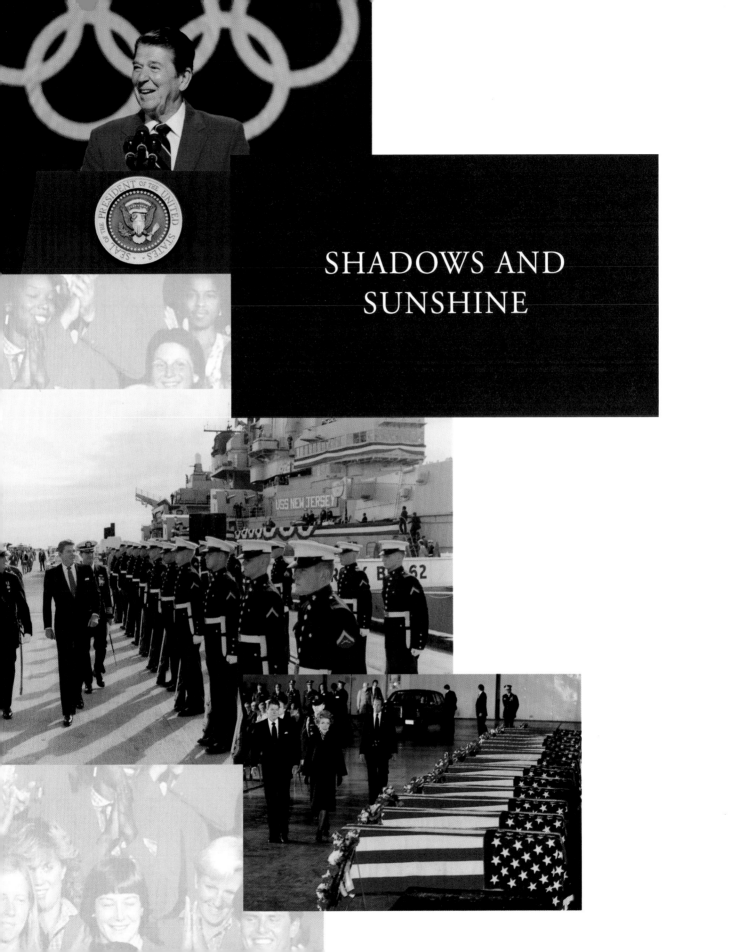

SHADOWS AND SUNSHINE

Late in his presidency Ronald Reagan sometimes told a version of an old fable about a scorpion that said it couldn't swim and asked a frog for a ride across a river. The frog was afraid the scorpion would sting and kill him. "That would be silly," replied the scorpion, "because if I stung you and you died, I'd drown." That made sense to the frog, who agreed to give the scorpion a ride. In midstream the scorpion stung him and the frog cried out, "Why did you do that? Now we're both going to die!" And the scorpion said, "This is the Middle East."

Reagan told the story to illustrate the treacherous nature of problems in the region, where he floundered, as have other administrations before and since. In most of his essential policies Reagan had a clear set of principles and knew what he wanted to accomplish. But in the Middle East, especially Lebanon, the Reagan administration lurched rudderless from side to side with too many hands on the tiller and no polestar to guide it.

When he became president, Reagan assumed the United States could rely on Israel. Over the years, Reagan had changed political positions and parties without ever abandoning his virtually uncritical support for Israel. In his Hollywood days he had refused to join a country club that discriminated against Jews, and he shared the film community's enthusiasm for Israel when the Jewish state was founded in 1948. Remembering vivid newsreels of the liberation of the Nazi death camps, Reagan sympathized with survivors of the Holocaust. Later, he valued Israel as a bulwark of freedom and an ally in the Cold War.

Because Reagan held this idealized view and had been told by Secretary of State Haig that the Israelis had limited interest in Lebanon, he was shocked when Israeli troops, under the direction of Defense Minister Ariel Sharon, marched to Beirut in the spring and summer of 1982. On June 10, Reagan, traveling in Europe, sent a message from Bonn to Israeli prime minister Menachem Begin urging ces-

sation of hostilities. Begin agreed to a cease-fire, but it lasted
only two days. When Begin visited the White House on
June 21, four days before Haig's resignation, he received a
cold welcome from Reagan, who told him that the Israeli

084430
CO 074

TOAST - LUNCHEON FOR P.M. BEGIN
JUNE 21, 1982

MR. PRIME MINISTER: *I am pleased to receive*
~~IT IS A PLEASURE FOR ME TO WELCOME~~
you once more at — this time
~~YOU BACK TO~~ THE WHITE HOUSE, TO HEAR YOUR

VIEWS AS WE CONSIDER THE VITAL ISSUES

THAT CONCERN BOTH OUR NATIONS.

WE FIRST MET LAST SEPTEMBER HERE IN

WASHINGTON, AT WHICH TIME WE WORKED HARD

TO CHART A COURSE FOR FULFILLING THE

POTENTIAL OF THE CAMP DAVID PEACE

PROCESS. THE UNITED STATES IS PROUD TO *HAVE*

WORK*ED* WITH ISRAEL & EGYPT TO REALIZE THAT

PROMISE. ~~AND~~ TOGETHER WE ~~ARE TAKING~~ *must take*

further ~~IMPORTANT~~ STEPS TOWARDS ACHIEVING

LASTING PEACE IN THE MIDDLE EAST.

MR. PRIME MINISTER, I KNOW THE DEEP

ANXIETY & TURMOIL ISRAEL EXPERIENCED IN

APRIL.

Welcoming remarks for Prime Minister Menachem Begin's visit

invasion had raised serious problems for the United States in the Arab world. Begin bridled at the word "invasion," saying that Israel was in Lebanon only to force the expulsion of the Palestine Liberation Organization (PLO).

Reagan was skeptical. And as Israeli planes bombed West Beirut for seven consecutive days in late July and the gruesome results were shown on television, Reagan and his advisers, especially Mike Deaver, were anguished. On August 4, Israeli armored units rolled into West Beirut in violation of a precarious truce, and Reagan sent a message to Begin urging him to stop. Begin replied that Israeli forces would continue their attacks until the PLO had withdrawn from Lebanon. On August 12, Israeli planes bombed West Beirut for eleven consecutive hours, and a disgusted Deaver told the president he was the only person who could stop the carnage. Reagan agreed. He instructed his secretary to place a call to Begin. An aide who monitored the conversation said it was the only time he ever heard the president become emotional.

"Menachem, this is a holocaust," Reagan said.

"Mr. President, I think I know what a holocaust is," Begin replied in a sarcastic voice.

But Reagan would not give ground. He bluntly told Begin about the bombing, "It has gone too far. You must stop it."

Twenty minutes later Begin called back and said he had ordered Sharon to stop the bombing attacks. Reagan thanked Begin, hung up the phone, and said to Deaver, "I didn't know I had that kind of power."

But power is illusory in the Middle East, even for an American president. Two days after this fateful phone call, Syria informed Philip C. Habib, the U.S. special envoy in the Middle East, that it was willing to withdraw its troops and PLO fighters under its command from Beirut. The next day the Israeli cabinet accepted Habib's plan for a multinational force (MNF) to oversee the expulsion of the PLO.

French and Italian military contingents arrived; they were joined on August 25 by 800 U.S. Marines, who were interposed between 30,000 Israeli troops and 15,000 Syrian and Palestinian soldiers. The vulnerability of the Marines worried Defense Secretary Weinberger and the Joint Chiefs of Staff, but by September 1 the last Syrian and PLO troops evacuated Beirut and a newly elected Lebanese government was poised to take control. Reagan interrupted a California vacation to make a nationally televised speech in which he said that the war in Lebanon, "tragic as it was, has left us with a new opportunity for Middle East peace."

Weinberger and the Joint Chiefs were not reassured. They advised Reagan that the Marines, having accomplished

Philip C. Habib conferring with the president

their primary mission of evacuating the PLO, should be withdrawn to nearby ships. On September 10, Reagan ordered their withdrawal over the objections of Habib and Secretary of State Shultz. Then on September 14, nine days before he was to assume the Lebanese presidency, Christian leader Bashir Gemayel was killed by a powerful bomb while speaking at the headquarters of his Phalangist Party in East Beirut. Israeli troops entered West Beirut and stood idly by for two days as Gemayel's militia entered Palestinian refugee camps at Sabra and Shatila and massacred more than 700 people, many of them women and children. Reagan spent the weekend of September 18–19 closeted in the White House family quarters and watching in horror the television accounts of Sabra-Shatila while his advisers blamed the Israelis and each other. Shultz and Habib contended that withdrawal of the Marines had created the conditions that led to the murder of Gemayel and the massacres and wanted them sent back into Lebanon. Weinberger thought this was "nonsense." How would a few hundred Marines deployed between two armies have prevented an assassination in Beirut? The Joint Chiefs joined Weinberger in opposing redeployment of the Marines. General John Vessey, chairman of the chiefs, said Lebanon was "the wrong place" for U.S. troops to be engaged. But Reagan was no longer listening to his military advisers. Sickened by Sabra-Shatila, he announced formation of a "new multinational force" and on September 20 sent the Marines back into Lebanon. "The scenes that the whole world witnessed this past weekend were among the most heart-rending in the long nightmare of Lebanon's agony," Reagan said. "There are actions we can and must take to bring that nightmare to an end."

Reagan's new goal for the multinational force was restoration of a strong central government and removal of all foreign troops—a far more ambitious undertaking than evacuating the PLO. Reagan said that U.S. troops would stay in Lebanon for a "limited period of time," which Vessey in his instructions to European commanders who were providing men and material for the deployment interpreted as sixty days. On September 20, Bashir Gemayel's older brother, Amin, was unanimously elected president in a rare display of unity for a parliament divided along religious lines. Amin lacked his brother's popularity and was viewed as a weak leader who was dependent on the United States. Nonetheless, there was peace in Lebanon for a few months. Syria used the lull to rebuild, with Soviet help, its air force and air defenses, which had been destroyed by Israel. Meanwhile, in Israel, a backlash against the Sabra-Shatila killings turned public opinion against a continued presence in Lebanon and led to the dismissal of Sharon.

Historians differ on whether a genuine opportunity for Lebanese stability existed; if it did, the Reagan administration did not take advantage of the deceptive peace. This was more the fault of Reagan's quarreling cabinet than of anything that was happening in Lebanon. Since his advisers were unable to reach a consensus, Reagan left the Marines in place, interposed between the Syrian and Israeli armies in an ill-defined and perhaps impossible mission. "I suspect that one of the reasons it was hard to win the argument to withdraw them was that everyone said, Look what happened when they went out," Weinberger told me years later. But Syria, which had long claimed Lebanon as a province, had no intention of allowing a U.S.-backed Christian government to remain in power. After the Israeli invasion of Lebanon, Syrian ruler Hafez Assad allowed units of the Iranian Revolutionary Guard into the strategic Bekaa Valley, where they served as a link to a radical Shiite faction known as Hezbollah (Party of God). Hezbollah was determined to expel the United States and Israel from Lebanon and had far more terrorist potential than the PLO, which was honeycombed with informants for U.S. and Israeli intelligence agencies. In contrast, Hezbollah—suspected of the bombing that killed Gemayel—was relatively invulnerable to such penetration. Hezbollah made its presence known on April 18, 1983, when a delivery van filled with explosives detonated on the grounds of the U.S. embassy on Beirut's waterfront. The midsection of the eight-story building collapsed, killing sixty-three people, including seventeen Americans. One of the dead was the respected Robert C. Ames, the chief CIA analyst of Middle Eastern affairs, who was convening a meeting of eight CIA officials when the bomb went off. All of the CIA officials were killed, depriving the United States of invaluable intelligence capability when it was most needed in Lebanon.

The destruction of the embassy should have led to the withdrawal of the Marines, but Reagan, as he would later put it, did not want to "cut and run." During the next six months his administration, led by Shultz, maneuvered to preserve the shaky Lebanese government and prod foreign troops to withdraw. The supposed high point of this diplomacy was an agreement on May 17 signed by Israel and Lebanon that called for Israeli troops to pull out of Lebanon within eight to twelve weeks providing Syrian forces did the same. But the agreement, as Weinberger observed, was worthless because Syria was not a party to it. On July 6, Shultz went to Damascus for a meeting with Assad he hoped would lead to Syrian withdrawal. He got nowhere. Later that summer the Syrian foreign minister predicted to his Lebanese counterpart that the United States would pull out after it lost a few Marines.

The May 17 agreement cost the Reagan administration the valuable services of Habib, who was declared persona non grata by Syria for negotiating it. Habib resigned and was replaced by the deputy national security adviser, Robert McFarlane. Like Shultz, McFarlane was a former combat Marine who believed in the usefulness of military power to accomplish diplomatic objectives. But McFarlane lacked the authority to do what he thought necessary, which was to have the Marines assist the untried Lebanese Army in occu-

pying strategic positions abandoned by the Israelis. In the
summer of 1982, the United States had been unable to persuade the Israelis to leave Lebanon. In the summer of 1983,
it could not persuade them to stay. The Israeli armed forces
were now under the direction not of the bellicose Sharon
but the realistic Moshe Arens, who knew the Israeli people
wanted them home. He promised to move the troops to safe
positions by the Jewish New Year in early September. As the
Israelis withdrew from the heights overlooking Beirut to a
southern defense line, their place was taken by rival militias
that sought to overthrow the Lebanese government.

Once again, the Reagan administration passed up an
opportunity to withdraw the Marines, who were now under
fire from the Syrian-supported Druze militia. The situation
was particularly perilous for the Twenty-fourth Marine
Amphibious Unit at the Beirut airport, which came under
near-constant artillery fire after the Israeli withdrawal. Two
Marines were killed in a rocket attack at the airport on September 5, and the U.S. destroyer *Bowen* fired its five-inch
guns in support of the Marines. Colonel Timothy Geraghty,
the Marine commander, was alarmed. He sent a report
warning that "the stakes are being raised weekly" and declaring that the U.S. "contribution to peace in Lebanon since 22
July stands at four killed and twenty-eight wounded." This
report received no response from Reagan or Shultz, who
were preoccupied with the Soviet downing of KAL Flight
007. Geraghty was opposed to shelling Druze positions or
using Marines to help the Lebanese Army, for he realized
that would make them participants in the Lebanese War.
But he eventually yielded to entreaties from McFarlane and
Lebanese commanders and permitted a bombardment of a
critical ridgeline. This temporarily restored the morale of a
Lebanese Army brigade but extinguished any remaining pre-

FOLLOWING FOUR PAGES: *KAL speech of September 5, 1983*

PRESIDENTIAL TELEVISION ADDRESS: FLIGHT 007
                                    MONDAY, SEPTEMBER 5, 1983

My fellow Americans, I am coming before you tonight about a
~~the Korean airline massacre~~
~~matter that continues to weigh heavily on our minds~~ -- the attack
~~last week~~ by the Soviet Union against 269 innocent men, women and
children aboard an unarmed Korean passenger plane. This ~~is a~~
crime against humanity MUST ~~we can~~ never ~~forget~~ BE FORGOTTEN, HERE OR THROUGHOUT THE WORLD,

Our prayers tonight are with the victims and their families
in ~~this~~ THEIR terrible time of grief. Our hearts go out to all of
them -- to brave people like Kathryn McDonald, the wife of a
Congressman, whose composure and eloquence on the day of her
husband's death are a tribute to the ideals he so courageously
represented. He will be sorely missed by all of us here in govt.

The parents of one slain couple wired me: "Our
daughter . . . and her husband . . . died on Korean Airline
Flight 007. Their deaths were the result of the Soviet Union
violating every concept of human rights." The emotions of these
parents -- grief, shock, anger -- are shared by civilized people
everywhere. FROM AROUND THE WORLD PRESS ACCOUNTS REFLECT AN
~~We are witnessing an~~ explosion of condemnation
BY PEOPLE EVERY WHERE,
~~throughout the world~~.
Let me STATE AS PLAINLY AS I CAN: ~~make one thing plain~~: There WAS ~~is~~ absolutely no
justification, either legal or moral, for what the Soviets did.
~~As~~ One newspaper in India said, "If every passenger plane . . .
is fair game for home air forces . . . it will be the end to
civil aviation as we know it."

~~Nor is~~ This *is not* the first time the Soviet Union has shot at and hit a civilian airliner when it overflew their territory. ~~As a matter of fact,~~ In 1978, ~~the Soviets~~ *They* positively identified one aircraft as a civilian airliner. The pilot *radioed* ~~said~~ the name on the side of the aircraft, and then was given a command to shoot it down. That plane escaped destruction by making a crash landing on a frozen lake, but *still* innocent civilians lost their lives — *killed by machine gun bullets.*

~~The United States Government does not fire on foreign~~ *Is this a practise of other countries in the world? The answer is no.* ~~aircraft over U.S. territory, even though~~ Commercial aircraft from the Soviet Union and Cuba ~~have~~ *on a number of occasions* overflown sensitive U.S. military facilities. *They weren't shot down.* We and other civilized countries believe in the tradition of offering help to mariners and pilots who are lost or in distress, on the sea or in the air. We believe in following procedures to prevent a tragedy, not to provoke one.

But despite the savagery of their crime, the universal reaction against it, and the evidence of their complicity, the Soviets still refuse to tell the truth. They have persistently refused to admit that their pilot fired on the Korean aircraft. Indeed, they have not even told ~~the Russian~~ *their own* people that a plane was shot down. The Soviet Government calls the whole thing an accident. I call it murder. Let me repeat the stark words of the Soviet pilot himself after signaling that his missile warheads were locked on the airliner: "I have executed the launch. The target is destroyed. I am breaking off attack."

The world must hear these words. Tomorrow the Security Council of the United Nations will hear them when a tape recording of the pilot's comments are played in public.

They have spun a confused tale of tracking the plane by radar until it just mysteriously disappeared from their radar screens;—that no one fired a shot of any kind.

But then they coupled this with charges that it was a spy plane sent by us and that their planes fired tracer bullets past the plane as a warning that it was in Soviet airspace.

Let me recap for a moment and present the incontrovertible evidence we have. The Korean airliner, a Boeing 747 left Anchorage Alaska bound for Seoul Korea on a course South & West which would take it across Japan. Out over the Pacific in international waters it was for a brief time in the vicinity of one of our reconnaissance planes a C-135 on a routine mission. At no time was the C-135 in Soviet airspace. The Korean Air Liner flew on and the 2 planes were soon widely separated.

The 747 is equipped with the most modern computerized navigation facilities but a computer must respond to input provided by human hands. No one will ever know whether a mistake was made in giving the computer the course or whether there was a malfunction. Whichever — the 747 was flying a course further to the West than it was supposed to fly — a course which took it into Soviet airspace.

The Soviets tracked this plane for 2½ hours while it flew a straight line course at 30 to 35,000 ft. Only civilian airliners fly in such a manner. At one point the Korean pilot gave Japanese air control his position as East of Hokaido Japan showing that he was unaware they were off course by as much or more than 100 miles.

The Soviets scrambled jet interceptors from a base on Sakhalin Island.

4

Japanese ground control recorded the ~~interceptors~~ interceptor planes
radio transmissions, their conversations with each
other and with their own ground control. We
only have the voices from the pilots, there is no
way ~~the JAPANESE~~ ground ~~control~~ could ~~record~~ ~~the~~ ~~can~~ ~~intercept~~ radio transmissions
from Soviet ground control. It is plain however
from the Pilots words that he is responding to
orders & querys from ~~ground control~~ HIS OWN.

~~I'm no playing you~~ Here is a brief
segment of the tape which we are going to play
in it's entirety for the U.N. Security Council tomorrow.
— Play 20 or 30 seconds of tape — That
was the voice of the Soviet pilot. In this tape ~~you hear the pilot~~ he describes
his search for what he calls the target. He
reports he has it in sight, indeed he pulls up
to within about a mile & a quarter of the Korean
plane, ~~he~~ mentions it's flashing strobe light and
that it blinked it's running lights. Then reports
he is ~~s~~ reducing speed to get behind the airliner;
gives his distance ~~at was~~ from the plane at
various points in this maneuver and finally announces
what ~~should~~ can only be called the Korean Airline Massacre.
He says he has ~~fitted~~ locked on the radar ~~control~~
which aims his missiles, has launched those missiles,
~~and~~ the target has been ~~has been~~ destroyed & he is breaking
off the attack.

Let me point out something here having to do
with his close up view of the Airliner on what we
know was a clean night with a $\frac{3}{4}$ moon. The 747
has a unique & distinctive silhouette unlike any
other plane in the world. There is no way a pilot
could mistake this for ~~anything else but a military plane~~ anything other than a civilian
airliner. And if that isn't enough let me point
out ~~the~~ our C-135 I mentioned earlier had been back
at it's base in Alaska, on the ground for an hour,
when the murderous attack took place over the Sea of Japan

tense that the Marines were a neutral, peacekeeping force in Lebanon.

By now, the nation's highest military men recognized that the Marines were in danger, but they did not press their case. "None of us marched in and told the president that the U.S. is going to face disaster if the Marines didn't withdraw," Vessey said later. Nor did they tell Congress. In September, when Congress debated a resolution to keep the Marines in Lebanon for another year and a half, Admiral James Watkins, the chief of naval operations, testified that withdrawing them "probably would have a devastating effect and could plunge Lebanon into anarchy."

At 6:22 A.M. on Sunday, October 23, at the Beirut airport, a smiling young man drove a yellow stake-bed Mercedes truck through the parking lot of the four-story steel and concrete headquarters where members of the First Battalion, Eighth Marine Regiment, were sleeping. The truck overran a barbed wire and concertina wire obstacle, passed two Marine guard posts without drawing fire, flattened a sandbagged booth at the building's entrance, penetrated the lobby, and exploded with the force of 12,000 pounds of TNT, the largest non-nuclear blast ever. The explosion ripped the building from its foundation. The building imploded, crushing or trapping most of its occupants beneath the wreckage.

Beneath the rubble were 346 U.S. servicemen, most of them Marines. A thick cloud of dust, pierced only by the cries and screams of the wounded, covered the scene. During the next six and a half hours, the bodies of 234 Marines were recovered from the wreckage. Another 112 Marines were pulled out alive, seven of whom died. Many of the survivors were permanently injured.

When the bomb destroyed the Marine headquarters, the

FOLLOWING FOUR PAGES: *Presidential address concerning the Beirut bombing*

My fellow Americans: Some 2 months ago we were shocked by the brutal massacre of 269 men, women and children, more than 60 of them Americans, in the shooting down of a Korean airliner.

Now in the past several days violence has erupted again, in Lebanon & Grenada. In Lebanon we have some 1600 Marines, part of a multinational force, that is trying to help the people of Lebanon restore order and stability to that troubled land. Our Marines are assigned to the southern part of the city of Beirut which includes the only airport in Lebanon. Just a mile or so to the North is the Italian contingent, and not far from them the French & a company of British soldiers,

This past Sunday at 22 mins. after 6 — Beirut time with dawn first breaking, a truck looking like a lot of other vehicles in the city, approached the airport on a busy main road. There was nothing in it's appearance to suggest it was any different than the trucks or cars that were normally seen on & around the airport. But this one was different. At the wheel was a young man on a kamikaze mission. The truck carried some 2000 lbs. of explosives. But there was no way our Marine guards could know this. Their first warning that something was wrong came when the truck crashed through a series of barriers including a chain link fence and barbed wire entanglements. The guards opened fire but it was too late. The truck smashed through the doors of the ~~Marine~~ H.Q. building in which 231 of our Marines were sleeping and instantly exploded. The 4 story concrete bldg. collapsed in a pile of rubble.

More than $\frac{3}{4}$ of the sleeping Marines were killed in that one hideous, insane attack. The others suffered injury and are hospitalized here or in Europe.

This was not the end of the horror. At almost the same instant another vehicle on a suicide & murder mission crashed into the headquarters of the French peace keeping force, an 8 story building, destroying it and killing more than 50 French soldiers.

Prior to this day of horror there had been tragedy for the men in the multinational force, attacks by snipers had taken their toll. Six times I had called bereaved parents and widows ~~to~~ of the sniper victims to express on behalf of all of us our sorrow and sympathy.

Sometimes there were questions and now many of you are asking, "why should our young men be ~~dying~~ dying in Lebanon. Why is Lebanon important to us?"

Well it is true Lebanon is a small country more than 6000 miles from our shores, on the edge of what we call the Middle East. Every President who has ~~held~~ occupied This ~~desk~~ office in recent years has recognized that the Middle East is of vital concern to our nation and indeed to our allies in Western Europe & Japan.

We have also been concerned because the Middle East

is a powder keg; four times it has gone to war in the last 3 decades and each time the world has teetered ~~on the brink~~ near edge of catastrophe.

The area is key to the ec. & pol. life of the West. It's strategic importance, it's energy resources, the Suez Canal and the vitality of the nearly 200 mil. people living there — all are vital to us & to world peace. If that key should fall into the hands of a power or powers hostile to the free world there would be a direct threat to the United States & to our allies. ~~There is another factor soon~~ We have another reason ~~to~~ to be involved. Since 1948 this nation has recognized & accepted a moral obligation to assure the continued existence of Israel as a nation. Israel shares our democrat. values and is a ~~stable~~ formidable force ~~in the area~~ an invader of the middle east ~~would have to reckon with. standing in the way of a potential conqueror.~~

~~A still our a year ago daily way~~

For several years Lebanon has been torn by internal strife. Once a prosperous peaceful nation it's govt. had become ineffective in ~~stopping~~ controlling the militias that warred on each other. ~~P.L.O. bands crossed the border into Israel on terrorist raids until finally Israel advanced into Lebanon all the way to Beirut. A year ago we watched on TV each night a war being fought within the city of Beirut~~

Only a year ago we were watching on our TV screens the shelling & bombing of Beirut which was being used as a fortress by P.L.O. bands. Hundreds & hundreds of civilians were being killed & wounded in the daily battles.

4

On ~~Lebanon~~ ~~eastern border~~ Syria which makes no secret of it's claim that Lebanon should be a part of a greater Syria had crossed the western border and occupied a large part of Lebanon Syria has become a home for ~~some~~ 7000 Soviet advisors & technicians who man a massive amount of Soviet weaponry including SS-21 ground to ground missiles capable of reaching targets in virtually all of Israel

A little over a year ago hoping to build on the Camp David accords which had led to ~~peace between Israel~~ & Egypt I proposed a peace plan for the Middle East to end the wars between the Arab states & Israel. It was based on U.N. resolutions 242 & 338. and called for a fair & just solution to the problem of the Palestinian refugees.

Before the ~~necessary~~ negotiations could begin it was essential to get all foreign forces out of Lebanon. To that end the multinational force was created to ~~a~~ help stabilize the situation in Lebanon until a govt. could be ~~established~~ and a Lebanese army ~~which~~ mobilized to ~~restore~~ Lebanons sovereignty over it's own soil as the foreign forces withdrew. Israel agreed to withdraw as did Syria but Syria then reneged on its promise. Some 5000 of the P.L.O. who ~~had been bringing~~ ruin down on Beirut however did leave the country.

Now to answer the question – why are we there – what is our mission? Well it is as I described it. Lebanon has formed a govt. under the leadership of Pres. Gemayel.

Reagans were asleep in the master suite of the six-bedroom
Eisenhower Cottage at the Augusta National Golf Club,
where they were spending the weekend. At 2:27 A.M., Reagan
was awakened by a call on his secure telephone from McFarlane, who was staying at an adjacent guest house. He
informed Reagan that there had been "a terrible attack on
the Marines with a substantial loss of life."

Years later, Reagan would remember the bombing as the
"saddest day of my presidency, perhaps the saddest day of
my life." Reagan was not a second-guesser. He became rec-
onciled to every other controversial decision of his presidency—including the secret sale of arms to Iran—but he
was never able to shake a deep sense of responsibility for the

Bodies returned from Beirut

(NSC/ROHRABACHER)   APRIL 23, 1983
                         6:45 P.M.

                                        1332935
               RETURN OF AMERICAN BODIES   *Pvt:*
                      FROM BEIRUT   *SP745*
                                             Cook

        IT IS ONE OF MY SADDEST DUTIES AS *FEDC*
PRESIDENT TO PAY TRIBUTE TO AMERICANS
WHO HAVE LOST THEIR LIVES WHILE SERVING
THEIR COUNTRY.

        TO THE FAMILIES OF THOSE WE HONOR
TODAY: I KNOW I SPEAK FOR ALL THE
AMERICAN PEOPLE WHEN, I EXTEND TO YOU MY
DEEPEST AND MOST HEARTFELT SYMPATHY. I
WOULD ALSO LIKE TO EXTEND MY
CONDOLENCES, THROUGH AMBASSADOR ITANI,
TO THE FAMILIES OF OUR LOYAL LEBANESE
EMPLOYEES WHO PERISHED IN THIS TRAGIC
EVENT, ALONG WITH THEIR AMERICAN
COLLEAGUES. WE OWE YOUR LOVED ONES A
GREAT DEBT. THEY SERVED THEIR NATION
WITH TALENT, ENERGY, COURAGE AND
COMMITMENT.

THEY HONORED US WITH THEIR DEDICATION,
AND WE OWE THEM OUR GRATITUDE AND
RESPECT. THE SORROW YOU FEEL IS SHARED
BY THE ENTIRE NATION. BUT SO, TOO, IS
YOUR PRIDE.

        THESE GALLANT AMERICANS -- AND YES
THEY WERE GALLANT -- THEY UNDERSTOOD THE
DANGER THEY FACED, YET THEY WILLINGLY
WENT TO BEIRUT. THEY WERE ATTACKED
BECAUSE THEY REPRESENTED US. THE BLAST
THAT ENDED THEIR LIVES WAS INTENDED AS
AN ASSAULT ON ALL OF US, ON OUR COUNTRY
AND OUR WAY OF LIFE. BUT FREE PEOPLE
ARE NOT DETERRED BY SUCH COWARDLY ACTS
OF TERRORISM, AND WE WILL NOT BE
DIVERTED FROM THE HONORABLE ENDEAVOR OF
PROMOTING PEACE, SECURITY, AND
FREEDOM -- WHICH IS THE REASON FOR OUR
PRESENCE IN THE TROUBLED COUNTRY OF
LEBANON.

Memorial service for Marines killed in Beirut

catastrophe in Beirut. "Part of it was my idea—a good part of it," he told me in 1990, speaking of the decision to send the Marines to Lebanon.

But on October 23, 1983, there was no time to mourn or reflect. The day before the bombing the Organization of Eastern Caribbean States, a group of six former British colonies, had requested U.S. military aid to restore "peace and stability" in the island nation of Grenada. A renegade faction of Premier Maurice Bishop's Marxist party had taken control of the government, held Bishop under house arrest for six days, and then, on October 19, murdered him. With Grenada in anarchy, its neighbors turned to the United States.

Long before Bishop's murder, Reagan had been worried about Grenada. During a visit to Barbados in April 1982, he was warned by Caribbean leaders that Grenada could become a communist beachhead in the region. Reagan responded with a bristling speech in which he said that Grenada "bears the Soviet and Cuban trademark, which means that it will attempt to spread the virus [of communism] among its neighbors." On March 23, 1983, the speech in which he unveiled the Strategic Defense Initiative, Reagan displayed an aerial photo of a 10,000-foot airport runway on Grenada that was being constructed by Cuban laborers. When the runway was finished, he said, it could be used by Libya and other U.S. foes to deliver arms to the Sandinista government in Nicaragua.

The request for assistance from the Caribbean countries gave Reagan a chance to do something about Grenada, and he jumped at it. Contingency planning had begun soon after Bishop's murder; a Marine battalion and naval task force led by the carrier *Independence* that was headed for Lebanon was diverted to Grenada. Reagan, back in Washington, approved plans for the intervention on October 24. After informing congressional leaders, he called British prime minister Margaret Thatcher, who strongly opposed the invasion. But Reagan had no intention of calling it off, not even for his most trusted international ally. At 5:36 A.M. on October 25, 400 Marines from the helicopter carrier *Guam* landed on Grenada's western shore. Thirty-six minutes later, U.S. Army Rangers parachuted onto the uncompleted runway on the southeastern tip of the 133-square mile island. The Rangers encountered unexpected heavy antiaircraft fire and resistance on the ground from Cuban soldiers and members of the labor battalion building the airstrip. It took two days to subdue these outnumbered Cubans; elsewhere there was little resistance. The attacking forces captured Bishop's killers and found an immense cache of arms. U.S. casualties were 19 killed and 115 wounded in a force of 5,000, while 59 of the 800 Cuban defenders were killed and another 25 wounded. The rest surrendered and were returned to Cuba. Forty-five Grenadians were killed and 337 wounded.

Reagan initially justified the invasion to Congress and the American people as a rescue of Americans on Grenada, especially the 800 students at the St. George's School of Medicine. Critics of the intervention ridiculed the notion that these Americans were in danger, but a majority of the American people, with the memory of the Iranian hostage crisis still fresh, accepted Reagan's explanation. So did the evacuated students, several of whom kissed the tarmac when they arrived in Charleston, South Carolina.

But while the action in Grenada was popular, Congress and many Americans remained in an uproar over Lebanon. Senator Ernest Hollings of South Carolina, a Democrat who had often given Reagan the benefit of the doubt, said that the Beirut bombing demonstrated the "stupidity of the original decision" to send the Marines to Lebanon. "They do not have a mission," he said. "If they were put there to fight, there are too few. If they were put there to die, there are too many." In the House, Speaker Tip O'Neill, who had supplied crucial bipartisan backing for deployment of the

Marines, changed his mind and called for their withdrawal. Polls showed that most Americans agreed with him. These Americans included the "two Bakers"—Reagan's White House chief of staff James Baker and Senate Majority leader Howard Baker—both of whom worried that the continued presence of the Marines in Lebanon would become a heavy political liability in the 1984 elections.

Reagan clung stubbornly to the view that the Marines were usefully deployed in Lebanon. In a nationally televised speech on October 27, he wove together the downing of the KAL plane, the Grenada action, and the Beirut bombing and blamed them all on the Soviet Union and its surrogates. Defying his critics, he said Lebanon was of "strategic importance" and described the U.S. mission as successful despite the loss of the Marines.

But Reagan's position was untenable in the face of three events and the increasing restiveness of Republicans who were up for reelection. The first event was a retaliatory air raid on a barracks in the Lebanese town of Baalbek that was the headquarters of the Iranian Revolutionary Guard. This was a problematic target—indeed, General Vessey warned that U.S. planes could be lost—but the options were limited. Reagan's advisers, led by Weinberger, opposed any retaliation likely to cause heavy civilian casualties, as the Israelis had inflicted in bombing Beirut, and the president agreed. So it became Baalbek or nothing. On December 4, twenty-three U.S. aircraft from the carriers *Independence* and *Kennedy* bombed the barracks. Syrian antiaircraft fire downed two A-6 bombers, killing a pilot and capturing a bombardier, who was later released. The Syrians lost only two gun emplacements and a radar building and scored a propaganda coup.

The next event was a report by Admiral Robert Long, who headed a Defense Department investigation of the Beirut bombing. The report blamed Marine commanders for lax security at the bombed-out headquarters building. It skirted direct criticism of the president but said the administration had relied too much on military options without paying "clear recognition" to changing political conditions in Lebanon or the threat of terrorism—a point that critics of the deployment had made before the bombing. The White House delayed this report for several days before releasing an edited version on December 28, just after Christmas. But in any version on any day the Long report was ammunition for those who wanted the Marines withdrawn from Lebanon.

The final event was the disintegration of the Lebanese Army and the collapse of Amin Gemayel's government. On February 2, Shiite militia overran two Lebanese Army positions. On February 5, the government fell. Reagan left the next day for a sentimental journey to Dixon, Illinois, and a celebration of his seventy-third birthday. From there, he headed to Las Vegas, Nevada, for two speeches prior to a vacation at his ranch. In his absence, Vice President Bush on February 7 chaired a National Security Planning Group meeting in the White House, where Weinberger argued that the remaining Marines in Lebanon faced the danger of new terrorist attacks. The situation in Lebanon was now becoming worse by the hour, and Weinberger finally had the support he needed in his long campaign to "redeploy" the Marines. James Baker backed him. So did McFarlane, who had replaced William Clark as national security adviser, and become disillusioned with the unwillingness of the Lebanon Army to fight. Bush went along, leaving Shultz as the only holdout. After Reagan's second speech in Las Vegas, he went to a holding room at the airport, where Bush reported to him on the meeting and presented the withdrawal of the Marines as a "redeployment." Reagan agreed, reluctantly, that there was no other choice.

Reagan never did use the word "withdrawal." A White House statement said the Marines were being redeployed from Beirut "to their ships offshore." But the ships sailed away, never to return, after a farewell bombardment by the battleship *New Jersey*, which fired 288 shells from its 16-inch guns on Shiite camps, towns, and hillsides. The bombing—inaccurate because there were no forward spotters on the ground—killed an undetermined number of civilians and infuriated Shiite militants, who vowed revenge.

The removal of the Marines from harm's way eliminated the most substantial barrier to Reagan's reelection. The nation was prosperous—it was "Morning Again in America," according to the Republican campaign theme—and Reagan was popular. In fact, he was the only president since Dwight Eisenhower in 1956 who was unopposed for nomination. The Democrats were not similarly united. Walter Mondale of Minnesota, a traditional Democrat and vice

The New Jersey *the year before going to the Middle East*

president under Jimmy Carter, faced a stronger than anticipated challenge from "new Democrat" Gary Hart, a Colorado senator. Mondale prevailed after losing several crucial
primaries, including Ohio and California. In his acceptance
speech at the Democratic National Convention in San Francisco, Mondale promised to raise taxes if he was elected. He
hoped to make the point that a tax increase would be necessary no matter who won; instead, he painted himself as a
tax-increaser and made himself an easy political target for
Republicans.

Reagan's campaign meanwhile took advantage of his
performing skills upon the presidential stage. His campaign
rallies featured youthful flag-waving audiences that interrupted his speeches with chants of "U.S.A.! U.S.A.!" in emu-

At the Olympic Games in Los Angeles, July 28, 1984

lation of that summer's patriotic refrain at the Olympic Games in Los Angeles. But Reagan's most celebrated—and carefully staged—event was not a campaign rally but a June 6 commemoration in Normandy, France, of the D-Day landings forty years earlier in which the Western allies took the first bloody steps in liberating Western Europe from Nazi rule. Equipped with a superb speech crafted by speechwriter Peggy Noonan, Reagan spoke at Pointe du Hoc to aging U.S. Rangers who in 1944 had scaled the 130-foot cliff with grappling hooks and ladders borrowed from the London Fire Department:

> Behind me [Reagan said] is a memorial that symbolizes the Ranger daggers that were thrust into the top of these cliffs. And before me are the men who put them there. These are the boys of Pointe du Hoc. These are the men who took the cliffs. These are the champions who helped free a continent. These are the heroes who helped end a war.

Many of the Rangers wept when they heard these words, and a number of reporters and Secret Service agents also made no attempt to hide their feelings. Reagan hit every grace note, paying tribute to the other Allied soldiers who had died in France and recalling the "great losses suffered by the Russian people." Later, he knelt in prayer with Nancy Reagan at the Omaha Beach chapel and toured the Normandy American cemetery, where a sea of white crosses and Stars of David mark the graves of 9,386 U.S. servicemen. Then he gave another speech at Omaha Beach, where he quoted General Omar Bradley as saying that every man who set foot on the beach that day was a hero. Reagan read from a letter written by an Army veteran who was in the first assault wave and survived. He had hoped to return after the war but never did. When he was dying of cancer three decades later, his daughter had promised her father she would return and put flowers on the graves. She had done

that this day. When Reagan read from the letter, it was his
turn to fight back tears.

.   .   .

Reagan's reelection was rarely in doubt after D-Day,
1984. His poll numbers soared after his appearance
in Normandy, and Mondale could not cut into the lead. The
Democratic nominee argued that Reagan had a "secret plan"
to raise taxes and sniped at the Strategic Defense Initiative;
Reagan wanted to respond to him but at the advice of his
strategists stuck to his "Morning Again in America" script
and ignored his opponent. Reagan had, however, agreed to
two debates. The Democrats saw these encounters as their
only chance to change the dynamics of the campaign.

The first of the debates was on October 7, a Sunday, in
Louisville, Kentucky. That morning Reagan pollster Richard
Wirthlin's private trackings and *The Washington Post*–ABC
poll gave the president identical 55–37 percent leads.
Reagan was confident. He had, after all, secured the nomi-
nation in 1980 in large part because he had demolished
George Bush at the Nashua debate, and he had clinched the
election in his debate with Jimmy Carter. But, unlike 1980,
Reagan was sequestered and out of practice in 1984, while
Mondale was sharp because he had been debating Hart and
other candidates in the Democratic primaries. In the
Louisville debate Mondale combined aggressiveness with
occasional expressions of deference to Reagan and the presidency, the way one might treat a valued uncle who was no
longer up to his job. He even borrowed the line that Reagan
had used so effectively against Carter—"There you go
again"—in the process of accusing Reagan of trying to cut
$20 billion from Medicare. The charge was inaccurate, since
Reagan had barely touched the program, but it shook him
nonetheless. Throughout the debate, Reagan seemed off
stride and had difficulty marshaling facts and figures. When
the candidates left the stage, both of them knew that Mon-

dale had succeeded in raising the issue of whether Reagan
was too old to be president for the first time since the 1980
primaries.

One of Reagan's great strengths as an actor and a politician was that he never fooled himself about his
performances. While his press agents were
circulating among the media in Louisville
trying to convince reporters that Reagan
had done just fine, the president was
telling his strategist, Stuart Spencer, that
he had been a "terrible" flop. Reagan's
assessment was promptly confirmed by a
number of focus groups. On October 9, the lead
story in the *Wall Street Journal* was headlined: "New
Question in Race: Is Oldest U.S. President Now Showing
His Age?"

In this crisis, Nancy Reagan once again came to the
rescue. Knowing that her husband needed his confidence

Debating Walter Mondale

restored, she put the blame on Reagan's briefers for his performance. She realized that her husband had not mastered
his briefing books but believed that his aides took credit
when he did well and ought to accept responsibility when he
did not. In preparation for the second debate, Spencer and
Paul Laxalt spent private time with Reagan, telling him how
good he was. Richard Nixon also wrote an encouraging letter and, since the subject of the second debate was foreign
policy, sent a long memo that Reagan found useful. Finally,
media consultant Roger Ailes, known as "Dr. Feelgood" to
the staff, was brought in to reassure Reagan.

It was just what Reagan needed. At his second debate
with Mondale, in Kansas City on October 21, Nancy
Reagan smiled at him from her first-row seat, and Reagan
was his usual, confident self. He held his own in discussing
foreign policy. Then, thirty minutes into the debate, Henry
Trewhitt of the *Baltimore Sun* recalled that President
Kennedy had functioned for days with little sleep during the
Cuban missile crisis and asked Reagan if he had any doubt
he could function in such circumstances.

"Not at all, Mr. Trewhitt," Reagan answered with a trace
of a smile, "and I want you to know that also I will not
make age an issue of this campaign. I am not going to
exploit, for political purposes, my opponent's youth and
inexperience."

Everyone laughed, including Mondale, but any lingering
suspense about the outcome of the campaign was over. As
David Broder observed the next day in *The Washington Post,*
"It well may have been that the biggest barrier to Reagan's
reelection was swept away in that moment."

On election day, in one of the great political landslides
in history, Reagan won 59 percent of the popular vote and
525 electoral votes to 10 for Mondale, who carried only the
District of Columbia and (narrowly) his home state of Minnesota. Reagan won a majority in every region and age
group, in cities, suburbs, towns, and rural areas, and in every
occupational category except the unemployed. He won the

votes of 62 percent of men and 54 percent of women, the
latter an improvement from his 47 percent showing in 1980,
even though Mondale set a precedent by choosing Geraldine
Ferraro as his running mate. The "gender gap" about which
Democrats had talked during the campaign proved damag-
ing to Mondale, who had more troubles with male voters
than Reagan did with female voters. Six of every ten independents voted for Reagan, as did one in four registered
Democrats. Reagan won a majority of Protestants,
Catholics, and every ethnic group except Hispanics, where
his 44 percent showing was the best ever for a Republican
presidential candidate. Two of every three Jewish voters cast
their ballots for Mondale, as did nearly nine of ten African
Americans.

To the Democrats, the most surprising result was
Reagan's overwhelming popularity among the youngest voters, those 18 to 24. He won 60 percent of this group, again
a record showing for a Republican presidential candidate.
Several political analysts decided that Reagan's popularity
among young voters reflected his unbending optimism. In
his campaign speeches Reagan talked of "going to the stars"
and said that America's best days were in the future, not the
past. He was the nation's oldest president, but he had a
young man's view of America.

Reagan's optimism pervaded America in 1984, the best
in history for incumbent politicians. Republicans retained
control of the Senate and added seventeen seats in the
House, wiping out most of the Democratic gains of 1982.
The nation was prosperous and at peace, and Americans of
all persuasions talked of possibilities rather than failures and
limits. In his 1980 campaign, Reagan had effectively borrowed a line from Franklin D. Roosevelt: "Are you better off
now than you were four years ago?" Reagan's opponents did
not ask this question in 1984. They knew the answer.

10

Some 37 new military bases have been built — there were only 13 during the Somoza years.

Nicaragua's army numbers 25,000 men supported by a militia of 50,000. It is the largest army in Central America supplemented by 8000 "quote" Cuban advisors. It is equipped with the most modern weapons, Soviet tanks, planes, armored vehicles, artillery, helicopters. There are additional hundreds of advisors from the Soviet U., East Germany, Libya & the P.L.O. We have 55 mil. trainers in El Salvador.

The history of Central America has been one of revolutions in which the revolutionary forces simply exchange one set of rulers for another and the peoples plight remains the same; hopeless, HELPLESS, hungry. This is true of the Sandinista revolution in Nicaragua. Everyone had reason to believe it would be otherwise because the people at virtually all levels came together in support of the revolution. But no sooner was victory achieved than a small clique ousted others who had been part of the revolution from having any voice in govt.

Humberto Ortega declared Marxism-Leninism would be their guide and so it is. Contrary to propaganda the Guerillas are not die hard Somoza survivors. They are led by and for the most part are participants in the Sandinista revolution who have been denied any part in governing apparently because they truly wanted democracy for Nicaragua & still do. Others are Miskito Indians (fighting for their lives.) By contrast the govt. of El Salvador duly elected by the people and making every effort to guarantee democracy, free labor unions, freedom of religion, & a free press is under attack by Guerillas dedicated to the same philosophy that prevails in Nicaragua, Cuba & the Soviet Union. It is the ultimate in hypocrisy for the unelected Nicaraguan govt. to charge that we seek their overthrow when they are doing everything they can to bring down the elected govt. of El Salvador.

If the story of the Sandinistas sounds familiar

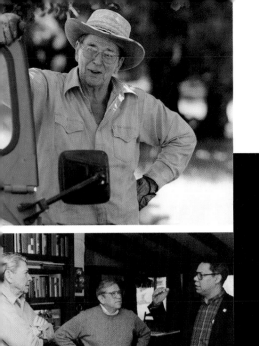

THE TEST OF
TERRORISM

P ower is poison," wrote Henry Adams nearly a century
ago, with President Theodore Roosevelt in mind. "Its
effect on Presidents [has] been always tragic, chiefly as an
almost insane excitement at first, and a worse reaction after-
wards; but also because no mind is so well balanced as to
bear the strain of seizing unlimited force without habit or
knowledge of it." The illusion of power is greatest after a
one-sided election, which is perhaps why presidential landslides are often unkind to the winners. Riding high after his
first reelection in 1936, Franklin Roosevelt tried to expand a
Supreme Court that had been invalidating New Deal laws.
After Lyndon Johnson's landslide victory in 1964, he sent
half a million troops to Vietnam. Richard Nixon's landslide
in 1972 encouraged the Watergate cover-up. And the Iran-
contra affair was in some ways a byproduct of the Reagan
landslide of 1984.

The first result of Reagan's 1984 landslide was an
improbable changing of the White House guard. It was
spurred by Treasury Secretary Donald Regan, who suspected
the White House staff of undermining his plan for tax
reform. With Reagan's blessing, White House chief of staff
James Baker visited the Treasury to soothe Regan's feelings.
This led to a conversation in which Regan and Baker sur-
prisingly agreed to swap jobs. Reagan passively accepted the
arrangement. In addition to Baker, Reagan would soon lose
his closest aide, Mike Deaver, who left the White House to
become a lobbyist.

These changes deprived Reagan of key advisers who had
been instrumental in the successes of his second term as governor and his first as president. The original White House
"troika" of Baker, Deaver, and Ed Meese had complimented
one another. Baker was focused and political, Deaver understood the Reagans, and Meese had a knack for explaining
complex issues to Reagan in plain terms. Meese was gone,
too. Reagan had named him to replace Attorney General
William French Smith, who had spent the first term living

in a Washington hotel and wanted to return to his law firm
and Los Angeles lifestyle. William Clark, another Californ-
ian upon whom Reagan depended, had in 1984 replaced
Secretary of Interior James Watt, who resigned under fire
after insulting disabled people and various ethnic groups.
Clark did a capable job at Interior, but he and Meese had
their hands full in their cabinet posts—as did Baker at Treasury—and none was available for daily counsel to Reagan.
The upshot was a White House staff with limited knowledge of Reagan's modes of behavior—a staff the president
barely knew.

The limitations of the new staff became apparent in an
early symbolic stumble that ironically stemmed from the
symbolic triumph of the 1984 D-Day commemorative cere-
monies in Normandy. German Chancellor Helmut Kohl
was unhappy that he had been excluded from this ceremony.
When he visited the White House on November 30, 1984,
Kohl gave a tearful account of how he and French President
François Mitterrand had visited the graves of German and
French soldiers who had fallen at Verdun in World War I.
Kohl asked Reagan to participate in a similar ceremony of
reconciliation honoring the military dead of World War II,
and the president agreed. The ceremony was tentatively set
for May 8, 1985, the thirtieth anniversary of the Nazi sur-
render in Europe.

The devil was in the details of this plan. Kohl left the
choice of a cemetery to the Reagan administration. In February, an advance team led by Deaver on his final White
House trip found a picturesque cemetery at Bitburg, where
snow covered the graves of German and allied soldiers.
Deaver instructed the U.S. embassy to determine that the
cemetery contained "nothing embarrassing"; the German
chief of protocol in turn assured the embassy that "no war

FOLLOWING TWO PAGES: *Taking time out for an exchange of views on disaster relief*

Andy Smith

400 London Pride Road

Irmo, South Carolina   29063

April 18, 1984

Dear Mr. President,

   My name is Andy Smith. I am a seventh grade student at Irmo

Middle School, in Irmo, South Carolina.

   Today my mother declared my bedroom a disaster area. I would like

to request federal funds to hire a crew to clean up my room. I am

prepared to provide the initial funds if you will privide matching funds

for this project.

   I know you will be fair when you consider my request. I will be

awaiting your reply.

Sincerely yours,

Andy Smith
Andy Smith

To Andy Smith 400 London Pride Rd.
Irmo So. Carolina 29063

Dear Andy,

I'm ~~sorry~~ to be so late in answering your letter but as you know I've been in China and found your letter here upon my return.

Your application for disaster relief has been duly noted but I must point out one technical problem; the authority declaring the disaster is supposed to make the request. In this case your mother.

However setting that aside I'll have to point out the larger ~~part~~ problem of available funds. This has been a year of disasters, 53? hurricanes as of May 4th and several more since, numerous floods, forest fires, drought in Texas and a number of earthquakes. What I'm getting at is that funds are dangerously low.

May I make a suggestion? This administration, believing that govt. has done many things that could better be done by volunteers at the local level, has sponsored a Private Sector Initiative Program, calling upon people to practice volunteerism in the solving of a number of local problems.

Your situation appears to be a natural. I'm sure your Mother was fully justified in proclaiming your room a disaster. Therefore you are in an excellent position to launch another volunteer program to go along with the more than 3000 already underway in our nation's — congratulations.

Give my best regards to your Mother
Ronald OR

criminals" were buried there. It was a misleading assurance. Among the dead at Bitburg were forty-nine SS soldiers, including SS Staff Sergeant Otto Franz Begel, who had been awarded the German Cross for killing ten American soldiers. When the media reported in April that SS soldiers were buried in Bitburg, outraged Jewish and veterans groups urged Reagan to cancel the visit. They were joined by Reagan's good friend, Charles Z. Wick, director of the U.S. Information Agency, who warned that the Soviets would exploit the visit for propaganda purposes.

Reagan was sensitive to these concerns and might have extricated himself from Bitburg had he been surrounded by adept advisers. Reverend Billy Graham told me that Reagan asked him if he should go through with Bitburg; Graham suggested he find an alternative site. But Regan and White House communications director Patrick Buchanan insisted that the administration should not give in to what Buchanan described as "pressure of the Jews." Realizing that Reagan was wavering, Kohl called the White House on April 19 to make the case for Bitburg. Instead of protecting Reagan, as Jim Baker would have done, Regan handed him the telephone. Kohl became emotional, and Reagan told the German chancellor he would honor his commitment. The same day, Reagan awarded the Congressional Gold Medal to Holocaust survivor Elie Wiesel, who urged him to find an alternative site, saying, "Your place is with the victims of the SS." Reagan was moved by the plea, but he had given his word to Kohl, and he would keep it.

In retrospect, it is clear that Kohl took advantage of Reagan and his inexperienced staff. Kohl knew all along, as Reagan did not, that members of the Waffen SS, the SS forces attached to military units, were buried in virtually every German military cemetery. One of the few genuine alternatives (suggested to Reagan by Reverend Graham, who attributed the idea to NBC's John Chancellor) was a visit to the Konrad Adenauer memorial, but Kohl rejected this sen-

sible compromise. Kohl and the White House staff had
handed the president a public relations disaster and left
Reagan to do his best to redeem it.

Reagan almost did. At Deaver's suggestion he visited
Bergen-Belsen, a Nazi concentration camp where 60,000
persons, half of them Jews, had died. Reagan was shaken
as he toured the camp and saw photographs of stacks of
bodies—he kept his arm around Nancy Reagan, a reporter
wrote, "partly to steer her, and, partly, it appeared, to derive
some support from her presence." Afterward, he gave a life-
affirming speech written by Ken Khachigian, who had been
brought in from California. Reagan read from the diary of
Anne Frank, who had died at Bergen-Belsen and mourned

Visiting Bitburg

the death of Jews who were killed "for no reason other than their existence":

> Everywhere here [Reagan said] are memories—pulling us, touching us, making us understand that they can never be erased. They beckon us through the endless stretches of our heart to the knowing commitment that the life of each individual can change the world and make it better.
>
> We're all witnesses; we share the glistening hope that rests in every human soul. Hope leads us, if we're prepared to trust it, toward what our President Lincoln called the better angels of our nature. And then, rising above all this cruelty, out of this tragic and nightmarish time, beyond the anguish, the pain, the suffering for all time, we can and must pledge: Never again.

Reagan gave this speech on May 5. The same day he was joined by ninety-year-old General Matthew Ridgeway for the wreath-laying ceremony at the Bitburg cemetery. Ridgeway had led the U.S. Eighty-second Airborne Division in the war against Nazi Germany and volunteered to help lay the wreath. His presence did not silence the critics, but it made the ceremony easier for Reagan to endure.

.   .   .

Reagan faced two significant foreign policy challenges at the beginning of his second term. The first, and more significant, was cashing in on the U.S. military buildup by engaging the Soviet leadership in negotiations. The second, and more frustrating, was international terrorism, some of it

FACING PAGE: *The speech at Bergen-Belsen sent to Archbishop O'Connor*

THE WHITE HOUSE

Office of the Press Secretary
(Bitburg Air Base, Federal Republic of Germany)

For Immediate Release   May 5, 1985

REMARKS OF THE PRESIDENT
AT BERGEN-BELSEN CONCENTRATION CAMP

Federal Republic of Germany

...ellor Kohl and honored guests. This
... more than remind us of the
... at we have seen makes
... f us can fully
... ed by the victims of

...ond anything that we can
...nan, an evil that
...on, was uniquely
... grim abyss of these

...se death was inflicted for
... Their pain was borne only
...he God in their prayers.
...lics and Protestants.

...d his evil were
People were brought
To go unfed when
...he whim struck --
...e was around them

...oughts. And that
...stalag? All was
...th of life's
...endid ache of
... Try to think of
... emotional and

the commandant of
...e all, we're struck
...ehensible horror.
...ver understand as
... we feel what the
...l as long as they
live.

Your Excellency

I'm taking the liberty of sending you copies of the talks I gave at Belsen Concentration Camp & at our airbase in Bitburg. Making that trip was something I felt I had to do.

Nancy's brother Dr. Davis has told us of your very kind words about us & your prayers. Please know how very grateful we are. Sincerely Ronald Reagan

What we've felt and are expressing with words cannot
convey the suffering that they endured. That is why history will
forever brand what happened as the Holocaust.

state-sponsored, against which Reagan had promised swift
and effective retribution. A little more than a month after
Bitburg this resolve was put to the test. On the morning of
June 14, 1985, TWA Flight 847 took off from Athens,
bound for Rome, with 153 passengers and crew aboard,
including 135 Americans. Once aloft, the plane was
hijacked by two grenade-wielding Arabs, who shouted,
"Marines" and "New Jersey." This was not a reference to the
state, as terrified passengers assumed, but to the deadly
shelling of Shiite positions by the battleship *New Jersey* as the
Marines pulled out of Lebanon in 1984. The hijackers
forced the pilot to fly the plane to Beirut, then Algiers, then
back to Beirut, where they brutally beat and shot to death
U.S. Navy diver Robert Dean Stethem, whose body was
dumped on the airport tarmac. After refueling, the plane
was flown again to Algiers and then a final time to Beirut.
Most of the passengers were released in one city or the other,
but when the terror-filled odyssey of TWA 847 ended on
June 16, thirty-nine passengers and crew were held as
hostages in Lebanon, most of them under control of Amal
Shiite leader Nabih Berri.

   The hijackers were not mindless terrorists. Their mission
was to force Israel to release 700 young Shiites who had
been taken captive for "security offenses" during the Israeli
invasion of Lebanon and held in a prison in Haifa in violation of the Geneva Convention. The hijackers had struck at
the United States, Israel's ally, because lax security at international airports made Americans vulnerable targets. To
Reagan, the captivity of the TWA 847 hostages was a potent
reminder of how President Carter had been manipulated by
the takeover of the U.S. embassy in Tehran. Both events had
been media spectaculars, dominating the news. Reagan had
a sure-footed sense of what to do when in the public spotlight; he decided that, unlike Carter, he would maintain his
normal schedule. Privately, however, Reagan was seething at
the murder of Stethem. He also identified with the hostages,

who sent the president a letter urging him not to take military action but to pressure the Israelis to free the 700 Shiite prisoners held in Haifa.

The letter put Reagan on the spot. Any military action in Lebanon was risky and probably unnecessary, since Israel was willing to free the Shiite prisoners if asked to do so by the United States. Reagan left negotiations to the diplomats and continued his business-as-usual campaign. This took him, on June 28, to Illinois, where he gave two speeches at a high school in Chicago Heights. As an add-on, the White House staff scheduled a meeting in the school library between Reagan and family members of the TWA hostages, who had been clamoring to see the president. Don Regan was oblivious to the risks of this meeting, which increased when the White House yielded to the demands of a local Republican congressman and allowed relatives of Father Lawrence Jenco to attend the gathering. Jenco, a member of a closely knit Catholic family, had been taken hostage in Lebanon on January 8, 1985, the same day Regan and Baker had agreed to swap jobs. The State Department had kept the Jencos away from the president, but they made the most of their opportunity this day. Two of Jenco's brothers asked Reagan why he was willing to deal with Israel to free the TWA hostages but not their brother. Reagan, defensive and uncomfortable, said he was doing the best he could. After a half hour of this, the son of a TWA hostage said to Reagan, "Mr. President, I don't know how you can stand your job." On that plaintive note, Regan finally pulled the president away.

The TWA hostages were released two days later after diplomatic pressure that included the intervention of Syrian President Hafez Assad, whom Reagan had phoned and written, and blunt suggestions from national security adviser Bud McFarlane to Berri, a lawyer who had lived in the United States, that he would be held accountable if the hostages were harmed. But Reagan's encounter in the school library had started him thinking about the plight of the seven Americans, including Father Jenco, who had been kidnapped one by one in Lebanon in 1984 and early 1985. On July 2, Reagan laid a wreath on Stethem's grave at Arlington National Cemetery. Then he went to Andrews Air Force Base to welcome home the TWA passengers and pledge that Stethem's killers would be brought to justice and the seven Americans held hostage in Lebanon freed. "The homecoming won't be complete until all have come home," the president said.

This was easier to say than to do. The United States had identified Stethem's killers, but they had escaped into Lebanon. Other terrorists were also beyond reach. On June 19, Salvadoran guerrillas attacked a sidewalk café frequented by off-duty U.S. servicemen in San Salvador, killing thirteen people, among them four U.S. Marines. The same day a bomb went off in the airport in Frankfurt, West Germany, killing three people and wounding forty-two. At a news conference the day before the San Salvadoran attack Reagan put himself on record against killing civilians to combat terrorists, saying this would be "an act of terrorism" itself. After the Marines were killed, Reagan's political advisers nonetheless urged him to retaliate. The president asked McFarlane if there were guerrilla staging areas that could be targeted in El Salvador. Not without causing large-scale civilian casualties, McFarlane told him. Reagan refused to allow retaliation.

Reagan did not respond militarily to terrorism until April 14, 1986, when U.S. Air Force and Navy bombers based in England struck the Libyan cities of Tripoli and Benghazi in retaliation for the bombing of a West Berlin disco where a U.S. serviceman had died. An intelligence intercept had identified Libya as responsible. The planes dropped ninety 2,000-pound bombs, at least two of which hit the barracks of Libyan strongman Moammar Qaddafi, killing Qaddafi's adopted two-year-old-daughter and wounding two of his sons. The Libyan leader was sleeping in

a tent outside and escaped unharmed. The raid was popular
in the United States but killed scores of civilians. Reagan, a
reluctant warrior when military action endangered civilian
life, did not order any follow-up attacks. The Libyan bombing, never repeated, was an exception in a presidency notable
for its respect for human life. In 1988, as the United States
maneuvered to oust Panamanian dictator Manuel Noriega,
Reagan vetoed an invasion he said would lead to heavy U.S.
and civilian casualties. The invasion, carried out in 1989 by
President Bush, proved Reagan right.

But Reagan's scruples were no guide to freeing the
Americans held hostage in Lebanon in 1985. Their fate was
entangled with U.S. policy toward Iran, which was engaged
with Iraq in a bloody war. U.S. policymakers, including Secretary of State Shultz and Defense Secretary Weinberger,
tilted toward Iraq, fearing that an Iranian victory would
interrupt the flow of oil from the Persian Gulf. With the
State Department taking the lead, the administration on
December 14, 1983, launched Operation Staunch to discourage other nations from sending arms to Iran. This was a
boon to Iraq, which had ample Soviet weapons. By the summer of 1984, war losses and the pressure of Operation
Staunch had made Iran desperate for weapons. The CIA was
flooded with offers from Iranians and Iranian exiles offering
intelligence information in return for antitank missiles or
helicopter gunships. These offers intrigued William Casey,
the director of central intelligence.

Casey had a strategic view of Iran. As a student of history, he was familiar with the CIA's role in toppling an Iranian national leader in 1953 and bringing the shah to power.
Casey wanted to revive that influence. He was also concerned with the fate of William Buckley, the CIA station
chief in Beirut, who had been kidnapped on March 16,

FOLLOWING TWO PAGES: *Deaver's resignation*

THE WHITE HOUSE

WASHINGTON

May 10, 1985

Dear Mr. President:

It is with sincere mixed emotions that I write this
letter of resignation as Deputy Chief of Staff of
the White House.

During these four and one half years I've experienced
the most personally rewarding and satisfying time
of my life.

Probably the most exciting part of this experience
for me has been the thrill of seeing you, Mr. President,
rise to the great challenges under difficult circumstances and achieve success.

To say I'm grateful for this opportunity falls way
short of my true feelings. I'll always remember these
years with fondness and pride.

Please remember, I'm always there if either you or
Nancy need me.

God bless you both.

                              Sincerely,

                              Mike

                              MICHAEL K. DEAVER
                              Assistant to the President
                              Deputy Chief of Staff

Dear Mike

You know I've accepted your resignation ~~verbally~~ orally but suppose I have to put something down on paper — after all this is Wash. The only place I haven't accepted it is in my heart and there I never will.

I've come to the conclusion that Nancy & I will both agree you will ~~forcibly~~ leave the West Wing. You will no longer bear a govt. title. You will not actually handle such things as schedule, trips etc. But that's as far as we go. You will continue to be a part of our lives. We will have concern one for the other and refuse surgery that would in any way remove you from a relationship that is part of our life support system. In return we will continue to be eternally grateful.

Sincerely Ron

1984, and was one of the Americans being held in Lebanon. Casey feared that Buckley was being tortured to reveal secrets, including the names of CIA agents in the region. This concern made Casey receptive to any initiative that might result in his release.

Meanwhile, national security adviser McFarlane was exploring a deal in which the United States would secretly supply weapons to a shadowy group of supposedly "moderate" Iranians in return for their influence in securing the release of the hostages. McFarlane knew that the deal involved a certain amount of wishful thinking, but no one seemed to have a better idea, and the national security adviser also shared Casey's view that the United States and Iran could ultimately forge a strategic relationship. He was encouraged by the Israelis, who in turn were motivated by a concern that Iraq, their most dangerous enemy, might win the Iran-Iraq war. These strands of national self-interest, power politics, and humanitarian concerns were woven together in an initiative that became the "Iran" part of the Iran-contra affair.

Shultz and Weinberger opposed the initiative. They made three arguments: that it could damage relations with U.S. allies by doing what the Reagan administration had asked them not to do in Operation Staunch; that trading hostages for weapons would encourage additional hostage-taking; and that if the deal became public it would seem as if Reagan were reneging on his promise not to negotiate with terrorists. Reagan conceded the first point but disagreed on the other two. In his mind, dealing with middlemen to secure the release of the hostages—which is how McFarlane presented the plan to him—was different from dealing directly with the kidnappers. Later, Reagan said in his diary that Shultz and Weinberger were right but that he had not believed them at the time.

The initiative was kept alive with many twists and turns until December 1985 when McFarlane, exhausted from

THE WHITE HOUSE
WASHINGTON

MEETING WITH CAROLINE KENNEDY AND JOHN F. KENNEDY, JR.

    DATE: Monday, March 11, 1985
    LOCATION: Oval Office
    TIME: 4:30 p.m. (15 minutes)
    FROM: Max L. Friedersdorf
              M. B. Oglesby, Jr.

I. Purpose

    To comply with the request of Senator Edward (Ted)
    Kennedy (D-MA) that you meet privately with the two
    children of the late President John F. Kennedy,
    Caroline and John, Jr.

II. Background

    Senator Kennedy spoke to the Vice President about his
    desire that his niece and nephew be allowed to meet
    privately with you to discuss the John F. Kennedy
    Library.

    Although the Senator elaborated no further, be advised
    that last June Caroline Kennedy was named to the
    library board of directors as the museum and exhibits
    chairperson. She is in charge of an effort to raise an
    $8 million endowment to update the library's exhibits.
    The library is operated by the Federal Government,
    under the auspices of the National Archives. While
    Federal funds pay for library operations and salaries,
    there is no endowment. The goal announced last June is
    to raise $8 million over 5 years. At the time of the
    announcement the library had $2.4 million already in
    hand and hoped to raise an additional $2.6 million by
    the end of this year. If the Kennedy children are here
    to ask for your assistance in this fundraising effort,
    you should make no commitment, but tell them you will
    seriously consider their request.

III. Participants

    The President
    Caroline Kennedy
    John F. Kennedy, Jr.
    Max Friedersdorf

Attachment A

SUGGESTED TALKING POINTS FOR THE MEETING
WITH CAROLINE KENNEDY AND JOHN KENNEDY, JR.

-- Caroline, John, how very good to see you.

-- Your uncle, Ted, told me you wanted to meet with me
    privately to talk about your Father and the
    Presidential library.

-- As you know, I am an admirer of the late President, and
    am pleased for this opportunity to talk with you.

    (Open discussion.) (If any assistance is requested on
    the fundraising effort for the endowment, you should
    give no commitment, but indicate you will give the
    request every condiseration.)

-- Thank you for coming to Washington to see me. I
    remember fondly my meeting with your grandmother in
    November of 1981.

                                                        -2-

IV. Press Plan

    White House photographer only.

V. Sequence of Events

    Caroline and John, Jr. arrive thru the west basement
    and are escorted to the Oval Office. The President
    greets his guests and they are seated in front of the
    fireplace for an informal discussion.

Attachment A: Talking Points

THE WHITE HOUSE
WASHINGTON

March 12, 1985

TO: DONALD REGAN
           MIKE DEAVER

FROM: MAX L. FRIEDERSDORF

SUBJECT: Presidential Meeting with
           Caroline and John Kennedy, Jr.

The purpose of yesterday's meeting between the children of
the late President and President Reagan was to invite the
President to attend a fundraiser for the Kennedy Library
endowment. The President indicated some interest in the
request and said he'd take a look at his schedule.

Caroline and John, Jr. propose holding the fundraiser at
their uncle's (Ted Kennedy) home in McLean, Virginia, and
raised the dates of June 10, 11 and 24. The President told
them to keep in touch with me, and we'd see what could be
worked out. It was my feeling that the President would
like to do this.

cc: M. B. Oglesby, Jr.
     Fred Fielding
     Fred Ryan
     Pam Turner

March 12, 1985

Dear President Reagan,

I would just like to thank you
for granting my sister and I an
opportunity to meet with you
and invite you to the library fundraiser.
    I know that you have many more
urgent matters that require your
attention so we both deeply appreciate
the time you gave us.
    I received the wonderful news today
that you will be able to come. Since
I know it was not our flawless sales
pitch that made the difference — thank
you for your sensitivity to the issue. Your
presence at the event, even for a few

minutes will help so much.
    President Reagan, you have been
enormously kind to my family over the
years. I speak on behalf of all of
us in conveying our sincere gratitude
for all you've done. This means a
great deal.

                    Sincerely yours,

                    John Kennedy

P.S. I was not one of the "invited
democrats" when you quoted my
father. I thought it was great!
Please, quote him all you want!

An example of the stages one goes through to see the president

work and differences with Don Regan, resigned. He was replaced by his deputy, Admiral John Poindexter, a former commander of a missile cruiser who disdained politics, kept the door to his office closed, and dealt with others, if at all, through his deputies or by computer message. Poindexter's inaccessibility in effect turned the initiative over to Oliver North, an adventurous Marine on the NSC staff with dreams of glory. By December 6, North had worked out a plan at once fantastic and precise that called for supplying the Iranians with 3,300 antitank missiles (known by their acronym of TOWs) and 50 HAWK antiaircraft missiles. The first American hostage would be released after receipt of the first 300 TOWs, and weapons would continue to be delivered in increments until every hostage was freed.

This plan, endorsed by McFarlane, was on the table when Reagan met with his national security advisers in the family quarters of the White House on December 7, a Saturday morning. McFarlane chaired the meeting for the last time. Also attending were Shultz, Weinberger, Regan, Poindexter, and Casey's deputy, John McMahon. Casey was traveling; so was Vice President Bush, who had opted to attend the Army-Navy football game rather than this meeting. Shultz said the initiative would "negate the whole policy" of not making "deals with terrorists." Weinberger made a lawyer's case that the plan would violate the U.S. embargo on arms to Iran as well as the Arms Export Control Act. McMahon was not authorized to make a formal recommendation, but he was openly skeptical and took particular issue with McFarlane's claim that he was dealing with Iranian "moderates." Even Don Regan, who had thought the initiative worth a try and would swing back to this view, at this crucial moment gave good advice. "Cut your losses," he said to the president.

In response to this near-united appeal to drop an ill-conceived initiative, Reagan displayed an awesome stubbornness. He was widely described as a passive president, but on

matters that he visualized in personal terms, he could show
passionate commitment. Reagan remembered his meetings
with the TWA hostages and the Jencos. He thought of
chained Americans rotting in Lebanese cells and of Buckley
being tortured. As Reagan saw it, he had a duty to free these
Americans, or at least a duty to try. Still, he made no formal
decision at this meeting other than to send McFarlane to
London to meet with North and Iranian go-betweens.
Weinberger left the White House convinced, as he told an
aide, that he and Shultz had prevailed and "this baby had
been strangled in its cradle." Shultz thought that Reagan,
while still undecided, was annoyed that he and Weinberger
had so persistently opposed the initiative.

The secretary of state was right. Over the next six weeks,
as even McFarlane began to doubt the intentions of the
Iranian "moderates," Poindexter and North kept the initiative alive. They were helped by Amiram Nir, who advised
Israeli Prime Minister Shimon Peres on issues of terrorism.
Nir's idea, endorsed by the Peres government, was that Iran
might influence Hezbollah to release the American hostages
in Lebanon if Israel agreed to release Shiite prisoners held by
the Israeli-backed Southern Lebanon Army. This was similar
to the deal that had won release of the TWA hostages, and it
intrigued Reagan. On January 6 he signed a finding prepared by Poindexter that authorized covert action to permit
the sale of weapons to Iran and the initiative secret from
Congress. On January 17 Reagan wrote in his diary that he
had "agreed to sell TOWs to Iran."

McFarlane left the White House payroll at the end of
the year, taking with him a computer that kept him elec-
tronically linked from home with Poindexter and the NSC
staff. In their farewell meeting, Reagan told McFarlane he
would like to call on him if anything came of the Iran initiative. By May 25, everything seemed ready. Bearing fake Irish
passports, McFarlane and North flew to Tehran from Tel
Aviv in an unmarked Israeli 707 loaded with one of the

Top: The president watches television reports of the Challenger *space shuttle disaster; bottom: the Peggy Noonan speech delivered January 28, 1986*

twelve pallets of HAWK spare parts that the United States had agreed to provide in return for the hostages. With them were George Cave of the CIA, an NSC staff member, a CIA radioman who set up a coded satellite link with Washington, and Amiram Nir, posing as an American. Cave, the agency's former Tehran station chief, went along because of his fluency in Farsi, the Iranian language. The delegation brought gifts of two .357 pistols and a chocolate layer cake decorated with a brass key, plus maps for conducting intelligence briefings on Iraq. Cave was reluctant to share this information but was under Casey's orders to do so.

Expectations were high after eight years of U.S.-Iran estrangement. McFarlane had been led to believe that the delegation would meet with the three highest-ranking Iranian officials below Khomeini, including Hashemi Rafsanjani, the speaker of the Iranian parliament. But no one met the plane at the airport. After an hour, an Iranian arms buyer showed up with a detachment of young Iran Revolutionary Guards, who unloaded the spare parts, took the gifts, and ate the cake. The Americans were taken downtown and lodged in the top floor of a run-down hotel that was formerly the Tehran Hilton. In four days of negotiations they never met a high-ranking official. When McFarlane demanded to speak with someone of authority, the Iranians produced Hossein Najafabadi, a member of Parliament and adviser to Rafsanjani. He said that those holding the hostages were now demanding release of seventeen terrorist bombers held in Kuwait plus Israeli withdrawal from southern Lebanon and the Golan Heights as a condition of releasing the American hostages. The delegation lacked the authority to do this, even if it had been so minded. On the final morning in Tehran, May 28, the Iranians came up with a proposal to release two hostages in exchange for the other eleven pallets of HAWK spare parts, which would be followed by release of the other hostages. While McFarlane slept, North agreed to this plan, and the plane with the spare

parts was en route from Israel even though no hostages had
been freed. When McFarlane awoke, he countermanded
North's order and sent the plane back in midflight. Release
all the hostages, McFarlane said, and the spare parts would
be sent. The Iranians refused, and the U.S. delegation flew
out of Tehran for Tel Aviv. "It was a heartbreaking disappointment for all of us," Reagan wrote in his diary.

It was during the layover at Tel Aviv before returning to
the United States that McFarlane learned that more was
involved in the Iran initiative than arms or hostages. "Don't
be too downhearted," North told him. "The one bright spot
is that we're using part of the money in those transactions
for Central America." The "bright spot" was the "contra"
side of the Iran-contra affair.

By now, the small covert force that Reagan in 1981 had
authorized at Casey's request had grown into a guerrilla
army of 7,500, operating largely in northern Nicaragua.
Reagan routinely called them "freedom fighters" and, in a
speech to a conservative conference in Washington on
March 1, 1985, hailed them as the "moral equal of our
Founding Fathers." Others,
even those who agreed with
Reagan's assertion that "Sandinista rule is a Communist
reign of terror," questioned
contra capability. Colin
Powell, then in the Pentagon and later Reagan's
national security adviser,
coolly described the contras
to me as a "highland fighting force" unlikely to
threaten Sandinista rule.
But the contras were a
favorite conservative
cause—and an equally

With William Casey

favorite target of liberal Democrats in the House, which twice cut off their funding. The second time this happened, McFarlane said, Reagan told him to keep the contras together "body and soul," which he took to mean encouraging other countries and private donors to contribute. In seven years of existence during the Reagan presidency, the contras received $306 million from the United States in funds approved by Congress and $48 million from other countries. Saudi Arabia was by far the biggest contributor with $32 million.

In comparison, the contras received a pittance from the Iran arms sales, which were channeled through The Enterprise, a covert network of dummy corporations, Swiss bank accounts, and aircraft operated by retired U.S. Air Force Major General Richard Secord and Albert Hakim, an Iranian-born U.S. businessman. By vastly overcharging the Iranians for weapons and spare parts, they diverted at least $3.8 million to the contras, less than the $4.4 million they and associate Thomas Clines pocketed in "commissions."

Reagan became enraged when he learned, months later, of this profiteering. But in the summer of 1986, he still harbored hope that the hostages would be freed. This hope burned brightest on July 26, when a blindfolded Father Jenco was released on the side of a highway. In September and October, however, three more Americans were kidnapped in Lebanon. After 500 TOWs were delivered to Iran on October 30 and 31, hostage David Jacobsen was freed on November 2. Two other hostages were also released, but another three Americans in Lebanon were kidnapped in January 1987. In addition, Reagan was informed that hostage David Kilburn, the former librarian at the American University in Beirut, had been killed on April 14, 1986, in apparent retaliation for the U.S. raid on Libya and that William

FOLLOWING TWO PAGES: *Excerpts from presidential addresses on Nicaragua*

Just some thoughts around the spots I've
marked. I don't submit these as word for word inserts
but possibly ideas to counter the general misinformation.

Insert. (5 Now I know many of you look at the
comparative size of Nicaragua & the U.S and ask
how could that tiny country be a threat to us? Well
in the sense of Nicaragua making war on the U.S.
it couldn't. But picture Nicaragua, which has a military
power greater than all it's Central American neighbors
combined and which right now smuggles arms to
communist guerillas in those neighboring countries, spreading
communist revolution by way of those guerillas to the
takeover of neighboring countries which could include the
Mexico to the North & Panama to the South. Then
with the great bulk of our shipping going through the
canal & the Caribbean they could one day provoke us
to the extent we'd have to protect our very real
interests and at such a time that would mean
military action.

also says not to use "flood of
refugees across our borders"
theme — offensive to Hispanics
OK to say "they are being driven from
their country" etc.

11

WHEN I WAS A YOUNG MAN BACK IN THE
1930's A WAR WAS SIMMERING IN EUROPE,
AND ENGLAND WAS IMPERILED, AND ITS GREAT
LEADER LOOKED ACROSS THE SEA FOR HOPE.
CHURCHILL ASKED FOR MILITARY ASSISTANCE.
HE SAID IF YOU GIVE US THE TOOLS THEN WE'LL
DO THE JOB. AND WE GAVE THEM THE TOOLS,
TO OUR EVERLASTING CREDIT.

TODAY ADOLFO CALERO, ALFONSO ROBELO,
AND ARTURO CRUZ LOOK TO US FOR HOPE —
AND WE MUST HELP THEM. HISTORY WILL KNOW
WHAT WE DID, AND IT WILL KNOW WHAT WE DIDN'T
DO, AND HISTORY WILL JUDGE. I HAVE MADE
MY POSITION CLEAR. I NEED YOUR HELP AS MUCH
AS THE CONTRAS NEED OUR HELP. I NEED FOR
THE CONGRESS TO KNOW THAT YOU WANT TO HELP
THE FREEDOM FIGHTERS.

IF U KNOW U CARE - WE WIN. IF U THINK
U DONT CARE - WE LOSE. ITS THT. SIMPLE.
ITS UP - U. PLS. HLP. THNK U &
GOD BLSS U.

Buckley, the former CIA station chief in Beirut, had died in captivity from medical neglect. A year after Reagan signed his finding approving the covert arms deal, two hostages were dead and seven Americans were held captive in Lebanon. The Iran initiative had provided more incentive for kidnapping Americans than releasing them.

Poindexter, however, was so encouraged by Jacobsen's release that he dropped hints to a White House political strategist that other hostages might be freed before the midterm elections of November 4, 1986. Politics was not Poindexter's strong suit; it seems never to have occurred to him that the last thing Republican candidates needed was the revelation of an arms-for-hostages swap. As it was, the election was a setback for the GOP, with negative consequences for the final two years of Reagan's presidency. This was not Reagan's fault; to the contrary, his strenuous campaigning helped several Republican candidates close wide gaps in the days before the election. But in contrast to 1980, when Republicans had won the close contests, they lost nearly every close race in 1986, and the Democrats regained control of the Senate. The Iran initiative was not a factor; a sketchy account appeared in a Lebanese magazine on November 3, but the story did not break in U.S. newspapers until November 5, the day after the election. Even then, the media at first proceeded cautiously, out of reluctance to jeopardize a mass release of hostages. When it became apparent, however, that no such release was imminent, a firestorm of criticism erupted in the media and on Capitol Hill. Senate Republican leader Bob Dole expressed concern that the administration had rewarded terrorists, and Senate Democratic leader Robert Byrd demanded a full investigation.

Reagan was slow to recognize that he faced the seminal crisis of his presidency. On November 7, he presented a tired and distraught David Jacobsen to reporters at a ceremony in the White House Rose Garden with the comment that "a great many prayers have been answered by his presence in our country." Jacobsen said he had been released through the humanitarian intervention of Terry Waite, a special envoy for the Archbishop of Canterbury, who was "free of all governments and any types of deals." This was untrue, but Jacobsen, who had been treated badly in captivity, was only repeating what he had been told. He was not persuasive, nor was Reagan when he said that there was "no foundation" for the stories that arms had been swapped for hostages.

By mid-November the administration was back on its heels, with its participants quarreling among themselves. Shultz, who had been abroad when the story broke, sent a cable to Poindexter suggesting a White House statement that described the Iran initiative as "a special one-time operation based on humanitarian grounds" undertaken by the president in the national interest. This was unacceptable to Poindexter, who still nourished the hope of additional hostage releases. He told McFarlane in a computer message that it would be "absolutely stupid" to say anything and added, "we have a damned good story to tell when we are ready." With Poindexter refusing to face reality, matters went from bad to worse at the White House.

On November 11, with input from the CIA's Casey as well as Poindexter, the White House press office finally issued a statement, but it raised more questions than it answered. Reagan, flanked by Shultz and Weinberger, briefed congressional leaders the following day; the leaders told reporters in the White House driveway that the president's explanations were unconvincing. On November 13, Reagan made a nationally televised speech at the urging of Patrick Buchanan, who remembered how President Nixon's stonewalling had damaged him after the Watergate disclosures. Unfortunately for Reagan, the information for the speech came from Poindexter. Critics pounced on numerous misstatements, of which the most glaring was a claim that all the "defensive" weapons and spare parts to Iran "could easily fit into a single cargo plane." On November 19, Reagan

compounded his problems by making other misstatements
at a news conference that was the brainchild of White
House chief of staff Don Regan.

Nancy Reagan, who understood her husband's strengths
and weaknesses, had objected in vain to the news conference. She realized he was in no condition to answer questions. "He never had his integrity questioned before," Mrs.
Reagan told me soon after he left office. "And that really,
really bothered him." She had it right. Ronald Reagan was
willing to take unpopular stands; he had remained sanguine
when his approval rating fell to 35 percent during the
1981–83 recession. But at that time it was his policy, not his
integrity, that was at issue. After the November 13 speech on
the Iran initiative, a *Los Angeles Times* poll found that only
14 percent of Americans believed that Reagan's account was
truthful. Richard Wirthlin's reliable private polls produced a
similar finding.

Other blows followed. Attorney General Meese, acting
as Reagan's lawyer and friend, had been trying to assemble a
comprehensible chronology of the Iran initiative. While he
was doing this, Oliver North was busily shredding documents. But when his shredder jammed late Friday, November 21, North and his assistant Fawn Hall quit for the night.
While Reagan was giving his weekly radio speech from
Camp David the next day, Assistant Attorney General
William Bradford Reynolds was searching North's office in
the Old Executive Office Building when he came across a
document headed "Release of American Hostages in Beirut."
It was a detailed April 4, 1986, memo from North to
Poindexter that contained the sentence: "$12 million will be
used to purchase critically needed supplies for the
Nicaraguan Democratic Resistance Forces." As Reynolds
and an associate left the office to have lunch with Meese,
they ran into North, who was returning to shred more documents.

Meese was later faulted for failing to secure North's

office, as a prosecutor would have done. But the attorney general was smart enough to realize that a diversion of funds to the contras raised the possibility that Reagan could be impeached. On Saturday, Meese discussed the matter with Casey, who told him little. On Sunday, he interviewed North, who falsely said that the money from the arms sales went from the Iranians to the Israelis. But when Meese asked if the arms shipments were a trade for the hostages or had a strategic purpose, North told the truth. "It always came back to the hostages," he said.

On Monday, in the company of Don Regan, Meese told the president about the incriminating memo. "He blanched when he heard Meese's words," Regan wrote in his memoirs. "The color drained from his face, leaving his skin pasty white. . . . Nobody who saw the president's reaction that afternoon could believe for a moment that he knew about the diversion of funds before Meese told him about it."

On Tuesday, November 25, Reagan accepted Poindexter's resignation and fired North. Then he announced his actions in the White House briefing room, saying he was "deeply troubled that the implementation of a policy aimed at resolving a truly tragic situation in the Middle East has resulted in such controversy." On December 1, Reagan named a review board headed by former Senator John Tower—its other members were Brent Scowcroft and former Senator Edmund Muskie—to review the arms sales. On December 2 *The New York Times*/CBS poll recorded a drop in Reagan's approval rating from 67 to 46 percent, the sharpest one-month decrease in presidential approval since such polls began in 1936. A few days later Meese reluctantly agreed that an independent counsel should conduct a criminal inquiry. Lawrence Walsh, a former federal judge and lifelong Republican, was appointed on December 19. Meanwhile, Democratic leaders announced they would launch a joint Senate-House investigation when they took control of Congress in January.

In this low month of December, Nancy Reagan reached out to save the Reagan presidency. She knew nothing about the ins and outs of the Iran initiative or the contras. But she realized that her husband, even if he avoided impeachment, would be unable to regain his effectiveness as president without the trust of the American people. This required a new White House staff. It also meant a speech in which her husband apologized to the American people for selling arms to Iran.

Reagan didn't want to apologize. He stubbornly insisted he had done nothing wrong and blamed his troubles on partisan critics and the media. To change his mind, Nancy Reagan did what she had done in the crises of the 1980 and 1984 campaigns—and more. She brought in old loyalists Mike Deaver and Stu Spencer to talk to the president. Deaver was especially blunt but failed to budge Reagan. Nancy Reagan then brought in a potent reinforcement in the form of Robert Strauss, a Washington power attorney and former Democratic national chairman who had worked to reelect President Carter in 1980. Strauss was a dedicated Democrat, but he had a patriotic appreciation of the presidency, and did not want to see Reagan driven from office. He also had a score to settle with his conscience. Strauss had once been asked by President Johnson to give his opinion of the Vietnam War. Although Strauss knew the war was a quagmire, he kept his opinion to himself and told LBJ what he wanted to hear. Later, he resolved that if a president ever again asked him for advice, he would tell him the unvarnished truth.

And that is exactly what Strauss did on the evening of December 4 in the living quarters of the White House. He called the Iran-contra affair a "cancer" that was eating at the Reagan presidency. He told Reagan he was being badly managed and that the press conference had been a mistake "because you didn't have your facts right and you looked bad and you got bad advice." He told Reagan he needed to make changes in the White House and get "on top of the problem" by finding out what he didn't know. That struck a chord with Nancy Reagan. "Bob is just saying to you, Ronnie, that he thinks you're telling the truth as you see it and, number two, it's inaccurate," she said. "And he's saying to you that that's the worst of all worlds. If you're telling the truth and know it isn't the truth, that's bad enough. But when you tell what you believe is the truth and it's inaccurate, then you're really in trouble."

Reagan did not like what he was hearing, and Strauss left the White House thinking his visit had been useless. He drank two vodkas, had a bowl of soup, and went to bed. As he was falling asleep, he received a phone call from Nancy Reagan, warmly thanking him and telling him her husband was upset. "He heard what you said, even though you felt tonight it was just a waste of your time," she said. "Ronnie hears and he heard everything you said tonight. . . . He didn't eat his dinner. He was terribly troubled."

"I'm so sorry," Strauss said.

"No. I'm not," Mrs. Reagan said. "He needed to be troubled. He has to have his mind opened and his eyes open on this and see what's happening to him."

This was the beginning of the end for Don Regan, although it is unlikely he would have in any case survived the demands of congressional Republicans for his resignation or the findings of the Tower board. On February 26, 1987, a Thursday, the Tower board issued its report: it found the president had traded arms for hostages and blamed Regan "for the chaos that descended upon the White House" after the initiative was disclosed. Regan thought this judgment terribly unfair but told the president that he would resign the next Monday. He never had the chance. On Friday, Regan learned from a CNN broadcast that he had been replaced as chief of staff by Howard Baker. "My prayers have really been answered," Reagan wrote in his diary that night.

Reagan now had a capable new team at the White House, where veteran diplomat Frank Carlucci had succeeded Poindexter as national security adviser. But he still needed to explain his actions to the American people. Once again, Nancy Reagan played a decisive role by recruiting Landon Parvin, a soft-spoken White House speechwriter, to help her husband in this effort. Parvin realized that Reagan still found it difficult to apologize for sending weapons to Iran, but he hit upon a formulation that the president found acceptable. "A few months ago I told the American people I did not trade arms for hostages," Reagan said in a nationally televised speech on March 4, 1987. "My heart and my best intentions still tell me that's true, but the facts and the evidence tell me it is not."

This speech was a turning point. An overnight CBS poll showed a nine-point jump in Reagan's approval ratings, which would rise steadily in the months ahead. *The Washington Post,* which had been sharply critical of the arms-for-hostages trade, said editorially that Reagan had given "the right speech" and "pledged to redeem the damage in his final two years in office." By restoring public confidence in his presidency—and in the process his self-confidence—Reagan had freed himself to complete the crucial task of negotiating a reduction in nuclear arsenals with the Soviet Union.

The speech did not resolve the question of whether Reagan had prior knowledge about the contra diversion, an issue of more interest to the media and Congress than to the American people. Most Americans knew little and cared less about the contras—Wirthlin's polls found that many people did not even know which side they were on. But Americans had been

Delivering the Iran-contra speech of March 4, 1987

obsessed with Iran since the 1978 seizure of hostages at the U.S. embassy in Tehran. It was the "Iran" side of Iran-contra that had aroused the public.

Lawrence Walsh would investigate the Iran-contra affair for more than seven years. Republicans criticized him because the inquiry took so long; the Democratic-controlled Congress undermined him by granting legal immunity to Poindexter and North so they could testify before an investigating committee. Walsh had warned that such testimony would jeopardize prosecutions, and he was right. He obtained convictions of Poindexter, North, and other Iran-contra figures, but appellate courts overturned them on grounds that jurors may have been influenced by the congressional testimony.

As to Reagan, Walsh found that the president had "knowingly participated or acquiesced in covering up the scandal" but said there was "no credible evidence that the president authorized or was aware of the diversion of the profits from the Iran arms sales to assist the contras, or that Regan, Bush, or Meese was aware of the diversion." While he didn't say so in his report or publicly, Walsh told me in 1999 that he sympathized with Reagan because Congress had been too abrupt in cutting off aid to the contras and should not have done so while the Nicaraguan rebels were engaged in battle in the field. Even Reagan's most dogged pursuer acknowledged that his profound mistake in ignoring his own policy and authorizing the Iran initiative was an error of the heart based on his determination to free Americans who were held captive in a foreign land.

FOLLOWING TWO PAGES: *The address to the nation regarding Iran-Contra*

(Parvin-1/1/87)

ADDRESS TO THE NATION

My fellow Americans, I've spoken to you from this historic office on many occasions and about many things. The power of the presidency is often thought to reside within this Oval Office. Yet it doesn't rest here, it rests in you, the American people, and in your trust.

Your trust is what gives a President his powers of leadership and his personal strength, and it's what I want to talk to you about this evening.

For the past three months I've been silent on the revelations about Iran. I ~~know~~ You must have been thinking, "Well, why doesn't he tell us what's happening? Why doesn't he just speak to us as he has in the past when we've faced troubles or tragedies?" Others of you I GUESS were thinking, "What's he doing hiding out in the White House?"

The reason I haven't spoken to you before now is this: you deserved the truth, the whole truth. And, as frustrating as it's been, I felt it was improper to come to you with sketchy reports, leaked testimony and erroneous statements, which would then have to be corrected, creating even more doubt and confusion. There's been enough of that.

I've paid a price for ~~this~~ MY silence in terms of your trust and confidence. ~~but I have simply believed that the truth should not be rushed.~~

~~In November I told you everything I knew about this situation. Since then I've waited to have you know the complete story.~~

I have had to wait as have you for the complete story.

2

That's why I appointed Ambassador David Abshire as my special counselor to help get out the thousands of documents to the various investigations. And I appointed a special review board, the Tower Board, which took on the chore of pulling the truth together for me and getting to the bottom of things. It has now issued its findings.

I'm often accused of being an optimist, and it's true I had to hunt pretty hard to find any good news in the Board's report. As you know, it's well-stocked with criticisms, which I'll discuss in a moment, but I was very relieved to read this sentence, "...the Board is convinced that the President does indeed want the full story to be told."

And that will continue to be my pledge to you as the other investigations go forward.

I want to thank the members of the panel--former Senator John Tower, former Secretary of State Edmund Muskie, and former National Security Adviser Brent Scowcroft. They have done the nation, as well as me personally, a great service by submitting a report of such integrity and depth. They have my genuine and enduring gratitude.

I've studied the Board's report. Its findings are honest, convincing and highly critical, and I accept them. Tonight I want to share with you my thoughts on these findings and report to you on the actions I'm taking to implement the Board's recommendations.

First, let me say I take full responsibility for my own actions and for those of my Administration. As angry as I

THE NEW ERA

The seeds sown by the U.S. military buildup and Reagan's persistent challenges to the Soviet Union began bearing fruit in 1985 after Mikhail Sergeyevich Gorbachev succeeded Konstantin Chernenko. The Soviet leaders in Reagan's first term—Brezhnev, Andropov, and Chernenko—were traditional, older Communists who resented Reagan's denunciations of Marxist ideology and Soviet conduct. Andropov was the most creative of this trio, but he was in such ill health during his brief reign that he would have found it difficult to negotiate with an American president even if he had been so inclined.

Gorbachev, an Andropov protégé, was a vigorous, reform-minded man of fifty-four when he took the reins of power. While he described himself as a committed Marxist-Leninist, he was more open and innovative than his predecessors. Despite a rural background, Gorbachev had traveled widely for a Soviet leader and was well informed about the United States, which was prospering while Soviet living conditions were in decline. Gorbachev was also politically tolerant, perhaps because of his boyhood exposure to the Stalinist terror, when both his grandfathers had been imprisoned and narrowly escaped with their lives. He wanted to change living conditions in the Soviet Union and forge a constructive relationship with the West. On a brief visit to London in 1984, a few months before he assumed power, Gorbachev had charmed Margaret Thatcher, Reagan's closest foreign ally. "I like Mr. Gorbachev," she said. "We can do business together." Reagan, who wanted to make a new start with the Soviets, was encouraged by Thatcher's optimism. On March 11, 1985, when Gorbachev was named Soviet leader a day after Chernenko's death, Reagan dispatched Vice President Bush to the Chernenko funeral with a letter inviting Gorbachev to a summit meeting in the United States and assuring him of "serious negotiations."

Although not yet ready to agree to a summit, Gorbachev welcomed the message. On March 24 he sent a reply to Reagan that pledged "peaceful competition" with the United

States and stressed that he was committed to avoiding the "catastrophic consequences" of nuclear war. The letter said the Soviet leadership attached "great importance to contacts at the highest level," signaling Gorbachev's willingness to meet with Reagan.

This exchange of correspondence marked the beginning of what would become the most extraordinary relationship between a U.S. president and a Soviet leader since the World War II alliance between Franklin Roosevelt and Joseph Stalin—and one that endured much longer. During Reagan's second term he and Gorbachev exchanged more than a score of letters, held four formal summits, and another informal meeting. Long after both men left office, they continued to meet and exchange letters of mutual appreciation and respect.

But in the climate of U.S.-Soviet distrust that prevailed in 1985 it took time to achieve this rapport—or even an agreement to hold a summit. On March 24, the same day Gorbachev sent his first letter to Reagan, a Soviet sentry shot and killed Major Arthur D. Nicholson in East Germany, where a 1947 agreement permitted both sides to have liaisons in a no-man's-land near the borders of the two Germanys. The killing, as Shultz observed in his memoirs, was "barbaric." The Soviet soldier continued shooting after Nicholson was hit, pinning down a U.S. sergeant and preventing him from providing medical assistance, with the result that Nicholson bled to death. Reagan was outraged. But when my colleague David Hoffman and I interviewed Reagan on April 1 he made a point of saying that this brutal act had not changed his mind about a summit with Gorbachev. "I want a meeting even more [to] talk to him about what we can do to make sure nothing of this kind ever happens again," Reagan said.

Privately, neither Reagan nor Shultz blamed Gorbachev

FOLLOWING THREE PAGES: *A draft of an early letter from Reagan to Gorbachev*

10/30/85

T.R. MacFarlane

note 8.2

RR

DRAFT GORBACHEV LETTER

Dear Mr. General Secretary,

As I told Foreign Minister Shevardnadze in New York October 24, I have been giving careful consideration to your letter dated September 12. The issues you raise are important ones, the ideas you have put forward are in many ways interesting, and I have wanted to study them thoroughly before replying.

Many of the specific points you addressed in your letter have been or will be dealt with by our delegations in the Geneva arms control negotiations or by our Foreign Ministers. In this letter I will therefore focus on what I consider the most significant issues you have raised.

You suggested in your letter that I am opposed to the possibility of a military clash between our two countries, and that language to this effect be incorporated into a concluding document for our Geneva meeting. Foreign Minister Shevardnadze has since proposed specific language for our consideration. As I have repeatedly made clear, it is indeed my view that a nuclear war can not be won and must not be fought. I therefore see no reason in principle why it should not be possible to reach agreement on this point and have instructed Secretary Shultz to develop appropriate language while he is in Moscow.

I believe it is important, however, that as we address this and other elements which may figure in any documents we may issue in Geneva, we give the most careful consideration to our words. The experience of the past has been that overly vague or rhetorical language has led to expectations which, given the competitive aspect of our relationship to which you referred in your letter, can not be sustained.

If we are to avoid subsequent misunderstandings and disillusionment, our own statements should be clear and based on concrete achievements. I am convinced that there is substantial common ground on the range of areas we have been discussing in connection with our forthcoming meeting. I see no reason why we should not be in a position to announce agreements in a number of fields when we meet in November if the Soviet side is prepared to show the necessary flexibility.

You raised several specific areas in the security field where this might be possible. Secretary Shultz will be prepared to discuss all your ideas in concrete terms while he is in Moscow. I believe you will find that we are indeed prepared to go our fair share of the way to ensure our meeting is a productive one.

This be amended to state our proposal — now being tabled at Geneva

I do, however, want to address your response to the proposals we had previously made in the Geneva arms control talks, which was foreshadowed in your letter and which your delegation subsequently tabled in Geneva.

We have been carefully assessing your counterproposal over the last month. As I stated in my address to the United Nations on October 24, I believe that within it there are seeds which we should nurture and that in the coming weeks we should seek to establish a genuine process of give-and-take.

In order to foster such a process, I have approved a new and comprehensive proposal designed to build upon the positive elements of your counterproposal and bridge the positions of our two sides. This new proposal deals with all three areas under discussion in the Geneva negotiations. Its essence is a proposal for radical and stabilizing reductions in strategic offensive arms and a separate agreement on intermediate-range nuclear missile systems, both of which bridge US and Soviet ideas. We also propose that both sides reaffirm that their strategic defense programs are and will remain in full accord with the ABM Treaty. Such reaffirmation must be contingent upon a prior resolution of our current differences over compliance with the treaty.

We have designed our approach to provide for a mutually acceptable resolution of the range of nuclear and space arms issues; to take account of the interrelationship between the offense and the defense; and to address those concerns that you and your negotiators have described as being of great importance to you. I am convinced that this new proposal can provide the basis for immediate and genuine progress on the numerous and complex issues facing us in the nuclear and space area, and I look forward to discussing it with you in Geneva later this month.

We will also, of course, have the opportunity in Geneva to discuss the other areas which make up our relationship. Much work remains to be done if we are to be able to announce specific progress on regional and bilateral issues. I hope that Secretary Shultz's Moscow visit will be a stimulus to rapid progress in the weeks ahead.

Before closing, I would like to reiterate the importance I personally attach to some movement on the Soviet side in the human rights field by the time of our meeting. As you know, I stressed this point to Foreign Minister Shevrdnadze during our New York conversation. I understand your sensitivities and principles in this area and I do not ask you to compromise them. But there are many cases which it would be possible for you to resolve without your having to do so. I can not tell you what an impact this would have on popular perceptions of the Soviet Union in this country and, I believe, in the world.

I have asked Secretary Shultz to convey my best wishes, and my hopes for major progress in our preparations for the Geneva meeting during his visit and in the weeks remaining.

Sincerely,

Ronald W. Reagan

for the incident. They were angered, however, that the Soviets, after expressing regret for Nicholson's death, typically tried to shift the blame by accusing the U.S. officer of "espionage." Reagan sent Gorbachev another letter on April 4, objecting to the Nicholson shooting and criticizing the Soviet occupation of Afghanistan. But Reagan's letter ended with another call for a summit where the two leaders could discuss contentious issues face to face.

Gorbachev was in the meantime moving cautiously to consolidate his leadership. In his first months in office he ordered more than a hundred studies of various Soviet social and economic problems and presided at a summit of the six Warsaw Pact nations. Reagan moved cautiously, too. While buoyed by a huge popular mandate in the 1984 election, he faced deep differences of opinion within his own cabinet over whether he should abide by the nuclear-weapons limits in the SALT II treaty signed by President Carter and Soviet leader Leonid Brezhnev in 1979. As a presidential candidate in 1980, Reagan had called this treaty "fatally flawed" because it regulated an increase rather than a reduction in nuclear arsenals. Prodded by Congress, Reagan had observed the unratified treaty during his first term, an easy gesture because the high limits permitted by SALT II did not restrain the U.S. defense buildup. By 1985, however, the United States was bumping up against the SALT II limits. Conservatives in the administration led by Defense Secretary Weinberger and arms control specialists Richard Perle and Kenneth Adelman urged Reagan to renounce SALT II on grounds the Soviets were cheating on its provisions. The pragmatic Shultz, supported by the Joint Chiefs of Staff, did not want the SALT II dispute to chill the growing warmth of U.S.-Soviet relations and proposed that the United States scrap an aging Poseidon submarine to stay within the treaty limits. Reagan opted for a middle ground. On June 10 he announced that he would abide for the time being with the

SALT II limits while assailing Soviet lack of compliance with the treaty. "Apparently my decision was right—at least I'm being called a statesman by both the left and right," Reagan wrote in his diary.

Shultz meanwhile was trying to nail down an agreement to a Reagan-Gorbachev summit in talks with Soviet foreign minister Andrei Gromyko and Anatoly Dobrynin, the Soviet ambassador to the United States. Since Gorbachev was unwilling to come to Washington and Reagan was opposed to going to Moscow, a neutral ground was needed. Geneva, Switzerland, soon became the site of choice. On July 1, Dobrynin brought Shultz a message that the Soviets had agreed to a Geneva summit on November 19–20.

In the months after this announcement Reagan pre-

Geneva summit, November 19, 1985

pared more assiduously for his first meeting with a Soviet
leader than for any other event of his presidency. Reagan,
who was seventy-four years old in 1985, could be indifferent
to briefings on subjects that did not interest him, but he
remained a quick study on matters that engaged him, and
the U.S.-Soviet relationship was the number one priority of
his second term. In the run-up to the Geneva summit he
responded enthusiastically to a series of tutorials on the
Soviet Union organized by his national security adviser,
Robert McFarlane, and conducted by Jack Matlock, the
Soviet specialist on the NSC staff. Matlock, later U.S.
ambassador to the Soviet Union, prepared twenty-five papers
for Reagan that examined Russian culture and history and
discussed Soviet objectives, strategy, and negotiating tactics.

Chateau Fleur d'Eau, the lakeside villa where Reagan met Gorbachev at their first summit in November 1985

Reagan also held a series of meetings with Suzanne Massie, the author of *Land of the Firebird: The Beauty of Old Russia,* and read her book before the summit.

Gorbachev boned up on Reagan, too. In high school Gorbachev had displayed an interest in dramatics and was considered a promising actor before deciding to study law. "We are both actors; he is a good one," Gorbachev would say of Reagan at a later meeting. There were other resemblances. According to Gorbachev biographers Dusko Doder and Louise Branson, Gorbachev possessed "an almost blind faith in himself" and particularly valued personal experience. "He had grasped that any hardship could be endured if one had resources of one's own; he was stubborn to a fault, once he had made up his mind," they wrote. The same could have been said of Reagan.

Both leaders were confident when the summit opened at 10 A.M. on November 19 at Chateau Fleur d'Eau, a nineteenth-century lakeside villa on the western shore of Lake Geneva. Removing his overcoat, Reagan stepped out into the cold and waited at the top of the steps for Gorbachev, who was wearing a heavy topcoat and black fedora, which he doffed theatrically. "As we shook hands for the first time, I had to admit—as Margaret Thatcher and [Canadian] Prime Minister Brian Mulroney predicted I would—that there was something likeable about Gorbachev," Reagan wrote in his memoirs. "There was warmth in his face and his style, not the coldness bordering on hatred I'd seen in most senior Soviet officials I'd met until then." As Nancy Reagan later told me, Reagan sensed a "moral dimension" in Gorbachev the first time they met.

Gorbachev liked Reagan, too, and—despite his implacable opposition to the Strategic Defense Initiative—shared his concern that the relentless expansion of U.S.-Soviet nuclear arsenals had the potential for catastrophe. Unlike many of the president's domestic opponents, Gorbachev did not underestimate Reagan. Years later, Gorbachev's interpreter,

Pavel Palazchenko recalled that the Soviet leader had bluntly silenced a Soviet official who was berating Reagan during a strategy session at Geneva. "This is the president of the United States, elected by the American people," Gorbachev said.

The mutual respect felt by the two leaders produced a summit in which Reagan and Gorbachev honestly aired their differences on SDI and human rights. Initiating a practice he would follow at subsequent summits, Reagan gave Gorbachev a list of dissidents, most of them Jews, whom he said the Soviet Union should allow to emigrate. On this score, Reagan followed the "quiet diplomacy" of his predecessors in the belief that making a public issue of restrictive Soviet emigration policy would be counterproductive. But Reagan was outspoken and emotional in describing pictures he had seen of Afghan children disfigured by Soviet bombs and mines. In response, Gorbachev said he had learned of the invasion of Afghanistan on the radio, which Reagan took to mean that he bore "no responsibility and little enthusiasm" for the war. Shultz was particularly struck by Gorbachev's low-key, emotionless discussion of Afghanistan, which he suspected might presage a change in Soviet policy.

But Gorbachev became passionate on the second day of the summit in denouncing SDI. He told Reagan their discussions would come to a halt unless they could find a way "to prevent the arms race in space." In response, Reagan insisted that SDI was entirely defensive. "SDI isn't to conduct war in space," Reagan said. "There are nuclear missiles which, if used, would kill millions on both sides. Never before in history has the prospect of a war that would bring about the end of civilization been out there." When Reagan then said he wanted to end "the world's nightmare about nuclear weapons," Gorbachev interrupted, shouting, "Why don't you believe me when I say the Soviet Union will never attack?" This was the tensest moment of the summit. Reagan tried to answer, but Gorbachev cut him off, twice

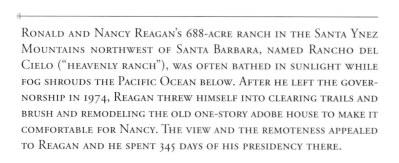

RONALD AND NANCY REAGAN'S 688-ACRE RANCH IN THE SANTA YNEZ MOUNTAINS NORTHWEST OF SANTA BARBARA, NAMED RANCHO DEL CIELO ("HEAVENLY RANCH"), WAS OFTEN BATHED IN SUNLIGHT WHILE FOG SHROUDS THE PACIFIC OCEAN BELOW. AFTER HE LEFT THE GOVERNORSHIP IN 1974, REAGAN THREW HIMSELF INTO CLEARING TRAILS AND BRUSH AND REMODELING THE OLD ONE-STORY ADOBE HOUSE TO MAKE IT COMFORTABLE FOR NANCY. THE VIEW AND THE REMOTENESS APPEALED TO REAGAN AND HE SPENT 345 DAYS OF HIS PRESIDENCY THERE.

repeating his question. Finally, Reagan was able to reply. "Look, no individual can say to the American people that they should rely on personal faith rather than sound defense," he said.

Gorbachev then became more conciliatory. He promised huge cuts in Soviet nuclear weapons if Reagan would scrap SDI. Reagan said he couldn't do it. After a long silence, Gorbachev said, "Mr. President, I don't agree with you, but I can see you really mean it."

By this time, late in the afternoon on the summit's second day, it was apparent there would be no agreement on strategic defense. Reagan and Gorbachev had already made progress, of a sort, the previous day when they met without their aides at a pool house on Lake Geneva before a roaring fire that would give the Geneva meeting its name: "the fireside summit." Walking back to the chateau after this meeting Reagan proposed what later would be seen as their most important achievement at Geneva—an agreement to hold future summits. Pausing in a parking lot before they reached the chateau, Reagan invited Gorbachev to a summit in Washington. Gorbachev accepted. He proposed a follow-up summit in Moscow, to which Reagan readily agreed.

But after the stormy discussions on SDI there were few other points of agreement to put in a joint statement. Negotiators worked through the night before finally reaching a compromise at 4:45 A.M. on Thursday, November 21. The statement ignored SDI and pledged that the United States and the Soviet Union would seek a 50 percent reduction in nuclear arms "appropriately applied." No one knew exactly what this meant, since the two sides counted nuclear arsenals differently, but it was sufficient for Reagan and Gorbachev to pronounce the summit a success. The joint statement also pledged acceleration of progress toward an "interim agreement on medium-range missiles in Europe." Later that morning Gorbachev and Reagan went to a press center where they read separate statements expressing a determination to curb the arms race and improve U.S.-Soviet relations. Just before they spoke, Reagan whispered to Gorbachev, "I bet the hard-liners in both our countries are bleeding when we shake hands."

The real accomplishments of Geneva were in personal relationships, not policy. Gorbachev appreciated Reagan's candor. Reagan discovered, as he later put it, that he shared "a kind of chemistry" with the Soviet leader. Dealing with Gorbachev reminded Reagan of his after-hours relationship with Tip O'Neill, because Gorbachev "could tell jokes about himself and even about his country." The Geneva summit also marked the blossoming of a fruitful relationship between Shultz and his Soviet counterpart, Eduard Shevardnadze, who had replaced Gromyko as foreign minister. Reagan had been pleasantly surprised when Shevardnadze, on a September visit to the White House in preparation for the summit, laughed at anti-Communist jokes that no other American president would have told a Soviet diplomat. Reagan had no way of knowing that Shevardnadze, a Georgian, was sharply critical of the communist system and had told Gorbachev at the time of his appointment that "everything is rotten" in the Soviet Union.

But Gorbachev wanted to save—and reform—the Soviet Union. He was determined to open up Soviet society ("glasnost") and restructure its economy ("perestroika"). To attain his goals, he needed Western economic credits and a reduction in Soviet military spending. The precondition for these objectives was a relaxation of international tensions and a constructive relationship with the United States. On January 1, 1986, following up on the summit, Gorbachev and Reagan exchanged simultaneous televised New Year's messages in which they talked optimistically to the citizens of each other's country about safeguarding peace. Two weeks later Gorbachev took the initiative on arms control by announcing a sweeping plan that called for halving U.S. and Soviet nuclear arsenals within five to eight years and elimi-

nating them entirely by 2000. He also discarded long-term
Soviet insistence that British and French nuclear weapons be
included in the count of Western medium-range missiles
capable of striking Soviet targets.

Gorbachev was then the rage of Europe. But in the early
morning of April 26, 1986, an explosion destroyed Reactor
No. 4 at the Chernobyl nuclear power plant in Ukraine,
killing more than thirty people and exposing as many as
100,000 to varying levels of radiation. As the fire inside the
reactor raged for days, scientists expressed fears it could lead
to an uncontrollable meltdown.

Gorbachev's first response to this worst disaster in the
history of nuclear power was to stonewall. Although abnor-
mal levels of radiation were soon detected in Sweden, the
Soviets refused to provide any information until sixty-seven
hours after the explosion and then only because Sweden was
about to issue a radiation alert. By the time of the terse
Soviet announcement, on the evening of April 28, a radiation cloud was spreading across Europe, where political leaders of all persuasions were expressing anger and fear at the
paucity of information provided by the Soviets. By May 3,
when the leaders of the industrialized democracies were
gathering in Tokyo for their annual economic summit, the
radioactive cloud had reached Japan. From Tokyo, Reagan
denounced the "stubborn refusal" of the Soviets to provide a
full account of the incident. This did not occur until May
14 when a haggard Gorbachev gave a television speech that
coupled a report on the disaster with attacks on the West for
conducting an "unrestrained anti-Soviet propaganda campaign." Although the speech contained neither an apology
nor an expression of regrets, Reagan nonetheless sent a sympathetic letter to Gorbachev.

Chernobyl was an epochal event that tarnished Gorbachev's bright image at a pivotal moment. While Gorbachev
never apologized for his handling of the incident, his biographers Doder and Branson believe he was changed by it.

"From that point on, natural disasters and man-made calamities would be reported promptly in the Soviet media," they wrote. Chernobyl also had an impact on Reagan, who was struck by a particular passage in Gorbachev's television speech: "Chernobyl showed again what an abyss will open if nuclear war befalls mankind." Reagan, who saw Chernobyl as a portent of Armageddon, totally agreed. In his memoirs he expressed the view that Gorbachev had been shaken by Chernobyl and that it "made him try harder to resolve Soviet differences with the West."

While Gorbachev spent the spring and summer of 1986 trying to regain the political initiative after the damage inflicted by Chernobyl, the Reagan administration was trying to resolve its persistent internal differences over the SALT II treaty. On May 27, after much discussion, Reagan finally scrapped U.S. adherence to SALT II but did so in a way that created confusion about his intentions. The president said the United States would no longer be bound by the treaty, which he accused the Soviet Union of repeatedly violating, but that it would remain in technical compliance for several months while two outmoded Poseidon submarines were being retired for budgetary reasons. If the Soviet Union took "constructive steps" during this period, Reagan added, "we will certainly take this into account."

Reagan's decision had little immediate effect, but it bothered the Soviets, who announced on June 1 they would not consider themselves bound by SALT II once the United States exceeded the treaty's weapons ceilings. The Soviets were even more disturbed—as were Democrats in Congress—by a contentious administration effort to reinterpret the 1972 ABM treaty to allow construction of a U.S. missile defense system. Typically, administration officials were themselves at odds. Reagan, who wanted to pursue SDI and was uninterested in the treaty's fine points, embraced a compromise by Shultz and his chief arms negotiator, Paul Nitze, which endorsed a broad interpretation of the ABM treaty but said the United States would abide by the traditional interpretation as a matter of policy. This straddle satisfied no one. On June 19, before a high school class in Glassboro, New Jersey, where President Lyndon Johnson and Soviet Premier Alexei Kosygin had begun the SALT process in 1967, Reagan urged Gorbachev to join him in reducing nuclear arsenals. But he also waxed glowingly on the potential of SDI, which he said "might one day enable us to put in space a shield that missiles could not penetrate, a shield that could protect us from nuclear missiles just as a roof protects a family from rain."

It was Reagan's persistence on SDI, more than anything else, which prompted Gorbachev to stall on his commitment to hold a follow-up summit in the United States. Viewed in historical hindsight, the reason for Gorbachev's obsessive opposition to SDI is no mystery. The numerous studies Gorbachev had commissioned had confirmed his worst fears about Soviet society. The Soviet Union was spending 25 percent of its gross national product on military needs and only 3 percent on health care. It ranked fiftieth in the world in infant mortality, behind some Third World countries. Other health statistics were equally alarming, and life expectancy was declining. So was Soviet economic performance. By 1987, at a plenum of the Communist Central Committee at the Kremlin, Gorbachev would describe the Soviet economic and social situation as a "crisis" and complain of corruption, waste, cynicism, alcoholism, drug abuse, and crime. To have any chance of turning things around, Gorbachev knew that he needed to transfer resources from military spending to domestic needs.

The Strategic Defense Initiative stood in his way. The real significance of SDI was not its military potential—either for defensive or offensive purposes—but the strain it put on the Soviet economy. Gorbachev's generals were confident they could overcome any defensive system, even if it became scientifically possible to deploy one, but warned they would need extra money to do it. SDI was not a single system. It was a research project involving an array of new technologies, some of them beyond Soviet capabilities. The Soviets had achieved nuclear parity by building an arsenal of gigantic ICBMs. They were not equipped for a more sophisticated competition that would diffuse their limited technological resources. And Gorbachev was not prepared, for any reason, to give his generals more money. He had already alienated the military by removing scores of high-ranking officers and putting others under strict party control. Now he wanted to cut the military budget, which he could never do if Reagan persisted in pushing SDI.

In the United States, where the economy was robust, Reagan was frustrated by lagging arms control negotiations and Gorbachev's reluctance to attend a second summit. Trying to get something started, Reagan signed off on a complex proposal that provided for elimination of U.S. and Soviet nuclear missiles in stages and for deployment of a missile defense system in which both sides would share the fruits of their defensive research. Reagan said in his diary on July 18 that the plan would "open the door to some real arms negotiations, if he [Gorbachev] is really serious." On July 25 he sent this proposal to Gorbachev in a lengthy letter in which Reagan reminded the Soviet leader of the commitment he had made to a follow-up summit at Geneva. Reagan invited Gorbachev to Washington to discuss his proposal and any other matters he had in mind.

Gorbachev did not respond until mid-September. By then, U.S.-Soviet relations had taken a turn for the worse. On August 23, the FBI arrested Gennady Zakharov, a Soviet physicist working at the United Nations, on a New York subway platform while he was exchanging money for classified documents. The Soviets retaliated a week later by arresting Nicholas Daniloff, the Moscow correspondent for *U.S. News and World Report,* and accusing him of being a spy. It was a classic Cold War gambit that raised doubts in

Washington about whether anything had really changed in the Soviet Union. Reagan sent a personal message to Gorbachev assuring him of Daniloff's innocence. When this brought no response, he publicly denounced the arrest as an "outrage," and the United States expelled twenty-five members of the Soviet mission to the United Nations as spies. The incident escalated further on September 19, when Shevardnadze delivered a letter from Gorbachev to the White House that chided Reagan for using the Daniloff incident to launch a "massive hostile campaign" against the Soviet Union and rejected the arms control proposal Reagan had made in his July 25 letter. The tone of the Gorbachev reply was stinging, with no hint of the warmth the Soviet leader had displayed at Geneva or in the New Year's day exchange of messages with Reagan.

The Gorbachev letter did, however, offer a ray of hope for the second summit that Reagan sought. In his letter Gorbachev said that the lagging arms control negotiations needed a "major impulse." He proposed a preparatory summit with Reagan in either Iceland or London to see if they could make progress in advance of a Washington summit. Reagan jumped at the idea, noting in his diary that he had "opted for Iceland." Formal acceptance was delayed until Shultz and Shevardnadze could work out a Zakharov-Daniloff swap, which the Soviets sweetened by allowing two prominent dissidents to emigrate to the United States. The summit was set for the second weekend in October in Reykjavik, the Icelandic capitol.

On October 11, Reagan and Gorbachev, accompanied by note-takers and interpreters, faced each other across a rectangular wooden table at Hofdi House, a reputedly haunted former ambassadorial residence overlooking the sea. As soon as they were seated, Gorbachev pulled a set of notes from his briefcase and presented what he called his "bold, unorthodox" proposals to limit strategic weapons, intermediate-range weapons, and weapons in space. Reagan was surprised.

Clearly, Gorbachev had come to Iceland for more than a preparatory summit. Reagan was not primed for such discussions, as he had been at Geneva. Neither his national security adviser John Poindexter nor his chief of staff Donald Regan had anticipated a full-dress summit, and this White House staff had no fallback position in case Reykjavik failed.

The conversation continued for fifty-one minutes with the voluble Gorbachev doing most of the talking. They were then joined by Shultz and Shevardnadze, and Gorbachev read his proposals aloud in the form of a directive that the two leaders would issue Sunday afternoon to their foreign ministers outlining the "principles" that would guide them in drawing up agreements to be signed at a Washington summit. Gorbachev's proposals were indeed bold. He proposed a 50 percent cut in strategic missiles and reiterated his idea of eliminating U.S. and Soviet intermediate-range missiles in Europe while allowing British and French missiles to remain. This, Gorbachev told Reagan, was "your own zero option." Gorbachev also proposed that both sides agree to abide by the ABM treaty for ten years during which SDI research was confined to the laboratory. This was a concession, since the Soviets had previously insisted on fifteen years.

When the meeting broke up, Gorbachev had spoken so long and said so much that Reagan could not remember all the specifics as he briefed the U.S. team in the "bubble," a tiny room of trans-

Reykjavik summit, October 11–12, 1986

parent plastic made secure from electronic eavesdropping.
But he had no doubt about Gorbachev's main objective.
"He's brought a whole lot of proposals, but I'm afraid he's
going after SDI," Reagan said to Shultz.

The leaders met again that afternoon, with Shultz and
Shevardnadze present from the start. Reagan reiterated his
view that SDI was not an offensive system—he compared it
to gas masks soldiers had used in World War I and said that
defensive systems would be an insurance policy for both
sides. He also proposed replacing the ABM treaty; Gorbachev replied that it should be strengthened. To resolve their
differences, Shultz proposed two working groups of experts,
one to deal with arms control and the other with human
rights and regional issues. Paul Nitze was named to head the
U.S. arms control group, facing off against a team headed by
Gorbachev's favorite general, Marshal Sergei Akhromeyev,
the chief of the Soviet General Staff. Beginning at 8 P.M., the
arms control group worked nonstop for six hours, with the
Soviets making substantial concessions on technical issues
and Akhromeyev impressing the Americans with his blunt,
direct way of speaking. At 2 A.M. on Sunday, October 12,
Akhromeyev requested a recess and the leaders of the working groups reported back to Shevardnadze and Shultz. An
hour later they returned for five more hours of discussions.
Again, the Soviets made concessions on nuclear weapons,
but the two sides, as Shultz put it, were at "a very serious
impasse" on missile defense.

The discussions resumed after lunch on Sunday, with
Shultz and Shevardnadze leading their respective teams. In
an effort to break the impasse, the Americans came up with
a creative proposal—devised by Richard Perle and Colonel
Robert Linhard, the arms control specialist on the National
Security Council staff—that redefined the ten-year period of
compliance with the ABM treaty proposed by Gorbachev.
During the first five years, strategic nuclear missiles on both
sides would be reduced by 50 percent. Both sides would

abide by the treaty for another five years if all ballistic missiles were eliminated during that time. After ten years each side would be free to deploy a strategic defense system. Shultz and Shevardnadze took this proposal to their leaders.

Reagan liked the idea. "He gets his precious ABM treaty, and we get all his ballistic missiles," he said to Shultz. "And after that we deploy SDI in space. Then it's a whole new ball game." When the president met Gorbachev again just before 3 P.M. on Sunday, the Soviet leader expanded the U.S. proposal by proposing to do away with all nuclear weapons in ten years. "It would be fine with me if we eliminated all nuclear weapons," Reagan said. But what was not fine was Gorbachev's insistence that SDI be confined to the laboratory during this time. When Gorbachev reiterated this position, Reagan became angry. "I've told you, if we find out that SDI is practical and feasible, we'll make that information known to you and everyone else so that nuclear weapons can be made obsolete," Reagan told Gorbachev. "Now with all that we have accomplished here, you . . . throw in this roadblock and everything is out the window. There is no we way we are going to give up research to find a defense weapon against nuclear missiles."

Both men stood their ground. Gorbachev said that Reagan's refusal to confine SDI to laboratory research would create irresistible momentum toward deployment of space weapons. Gorbachev said he would be regarded as "the village idiot" in Moscow if he agreed to massive cuts in Soviet offensive weapons without any concessions on SDI. Reagan said he had made a promise to the American people to develop SDI and intended to keep it. Noting how close they were to an agreement, Reagan asked Gorbachev to "give me this one thing."

Gorbachev wouldn't do it. He said he didn't believe that the United States would share the fruits of its SDI research, a comment that irritated Reagan. Night was falling. The two leaders had met for four hours on Sunday afternoon, with a brief recess, and neither would budge on SDI. After Gorbachev rejected Reagan's request to "give me this one thing," Reagan closed his briefing book and stood up. "The meeting is over," he said. "Let's go, George, we're leaving." Gorbachev was stunned. The Soviets had made it known they were willing to spend another day in Reykjavik, and Gorbachev had more to say. As Reagan put his coat on, Gorbachev said to him, "Can't we do something about this?" Reagan shook his head. "It's too late," he said.

And so ended the Reykjavik summit. Journalists from all over the world had spent the day in the summit press center, as rumors circulated that the two sides were about to reach a historic agreement. But when the reporters saw television pictures of the two leaders grimly leaving Hofdi House, they knew that something had gone wrong. Shultz arrived at the press center in a mournful mood and gave an unusually emotional briefing, making no effort to hide his own "great sense of disappointment." A two-line banner headline in *The Washington Post* the next day summarized the first judgment on Reykjavik: "Reagan-Gorbachev Summit Talks Collapse as Deadlock on SDI Wipes Out Other Gains."

With midterm elections approaching, the White House "spin patrol" tried to put a happy face on the summit. Reporters were skeptical of the claims of Don Regan and White House press aides that the summit had been a roaring success, but Reagan succeeded where his aides had failed by giving a candid nationally televised speech on October 13 in which he defended his refusal to restrict SDI. "I went to Reykjavik determined that everything was negotiable except two things: our freedom and our future," Reagan said. The explanation was persuasive. A *New York Times*-CBS poll taken the week after Reykjavik showed an 11 percent jump (to 72 percent) in the percentage of Americans who thought Reagan was successfully handling relations with the Soviet Union. Gorbachev was also doing his best. Although he castigated SDI in a post-Reykjavik news conference that was even bleaker in tone than Shultz's briefing, the Soviet leader saw portents of success. "We have reached agreement on many things," Gorbachev said. "We have traveled a long road."

In the immediate aftermath of Reykjavik, which Shultz called "the highest-stakes poker game ever played," the world saw the Iceland summit as a gallant failure in which both sides had negotiated earnestly but wound up empty-handed. Instead, as Don Oberdorfer observed in *The Turn,* a history of the end of the Cold War, Reykjavik "paradoxically would be a turning point in the relations" between the United States and the Soviet Union. Although Reagan and Gorbachev would never see eye to eye on SDI, the two sides had come so far in their discussions before the summit collapsed that an outline of an agreement to eliminate medium-range missiles in Europe had emerged.

Working out the specifics of the Intermediate Nuclear Forces (INF) treaty would take time, however. In 1987, Gorbachev was under pressure because of the deepening Soviet economic crisis; his government faced internal opposition from left and right. Reagan, meanwhile, was dogged by the Iran-contra disclosures, which caused his popularity to plummet and preoccupied him well into the spring of 1987. Like Gorbachev, he also faced an aroused political opposition. Democrats had won control of the Senate in the 1986 elections, limiting Reagan's freedom of maneuver.

As is usually the case, however, control of Congress by the opposition had greater impact on domestic policies than on foreign affairs. Reagan's appointments now came under close scrutiny from the Senate, which, after a fierce battle, in October rejected his nomination of Robert Bork to the Supreme Court. A year earlier, with Republicans in control, the nomination of Antonin Scalia, who had served on the

---

FOLLOWING TWO PAGES: *Talking points for a phone call to Judge Robert H. Bork*

THE WHITE HOUSE

WASHINGTON

MEMORANDUM FOR THE PRESIDENT

Recommended Telephone Call

TO: Judge Robert H. Bork

TELEPHONE: 202 862-1712 (Montpelier Room
                        at Madison Hotel; 1:30 p.m.
                        luncheon reservation)

                        ███████████ (home after the
                        luncheon)

DATE TO CALL: Friday, October 23, 1987

RECOMMENDED BY: Arthur B. Culvahouse, Jr.
                        Counsel to the President

PURPOSE: To thank him for all of his efforts
                        as the President's nominee as
                        Associate Justice of the Supreme Court
                        of the United States.

TOPICS OF
DISCUSSION: 1. I am saddened and very disappointed
                           that the Senate rejected Judge
                           Bork's nomination.

                       2. You are one of the finest judges in
                           America's history, a truly
                           distinguished jurist. However, your
                           nomination became a distorted,
                           unseemly political campaign.

                       3. Your courage in facing an uphill
                           battle to maintain the independence
                           of our judicial system is
                           remarkable.

                       4. Your willingness to press forward to
                           a final Senate Vote and not withdraw
                           under pressure was an all too rare
                           exercise of conviction and
                           principle.

5. I deeply appreciate your efforts.
    It was an honor to nominate you. I
    wish you and your family the very
    best. You will be vindicated by
    history.

DATE OF
SUBMISSION: October 23, 1987

ACTION _____ *Call made* _____

same appellate court as Bork and was more conservative on some issues, had sailed through the Senate. After Bork was rejected, Reagan was able to win unanimous Senate confirmation of Anthony Kennedy, who had avoided the numerous controversies into which Bork injected himself. The confirmation of Kennedy gave Reagan a successful overall record—three victories in four tries—in his selections to the high court. In 1981 he had kept a campaign promise to put a woman on the Supreme Court by nominating Sandra Day O'Connor. She was a first; so, too, was Scalia, who was the first justice of Italian descent.

With his domestic political clout diminished, Reagan became more determined than ever to secure agreement on a major arms-control accord. It didn't come easily. Neither U.S. allies in Europe nor the Joint Chiefs of Staff had any enthusiasm for the bold ideas tossed about by Reagan and Gorbachev at Reykjavik to eliminate strategic missiles. While there was more support for an INF treaty, which Gorbachev unlinked from other agreements and the SDI issue on February 28, problems remained on many questions, including medium-range Soviet missiles in Asia and shorter-range missiles in East Germany and Czechoslovakia. Then there was West Germany, which wanted to retain seventy-two aging Pershing 1-A missiles. At one point, alone in the Oval Office with his new chief of staff Howard Baker, a frustrated Reagan turned to him and said, "Howard, I think I'm the only person left in this government who wants to see the completion of an INF treaty with the Soviets." Baker told him that he was wrong, that "many people" wanted the treaty. One of them was Baker, who worked closely with Shultz and national security adviser Frank Carlucci in restoring the collegiality that had marked the administration's halcyon days.

In April, Shultz went to Moscow, where Gorbachev told him the Soviet Union would destroy its shorter-range missiles in East Germany and Czechoslovakia, leaving it to the

United States to persuade West Germany to scrap its missiles. On April 15, Shultz announced that the two sides had agreed to remove all medium-range missiles within four to five years and said an INF treaty must contain provisions for "very strict and intrusive verification." On June 12, appropriately in Reykjavik, NATO foreign ministers called for "global and effectively verifiable" elimination of all intermediate-range and shorter-range missiles. On July 23, Gorbachev accepted this concept, known as "double global zero," and said the Soviet Union would destroy their intermediate-range and shorter-range missiles if the United States would do the same. On August 26, Helmut Kohl announced that West Germany would dismantle its Pershing missiles.

Gorbachev's acceptance of the "double global zero" formula and particularly of on-site verification, which previous Soviet leaders had adamantly opposed, led to swift resolution of the remaining issues. On September 18 Shultz and Shevardnadze met in Washington and announced they had agreed in principle on an INF treaty. Shevardnadze brought other good news as well: he told Shultz that Gorbachev had decided to withdraw Soviet troops from Afghanistan within eighteen months and would make this announcement in December.

Reagan by now had recovered the habitual optimism that had deserted him in the aftermath of the Iran-contra disclosures. In June he made a ten-day tour of Europe that included participation in the economic summit in Venice and was capped by a visit to West Berlin where Reagan stood before the Brandenburg Gate, then the symbol of Europe's division, and made one of the most memorable speeches of his presidency. He challenged Gorbachev to create a new era of freedom in Europe. After asking whether the stirrings of "reform and openness" that had begun in the Soviet Union signaled "profound changes" or were merely "token gestures," Reagan said:

There is one sign the Soviets can make that would be unmistakable, that would advance dramatically the cause of freedom and peace.

General Secretary Gorbachev, if you seek peace, if you seek prosperity for the Soviet Union and Eastern Europe, if you seek liberalization: Come here to this gate!

Mr. Gorbachev, open this gate! Mr. Gorbachev, tear down this wall!

.   .   .

Gorbachev made one last attempt to link SDI to nuclear arms reduction. On October 21, at a meeting in Moscow with Shultz and Carlucci, the Soviet leader launched into a tirade about anti-Soviet attitudes in the United States and suggested there was no point to a Washington summit unless Reagan was willing to give ground on SDI or the ABM treaty. Shultz called his bluff, saying it was possible to sign and ratify the INF treaty without a summit, but that it would carry more weight if Reagan and Gorbachev signed it. For three days after the U.S. team left Moscow, the fate of the summit was in doubt. But on October 26, the Soviet foreign ministry asked for visas so that Shevardnadze and his team could come to Washington for summit preparations. "The Soviets blinked," Reagan wrote in his diary.

The INF treaty was signed in the East Room of the White House on December 8, 1987, the first day of the Washington summit. Sitting side by side at a table once used by Abraham Lincoln, Reagan and Gorbachev signed two copies of the treaty, one bound in slate-blue leather for the United States and the other in burgundy-red leather for the Soviet Union. Their action would lead to the destruction of 859 U.S. missiles and 1,836 Soviet missiles with a range of 300 to 3,400 miles—about 4 percent of the nuclear arsenals of the two superpowers. But the treaty's importance, as Reagan said at the signing ceremony, transcended numbers.

The INF treaty was the first U.S.-Soviet accord of any kind to provide for destruction of nuclear weapons and also the first to provide on-site monitoring of this action by representatives of the two nations.

The signing ceremony demonstrated the comfortable familiarity with each other that Reagan and Gorbachev had developed at Geneva and Reykjavik.

"We have listened to the wisdom of an old Russian maxim," said Reagan. "The maxim is *doverey, no proverey*—trust but verify."

Signing the INF treaty

The final moments of the signing of the INF treaty—the first U.S.–Soviet accord to reduce nuclear weapons

"You repeat that at every meeting," Gorbachev said
good-naturedly.

"I like it," Reagan said.

The private meetings did not go as well as the public
ones. The two leaders had a sharp exchange on human
rights, and Reagan told a shopworn anti-Soviet anecdote
that Gorbachev didn't like. In another session Gorbachev
asked Reagan to discontinue U.S. aid to the Afghan
mujahadeen once the Soviets began withdrawing from
Afghanistan, and Reagan asked Gorbachev to cut off military aid to Nicaragua. These actions would happen in time,
but neither leader was willing to commit to them at the
Washington summit. Nor was either leader willing to com-

Celebrating the signing of the INF treaty

mit to a strategic arms treaty, for the same reasons as at Reykjavik. Reagan remained wedded to deploying an antimissile system, while Gorbachev still wanted to confine SDI to the laboratory.

Outside the formal sessions, Gorbachev was the star performer in Washington, somewhat to the surprise of the Americans. The capital city, which usually takes visitors in stride, was gripped with what *Washington Post* columnist Tom Shales called "Gorby fever." On December 7, after arriving in Washington, Gorbachev told an applauding group of celebrities that "something very profound" was happening in U.S.-Soviet relations. By December 10, departure day, Gorbachev was behaving like an American politician, much to the consternation of the Secret Service and the KGB. Crowds lined the street to applaud him. On busy Connecticut Avenue he brought traffic to a halt by ordering his limousine to stop so he could get out and shake hands with well-wishers.

In a rainswept departure ceremony on the South Lawn of the White House, Reagan called the summit "a clear success." His own great contribution to this success would come after Gorbachev had returned home, and conservatives mounted a well-financed and sophisticated campaign against ratification of the INF treaty by the Senate, where a two-thirds vote was required. The pet conservative theory about Reagan, which ignored the fact he had favored a "zero option" INF treaty since 1981, was that he was so weakened by the Iran-contra affair that he had become overly accommodating to Gorbachev.

Borrowing the techniques that a left-liberal coalition had used successfully to stir up public opposition to the Supreme Court confirmation of Bork, the antitreaty forces generated 300,000 letters of opposition, distributed 5,000 cassette recordings of an attack on the treaty by former NATO commander General Bernard Rogers, and ran newspaper advertisements comparing Reagan to Neville Chamberlain, the gullible British prime minister who had signed an accord with Hitler and predicted "peace in our time." Reagan's ideological mentor, William F. Buckley, opposed ratification in the *National Review,* and said he couldn't understand Reagan's enthusiasm for a treaty that ignored "the larger question" of whether Europe would be safer without the missiles. Reagan invited Buckley to the White House for a friendly conversation but failed to persuade him of the treaty's merits.

Nor was opposition limited to the far right. Henry Kissinger, while professing support for the treaty, gave aid and comfort to its opponents by saying he had "grave reservations" about its effect on the East-West balance of power. Liberal Democrats, led by Senator Joseph Biden of Delaware, made an issue of what they saw as Reagan's loose interpretation of the ABM treaty. Biden sought to attach a reservation to the INF treaty that would have written into law the Senate's historic powers in treaty-making. After negotiations with Shultz and Senate Republicans he settled for a milder reservation banning future administrations from reinterpreting the INF treaty. But the Reagan administration was not out of the woods. Senate conservatives led by Jesse Helms of North Carolina, who called the INF treaty "an engraved invitation to cheat," proposed amendments that would have required Soviet compliance with other treaties to make the INF accord operable—known as "killer amendments" because they were unacceptable to the Soviets. After these amendments were rejected Helms led a filibuster against the treaty. Reagan told Senate leaders he did not want the embarrassment of arriving in Moscow for his fourth summit with Gorbachev with the treaty unratified. They agreed and choked off the filibuster. On May 27, 1988, two days before the beginning of the Moscow summit, the Senate approved the INF treaty by a 93–5 vote. It was a decisive triumph for Reagan. The conservative campaign to block INF might well have succeeded against a president with less impeccable anticommunist credentials, but the notion that Reagan had gone soft on the Soviet Union was not credible to most Americans. Polls showed that the public overwhelmingly supported the treaty and believed that Reagan had acted in the best interests of the United States.

The Moscow summit was a triumph, too. Previous Reagan-Gorbachev summits had been held in the late fall or winter gloom of Geneva, Reykjavik, and Washington. Now, as Reagan observed in his arrival remarks at the Kremlin, it was nearly summer and the seeds of their earlier meetings "are beginning to bear fruit." The Senate's nick-of-time ratification of the INF treaty made it possible for Reagan

Arriving in Moscow for the summit

and Gorbachev to exchange the documents of ratification, placing the treaty officially in force. But this was a formality. The significance of the Moscow summit had much less to do with the modest documents signed there than with the fact that Reagan was visiting the country he had labeled "the evil empire" and doing business with Gorbachev, whom he now called "my friend." Praising Reagan's "realism" on the eve of his arrival, Gorbachev said: "Who would have thought in the early eighties that it would be President Reagan who would sign with us the first nuclear-arms reduction agreement in history?"

Reagan had more in mind, however, than simply showing up. He looked upon a summit in Moscow as a unique opportunity to make the case for freedom that had been the cornerstone of his campaigns for the presidency and in a larger sense of his entire political career. At Reykjavik he had brought Gorbachev a list of 1,200 Soviet Jews who sought to emigrate. In Washington he had given the Soviet leader other lists of dissidents and members of separated families. In Moscow, he presented Gorbachev with a list of fourteen specific human rights cases on which he said the United States wanted action. When asked if he would act on the U.S. requests, Gorbachev became testy. "There are too many lists," he complained.

Reagan particularly wanted to dramatize the plight of Soviet Jews. With this in mind, Nancy Reagan suggested they visit a well-known Jewish refusenik family, the Ziemans, who had been waiting to emigrate since 1977. Soviet deputy foreign minister Alexander Bessmertnykh sent word that the foreign ministry was quietly arranging for their emigration to the United States but would be unable to accomplish this if the Reagans insisted on putting them in the

FOLLOWING TWO PAGES: *A 1981 letter to Brezhnev regarding a well-known Soviet dissident, Natan Sharansky. In a small way, it illustrates a long history of Reagan's work on behalf of Soviet Jews*

My Dear Mr. President

I'm sorry to be so long in answering your letter to me and can only offer as an excuse the problems of settling into a routine after my hospitalization. I ask your pardon.

I won't attempt a point by point response to your letter because I agree with your observation that these matters are better discussed in person than in writing. Needless to say we are not in agreement on a number of points raised in both my letter & yours.

There is one matter however which I feel I must bring to your attention. All information having to do with my govt's practices & policies past & present is available to me now that I hold this office. I have thoroughly investigated the matter of the man Scharansky an inmate in one of your prisons. I can assure you he was never involved in any way with any agency of the U.S. govt. I have seen news stories in the Soviet press suggesting that he was engaged in espionage for our country. Let me assure you this is absolutely false.

Recently his wife called upon me. They were married and spent one day together before she emigrated to Israel assuming that he would follow shortly thereafter. I believe true justice would be done if he were released and allowed to join her.

If you could find it in your heart to do this the matter would be strictly between us which is why I'm writing this letter by hand.

While on this subject may I also enter a plea on behalf of the two familys who have been living in most uncomfortable circumstances in our embassy in Moscow for three years. The _____ family & the _____ are pentecostal christians who feared possible persecution because of their religion. Members of that church in America would, I know, provide for them here if they were allowed to come to the U.S.

Again as in the case of Schoransky this is between the two of us and I will not reveal that I ~~requested~~ made any such request. I'm sure however ~~that~~ you ~~can~~ understand ~~how~~ that ~~much~~ such action on your part would ~~be~~ lessen my problems in future negotiations between our two countries.

Sincerely

spotlight. The Reagans reluctantly called off the visit and saw the Ziemans the following day at a reception at the U.S. embassy for refuseniks and dissidents. Subsequently, the Ziemans were permitted to emigrate to the United States, where they settled in Boston.

As a substitute for the Zieman visit on their first night in Moscow, the Reagans went for a Sunday stroll on the Arbat, a famous pedestrian mall lined with artisans' shops and cafés. When the Russians learned that the Reagans were in their midst, they surged forward to get a glimpse. Without provocation, KGB security formed a flying wedge and charged the crowd, hurling people aside and pounding on them with their fists. Reagan was shaken. That night he wrote in his diary: "It was amazing how quickly the street was jammed curb to curb with people—warm friendly people who couldn't have been more affectionate. In addition to our Secret Service, the KGB was on hand, and I've never seen such brutal manhandling as they did on their own people who were in no way getting out of hand."

To the surprise of Soviet authorities, Reagan was even more popular in Moscow than Gorbachev had been in Washington. Everywhere his motorcade went, crowds lined up to cheer. "The Russians loved him," wrote Gorbachev biographers Doder and Branson. Reagan's speeches to Soviet writers, intellectuals, dissidents, and students were dotted with Russian literary allusions supplied by U.S. Ambassador Jack Matlock and James Billington, the librarian of Congress. Gorbachev's biographers thought these speeches were among Reagan's "most spectacular performances and touched the deepest chords of the Russian psyche." They quoted a Muscovite as saying, "I'm not religious, but I was delighted to hear him end his speeches by saying, 'God bless you.' We never heard it said before on television."

On Monday, May 30, Reagan visited the Danilov Monastery, a spiritual oasis for Orthodox religious, and proclaimed his "hope for a new age of religious freedom in the Soviet Union." Then he spoke at Spaso House, the U.S. ambassador's residence, to ninety-six dissidents, who had come from all corners of the Soviet empire. Reagan said his human rights agenda was freedom of religion, freedom of speech, and freedom of travel for the Soviet people. "I've come to Moscow with this human rights agenda because . . . it is our belief that this is a moment of hope," Reagan said. To his audience's delight, he ended his speech with a quotation from the poet Aleksander Pushkin: "It's time, my friend, it's time."

On Tuesday, May 31, the third of his five-day visit, Gorbachev accompanied Reagan on a leisurely tour of Red Square, explaining its history and that of nearby St. Basil's Cathedral. The two leaders were approached by carefully screened groups, one composed of women, to whom Reagan said, "I have great admiration for the women of Russia. You are so courageous and contribute so much to Soviet society." This sentiment, rarely voiced by Soviet officials, pleased the women, and Reagan's statement was featured on the front page of *Pravda*.

When the two leaders returned to the Kremlin grounds, a reporter asked Reagan what had become of the "evil empire."

"I was talking about another time, another era," Reagan replied.

His remark was overheard by Gorbachev, who proudly quoted it later in the summit and afterward. When another reporter asked the two leaders if they were "old friends" after all their meetings, Gorbachev replied, "Da, da," without hesitation. "Yes," agreed Reagan.

The president's best performance in his role as freedom's advocate occurred that afternoon at Moscow State University, where he stood beneath a gigantic white bust of Lenin and addressed the students on the value of a free society. "Freedom is the right to question and change the established way of doing things," Reagan said. "It is the continuing revolution of the marketplace. It is the understanding that allows us to recognize shortcomings and seek solutions. It is the right to put forth an idea, scoffed at by the experts, and watch it catch fire among the people. It is the right to dream—to follow your dream and stick to your conscience, even if you're the only one in a sea of doubters." As the students listened raptly, Reagan explained that "Americans seek always to make friends of old antagonists," as they had done with the British after the War for Independence, among themselves after the Civil War, and with the Germans and Japanese after World War II. Now, he said, as the Soviet Union began its journey to freedom, it was time for Americans and the Soviet people to become friends:

> We do not know what the conclusion will be of this journey, but we're hopeful that the promise of reform will be fulfilled. In this Moscow spring, this May 1988, we may be allowed that hope: that freedom, like the fresh green sapling planted over Tolstoy's grave, will blossom forth at last in the rich fertile soil of your people and culture. We may be allowed to hope that the marvelous sound of a new openness will keep rising, ringing through, leading to a new world of reconciliation, friendship, and peace.

After the speech, a relaxed Reagan took questions from the students—another rarity in the Soviet Union. The students enjoyed the give-and-take and applauded and cheered his answers. As we left the hall, my colleague Gary Lee, then the Moscow correspondent for *The Washington Post,* overheard two women students chatting in Russian. He laughed. "What are they saying?" I asked. Lee told me that one of the students had praised Reagan's speech and that the other had responded: "You can see why he's called the Great Communicator."

In comparison to his speeches and informal exchanges,

three of Reagan's four private meetings with Gorbachev were pale and ceremonial. It was only at their final business meeting on June 1 that Gorbachev challenged Reagan, as he had done at their previous summits. This time the challenge came not over SDI but the text of a joint communiqué to which Gorbachev wanted to append a statement on "peaceful coexistence." Reagan did not object, but his advisers—Shultz, Carlucci (now secretary of defense), and national security adviser Colin Powell—thought the statement uncomfortably resembled Soviet propaganda dredged up from the depths of the Cold War. When Reagan said he couldn't sign it because his advisers opposed it, Gorbachev said, "Well, Mr. President, I don't understand why you're not for peace."

Reagan did not take the bait. He had come too far and accomplished too much to end the summit with a quarrel, and he repeated quietly that he couldn't sign it. Gorbachev fell silent for a moment, then brightened and put his arm around Reagan. "Mr. President, we had a great time," he said.

Reagan departed Moscow on June 2 after saying there had been "sizeable improvement" on human rights under Gorbachev, who had already freed 300 people on the various lists Reagan had given him. Another hundred dissidents, including many who had heard Reagan at Spaso House, would be allowed to emigrate within a few months. Tens of thousands of Jews would leave for Israel and the United States in the years to come as Gorbachev's government relaxed restrictions on emigration.

In a June 3 speech at Guildhall in London on his way home, Reagan celebrated the Moscow summit as a turning point in East-West relations. He said a "worldwide movement toward democracy" was ushering in "the hope of a new era in human history, and, hopefully, an era of peace and freedom for all." The speech echoed Reagan's prediction at Westminster six years earlier that "the tides of history were running in the cause of liberty."

Responding to his speech, British prime minister Margaret Thatcher paid tribute to Reagan for his persistent effort "to enlarge freedom the world over" and for his leadership of the Western alliance.

"God bless America," she said.

REAGAN REMEMBERED

The Reagan presidency casts a long shadow.

In foreign affairs the symbiotic relationship forged by Reagan and Gorbachev and the achievement of the INF treaty marked the beginning of the end of the Cold War and, as it turned out, of the Soviet Union itself. The demise of the Soviet Union in turn had domestic economic consequences for the United States, the most important of which was a sharp reduction in the record peacetime military spending of the early Reagan years. By the end of the twentieth century, U.S. military spending was 3 percent of the gross domestic product, the lowest level since Pearl Harbor. As discussed in "Staying the Course", this created a context in which a Democratic president and a Republican Congress were in time able to transform the accumulated budget deficits of the Reagan years into a string of surpluses.

The political legacy of the Reagan presidency was also far-reaching. When the Republicans won control of the House in 1994 after a hiatus of nearly four decades, they ran on a platform called the "Contract with America" devised by House Republican leader Newt Gingrich, who took many of its proposals from Reagan's final State of the Union address. That Gingrich received credit for the Republican victory wouldn't have troubled Reagan. Throughout his presidency he kept a sign on his desk in the Oval Office that said, "There's no limit to what a man can do or where he can go if he doesn't mind who gets the credit."

Credit aside, the 1994 election resulted in fifty-three new Republican House members, most of them Reagan disciples. Political historian Michael Barone has observed that there were more New Deal Democrats in 1958 than at any time during Franklin D. Roosevelt's presidency; similarly, there are more Reagan Republicans in Congress today than when Reagan was in the White House. Like his early hero FDR, Reagan became his party's enduring idol. And like FDR, he influenced the opposition party as much as his own. New Deal measures such as Social Security became so popular that Republican legislators who had fought them tooth and nail embraced them as a matter of political survival. A half century later, in the aftermath of the Vietnam War and Watergate, many Americans wanted to rein in a pervasive federal government that had lost their trust.

Reagan became their champion. He was so popular in the West and South, especially, that a number of Democratic legislators in these regions supported him on crucial issues for political reasons, as some Republicans had once gone along with Roosevelt.

With his landslide reelection victory in 1984 over a respected liberal—an election in which he won a majority among independents and obtained a fourth of the votes cast by Democrats—Reagan demonstrated to the Democrats that they had little hope of regaining the White House unless they moved to the center. In this way he exercised a rightward tug on the political system, cre-

ating the context for a Clinton presidency and such measures as the conservative federal welfare bill of 1996. Reagan also helped set the agenda for the Republican administration that followed the two-term Clinton presidency. George W. Bush's most conspicuous early success as president in 2001 was passage of a major income tax reduction that emulated the Reagan tax cut of 1981. In national defense Bush picked up the torch of missile defense that Reagan had lit in 1983.

At once self-confident and modest, Reagan never saw himself as bigger than the causes he espoused. His presidential farewell

Saying good-bye to the Oval Office

speech ranks with Eisenhower's for its notable humility. Nor was Reagan carried away with his reputation as the "Great Communicator," although he certainly spoke powerfully in crises such as the *Challenger* space shuttle disaster on January 28, 1986, when he gave a memorable, life-affirming speech to a grief-stricken nation. Reagan recognized, however, that the label of "Great Communicator" often was used to disparage his ideas by praising the way he presented them. Reagan, to whom ideas were important, knew better. As he said in his farewell address:

> I never thought it was my style or the words I used that made a difference: it was the content. I wasn't a great communicator, but I communicated great things, and they didn't spring full bloom from my brow, they came from the heart of a great nation— from our experience, our wisdom, and our belief in the principles that have guided us for two centuries. They called it the Reagan revolution. Well, I'll accept that, but for me it always seemed more like the great rediscovery, a rediscovery of our values and our common sense.

．　　．　　．

When Reagan left office in January 1989 the Berlin Wall still marked the division of Germany. Within the year, the barrier that Reagan had urged Gor-

bachev to tear down had been demolished, as Gorbachev subsequently said, by Germans exercising "their free choice." Germany was unified in 1990. On Christmas Day, 1991, Gorbachev stepped down and the Soviet empire expired, fulfilling Reagan's prophecy in his June 8, 1982, speech at the Palace of Westminster that "the march of freedom and democracy" would "leave Marxism-Leninism on the ash heap of history." Reagan had also been proved right in his first impression that Gorbachev was a different kind of Soviet leader, with a moral dimension that made him unwilling to shed blood to save the discredited political system he had sought to reform.

In the aftermath of these events, many viewed the Soviet breakup as inevitable, a natural product of fundamental and internal change. But even those who took this view recognized that the Cold War could have ended in violence, either through accident or miscalculation. Jack Matlock, the U.S. ambassador to the Soviet Union at the time of its passing, believes that the firm military and diplomatic policies of the Reagan administration were crucial to the outcome. In *Autopsy on an Empire,* Matlock wrote that the Cold War ended because of the coincidence of "a Western policy that combined strength and firmness with a willingness to negotiate fairly" and "a Soviet leadership that finally realized that the country could not go on as it had, that it had to change internally, but that it could do this only in cooperation with the outside world." Alexander Bessmertnykh, first deputy under

Shevardnadze and later Soviet foreign minister, said that the Cold War was "ended by human beings, by people who were dedicated to eradicating this part of history."

In February 1993, the Princeton Conference on the End of the Cold War brought together nine leading former U.S. and Soviet diplomats, including George Shultz and Bessmertnykh, as well as other analysts. While they differed on some details, they agreed that the Cold War had not ended automatically. All the participants gave credit to Reagan and Gorbachev, none more eloquently than Bessmertnykh. "As for the common things," he said, "I would say that those two men were very idealistic. They each had their own ideals which they had tried to follow all through their lives. Their ideals were not similar, but the dedication to those ideals was similar. They both believed

The president's desk as displayed at the Reagan Library

in something. They were not just men who could trim their sails and go any way the wind blows. . . . This is what they immediately sensed in each other, and why they made good partners."

Bessmertnykh scoffed at opinions in "the American press" after Reykjavik that Reagan had fallen short as a negotiator. "It was not true at all," he said. "Reagan handled negotiations very, very well. He might not have known all the details. He used little cards when he would come to details. He didn't like the formal part of negotiations. . . . He would try to rush through this formal part, and then he would throw away the cards and then he would start talking the direct way. I was across the table at all the summits and followed this president for all those years, and I personally admired the man very much. He was a good politician. He was a good diplomat. He was very dedicated. And if it were not for Reagan, I don't think we would have been able to reach the agreements in arms control that we reached later, because of his idealism, because he thought that we should really do away with nuclear weapons. Gorbachev believed in that. Reagan believed in that. The experts didn't believe, but the leaders did."

.   .   .

Ronald Reagan campaigned in 1988 for his vice president, helping George Bush win a decisive victory that some political analysts said partly reflected the longing of Americans for a third Reagan term. He returned to California from Washington without regrets on January 20, 1989, quipping to a welcoming rally at Los Angeles International Airport that he had been offered a part in a remake of *Bedtime for Bonzo,* "only this time they wanted me to play Bonzo." Reagan was happy to be home. "When you have to stay eight years away from California, you live in a perpetual state of homesickness," he said.

The Reagans resumed their comfortable Southern California lifestyle, settling into a spacious, three-bedroom ranch-style house on a wooded acre in Bel Air, close to old friends and a five-minute drive from Reagan's new office on the thirty-fourth floor of 2121 Avenue of the Stars in Century City. The office has a western window from which, on clear days, Reagan could glimpse the Pacific Ocean in the distance. Reagan, observed his wife, had a preference for heights. The Ronald Reagan Presidential Library was built on a mountaintop in Simi Valley, and Reagan's beloved 688-acre ranch (Rancho del Cielo or "Heavenly Ranch") was on a mountaintop northwest of Santa Barbara. Whenever he could, Reagan slipped off to ride at Rancho del Cielo, where, on May 3, 1992, he and Nancy Reagan hosted Mikhail and Raisa Gorbachev the day before he gave Gorbachev the first Ronald Reagan Freedom Award in a ceremony at the presidential library. Apart from his trips to the ranch, Reagan worked diligently in his Century City office on his memoirs. Following the habits of a lifetime, he cleared off his desk at the end of the day. He stayed politically active, making twenty-nine speeches or videotapings for Republican candidates in the 1990 elections.

But Reagan was slowing down. The first sign of difficulty came in July 1989, when he suffered a concussion after falling on his head during a riding accident. His recovery was less rapid than expected. During the next two years he sometimes faltered but remained engaged. He was lucid and reflective when I interviewed him for a story in *The Washington Post* on February 6, 1991, his eightieth birthday. That night he attended a fundraising dinner for the Ronald Reagan Presidential Library at which the featured speaker was Margaret Thatcher. When it was Reagan's turn to speak he praised Thatcher effusively but saved his best line for Nancy Reagan. "Put simply, my life really began when I met her and has been rich and full ever since," he said.

Reagan's last great performance came at the Republican National Convention of 1992 in Houston, where his generous and inspirational call to battle contrasted with the divisive and exclusionary rhetoric of many other speakers. Unwisely, the convention organizers did not use Reagan in prime time. Republican operatives also made less use of Reagan than he would have liked in the campaign that followed, which ended in a crushing Republican defeat. Bill Clinton, with an assist from Ross Perot, routed President Bush in California, which Reagan had

carried ten times in primaries and general elections for governor and president.

In 1993 Reagan's friends began to notice that he had become forgetful and was inclined to repeat himself. The public received an inkling of this when Reagan repeated a toast to Thatcher verbatim during a celebration of his eighty-second birthday at the Ronald Reagan Presidential Library. Afterward, public events on Reagan's schedule were reduced. In August 1994, the fears of the Reagans were confirmed at their annual visit to the Mayo Clinic, where Reagan was diagnosed with the mind-destroying neurological disorder known as Alzheimer's disease. In November the doctors made their findings public in keeping with the Reagans' longtime practice; he had disclosed clinical details of two cancer surgeries during his presidency and Nancy Reagan had been equally candid about her breast cancer in the belief that sharing her experience would encourage other women to take preventive measures.

The doctors' report was overshadowed by Reagan's poignant description of his plight. In a handwritten letter on November 5, 1994, he spoke to the nation for a final time, saying he had learned that he was one of the millions of Americans afflicted with Alzheimer's disease. "In opening our hearts, we hope this might promote greater awareness of this condition," Reagan wrote. "Perhaps it will encourage a clearer understanding of the individuals and families who are affected by it." Nancy Reagan called this farewell document "a typical Ronnie letter," and so it was. In it he expressed regret that he would become a "heavy burden" for his wife and said he wished he could "spare Nancy from this painful experience." Then he expressed the faith and confidence that had been a hallmark of his life and presidency:

> In closing let me thank you, the American people for giving me the great honor of allowing me to serve as your President. When the Lord calls me home, whenever that may be, I will leave with the greatest love for this country of ours and eternal optimism for its future.
>
> I now begin the journey that will lead me into the sunset of my life. I know that for America there will always be a bright dawn ahead.
>
> Thank you, my friends. May God always bless you.

The letter was signed: "Sincerely, Ronald Reagan."

Alzheimer's was indeed a heavy burden for Nancy Reagan, as it inevitably becomes for the principal caregivers of those who suffer from this disease. With the aid of a nurse, Nancy Reagan cared for her husband without complaint, guarding him from intrusion so that people would remember him as he had been before. When she was praised for her devotion, she often said he would have done the same for her. But it was hard and lonely nevertheless. "Not being able to share memories is an awful thing," she said.

But Reagan's letter did accomplish its declared purpose of promoting greater awareness. The letter was a boon to the Chicago-based Alzheimer's Association in its effort to increase understanding of the disease and raise money for its cure and treatment—a cause in which Reagan's daughter, Maureen, became active. By the end of the twentieth century, more than 4 million Americans suffered from Alzheimer's, and it was estimated that the number would grow to 14 million within fifty years unless a cure was found. But medical researchers have made progress in developing drugs that delay the onset of Alzheimer's and have been working assiduously toward developing a cure.

.   .   .

Reagan has for two decades placed high on the list of the nation's most popular presidents. His approval rating of 63 percent in the final Gallup poll of his presidency was the highest for any president leaving office since FDR died early in his fourth term, and *The New York Times*-CBS poll gave him an even higher rating of 68 percent. In a Gallup poll taken in February 2001, soon after Reagan's ninetieth birthday, Americans ranked Reagan as the greatest president of all time, slightly ahead of John F. Kennedy, with Abraham Lincoln third. Reagan's standing also has improved with academic historians and political scientists who tended to give him low marks during and just after his presidency. Reagan was ranked twenty-second among the-then forty presidents in one survey of these experts in 1989. More recently, four other such surveys have placed Reagan higher—anywhere from eleventh to third. Political historian James

MacGregor Burns, a Pulitzer Prize winner for his work on Franklin Roosevelt, wrote in *The Washington Post* on October 24, 1999, that Reagan will rank with FDR among the "great" or "near-great" presidents of the twentieth century.

Whatever his ranking, Reagan's contributions to America and to the cause of free-

RONALD REAGAN

Ronald Reagan's letter to the American people regarding the diagnosis of Alzheimer's

dom have been enormous. Writing about Reagan's achievements in his final month in office, Margaret Thatcher said he had "achieved the most difficult of all political tasks: changing attitudes and perceptions about what is possible. From the strong fortress of his convictions, he set out to enlarge freedom the world over at a time when freedom was in retreat—and he succeeded." On March 4, 2001, Ronald and Nancy Reagan's forty-ninth wedding anniversary, these words were echoed by President George W. Bush, at the dedication of the nuclear carrier *USS Ronald Reagan* at Newport News, Virginia. "As president, Ronald Reagan believed without question that tyranny is temporary, and the hope of freedom is universal and permanent," Bush said. "The strength of these beliefs gave strength to our allies and hope to political prisoners, and courage to average citizens in oppressed nations, and leadership to our military and to our country."

When Americans remember Ronald Reagan they are apt to recall his character, his principles, and his quintessential optimism. They remember him as The Gipper, who when asked if he could run with the football,

replied, "How far?" They remember that his sense of humor never deserted him—that he said in the hospital after he was shot, "All in all, I'd rather be in Philadelphia." They remember that Reagan stood tall in bad times as well as good, never quitting on his economic program or his dreams of peace.

Reagan was a mirror of America. "[He] does not argue for American values; he embodies them," wrote Garry Wills. Walter Lippmann once said of Charles de Gaulle that he was great not because he was in France but because France was in de Gaulle. Similarly, the greatness of Reagan was that he held a shining vision of America inside of him, a vision he carried all the way from Dixon, Illinois, to the White House.

On the eve of his election as president in 1980 a radio reporter asked Reagan what it was that Americans saw in him. Reagan, never one to brag, hesitated a moment before replying: "Would you laugh if I told you that I think, maybe, they see themselves and that I'm one of them? I've never been able to detach myself or think that I, somehow, am apart from them."

No one laughed, then or ever. Reagan and the American people were inseparable.

THE RONALD REAGAN PRESIDENTIAL LIBRARY AND MUSEUM

On November 4, 1991, an unprecedented gathering of five presidents—from Richard Nixon to George Bush—attended the dedication of the Ronald Reagan Presidential Library and Museum. "The doors of this library are open now and all are welcome," declared Ronald Reagan. "The judgment of history is left to you, the people. I have no fears of that. We have done our best. And so I say, 'Come and learn from it.'"

Set on a hilltop in Simi Valley, forty miles northwest of Los Angeles, the 153,000-square-foot library, two-thirds of which is underground, is built in a Spanish mission style. It commands a view of the Southern California hills that once served as a backdrop for Hollywood westerns when Reagan was a movie star.

The Library is made up of two distinct parts with separate, but complimentary, missions. The first is the museum with its permanent exhibit galleries and the special or temporary exhibit space. The permanent exhibit tells the story of President Reagan's American journey from childhood through the presidency. The exhibit includes an exact reproduction of the Oval Office, a piece of the Berlin Wall, a decommissioned Tomahawk Missile, interactive displays, gifts from around the world, and many personal items from President and Mrs. Reagan.

The temporary space features two to three exhibits per year that present important issues, themes and events related to President Reagan, the presidency, and/or leadership. These exhibits blend traditional museum experiences using historically significant objects with innovative production techniques and storytelling that create interest and excitement.

The *Spirit of America Series* is a recurring theme for many temporary exhibits. As president, Ronald Reagan restored national pride, patriotism, and re-ignited the spirit of America through his deep-seated belief in the American people. To honor that spirit, the Library created a series to celebrate and recognize great Americans—not only individuals, but also companies, events, entertainments, and locations that are uniquely American and represent our nation's distinct character.

The temporary exhibits are included in the museum admission charge. The museum is open every day except Thanksgiving, Christmas and New Year's day. The hours are 10:00 A.M.—5:00 P.M. For museum and exhibit information please call (800) 410–8354.

The second part of the Library is the

archive, which consists of material relating to the life and political career of Ronald Reagan. The mission of the archival staff is to arrange, preserve, and make available for research the approximately 50 million pages, 1.5 million photographs, 20,000 videotapes, 25,000 audio tapes, and 670,000 feet of film. The arranged and processed materials are available for research in the Library's research room, Monday through Friday from 9:00 A.M. to 5:00 P.M., and Saturdays by appointment.

While the vast majority of the records pertain to Ronald Reagan's two terms as president of the United States, the Library's archival collection also includes materials relating to his two terms as governor of California (1967–1974), as well as other pre- and post-presidential records.

SOURCES AND ACKNOWLEDGMENTS

This book is largely based on my accumulated writings about Ronald Reagan, which began in 1965 when he was a prospective candidate for governor of California and I was state capitol correspondent in Sacramento for the *San Jose Mercury-News*. During the next three decades I wrote more than two thousand articles or columns about Reagan, at first for the San Jose newspaper and then for *The Washington Post*, for which I was senior White House correspondent throughout the Reagan presidency. I also wrote three Reagan biographies: *Ronnie and Jesse: A Political Odyssey,* (Garden City, New York: Doubleday, 1969) *Reagan,* (New York: G.P. Putnam's Sons, 1982) *and President Reagan: The Role of a Lifetime* (New York: Simon & Schuster, 1991). The latter book, my most extensive, was updated and reissued in 2000 by PublicAffairs, the publisher of *Ronald Reagan: The Presidential Portfolio.* Some passages in this book are taken in slightly revised form from my previous books or articles.

The biographical essay in this book also draws upon some forty formal interviews and numerous informal conversations that I conducted with Reagan as governor, candidate, and president and on his post-presidential comments to Landon Parvin, a former White

House speechwriter, in *Speaking My Mind,* (New York: Simon & Schuster, 1989) a collection of Reagan speeches. Also useful were Reagan's early autobiography, *Where's The Rest of Me? Ronald Reagan Tells His Own Story* (New York: Dell, 1965) and his later memoirs, *An American Life* (New York: Simon & Schuster, 1990). The Public Papers of the Presidents issued by the U.S. Government Printing Office—a full fifteen volumes for the eight years of Reagan's presidency—were an indispensable resource.

In writing about the Illinois social context, Reagan's parents, Reagan's film career, and his experiences with General Electric, I frequently relied on *Reagan's America: Innocents at Home* (Garden City, New York: Doubleday, 1985) by Garry Wills, a Pulitzer Prize-winning historian. Also of benefit was Wills's article, "It's His Party," in the August 11, 1996, issue of *The New York Times Magazine.* I also consulted *The Films of Ronald Reagan* (Secaucus, New Jersey: Citadel Press, 1980) by Tony Thomas, the definitive book on Reagan's movie career.

The most valuable guide to the political context of the Reagan era is *Our Country: The Shaping of America from Roosevelt to Reagan,*

(New York: The Free Press, 1990) by Michael Barone, which I drew upon at several points. Michael generously shared his political insights for this book, as he has done on many occasions in the past. *The Rise of Ronald Reagan (*New York: Random House, 1968) by Bill Boyarsky provides a useful account of the 1966 gubernatorial campaign. The best and most detailed account of the 1976 presidential campaign is *Marathon: The Pursuit of the Presidency 1972–1976* (New York: The Viking Press, 1977) by Jules Witcover.

Among the many books by former Reagan aides, associates, or cabinet members, *Turmoil and Triumph* (New York: Charles Scribner's Sons, 1993) by George P. Shultz was especially useful. Also helpful were *Behind the Scenes* (New York: William Morrow, 1987) by Michael K. Deaver and *For The Record: From Wall Street to Washington* (New York: Harcourt Brace Jovanovich 1988) by Donald T. Regan.

I owe a special debt of gratitude to Martin Anderson and his wife, Annelise Anderson, both of whom played important roles in the Reagan presidency's early years. Martin Anderson's book, *Revolution,* (New York: Harcourt Brace Jovanovich, 1988) is the best account from a conservative perspective of the Reagan years. The Andersons and Kiron K. Skinner are the editors of *Reagan In His Own Hand,* (New York: The Free Press, 2001) a compilation of Reagan writings focusing on his radio speeches in the 1970s. I also thank the Andersons for their many insights and for providing the illustration of the Reagan speech, "Two Worlds," used in this book.

In discussing the tests from terrorism confronting the Reagan administration, *Best Laid Plans: The Inside Story of America's War Against Terrorism* (New York: A Touchstone Book, 1988) by David C. Martin and John Walcott was an essential text. On the Iran-contra affair, in addition to my own reporting, I relied upon *Iran-Contra: The Final Report,* (New York: Times Books, 1994) by Lawrence E. Walsh, the independent counsel who investigated it, and on an interview with Walsh that I conducted for the updated version of *President Reagan: The Role of a Lifetime.* Another useful book is *Special Trust* (New York: Cadell and Davies, 1994) by Robert C. McFarlane. I also consulted a May 15, 1988, article in *The Washington Post* by David M. Abshire, "Don Regan's Real 'Record'; Looking Out for Number One."

In writing about U.S.-Soviet relations, I consulted *The Turn: From the Cold War to a New Era* (New York: Poseidon Press, 1991) by Don Oberdorfer, my former colleague at *The Washington Post.* It is the best book about how and why the Cold War ended. Also useful were *Autopsy on an Empire: The American Ambassador's Account of the Collapse of the Soviet Union* (New York: Random House, 1995) by Jack F. Matlock, Jr., *Gorbachev: Heretic in the Kremlin* (New York: Viking Penguin, 1990) by Dusko Doder and Louise Branson, *Gorbachev: On My Country and the World* (New York: Columbia University Press, 2000) by Mikhail Gorbachev, and *Witnesses to the End of the Cold War,* (Baltimore: the Johns Hopkins University Press, 1996) edited by

William C. Wohlforth. The latter book is based upon the transcripts of the Princeton Conference on the End of the Cold War, held in February 1993.

The idea for the PublicAffairs Presidential Library series originated with Edwin Schlossberg. This book, the second in the series, was the brainchild of Peter Osnos, the publisher of PublicAffairs, and was carried to fruition by Robert Kimzey, my able and supportive editor. I owe an immense debt of gratitude to my wife and researcher, Mary Cannon, who once again carefully reviewed every page and made many corrections and helpful suggestions. My oldest son, Carl Cannon, the White House correspondent for *National Journal,* also read the manuscript and made good suggestions for improving it. My esteemed agent, Kristine Dahl of ICM, encouraged me to write this book with her customary cheerfulness and professionalism. Many people at PublicAffairs made valuable contributions to the final product, including page designers Jenny Dossin, Joan Greenfield, and Mark McGarry, production consultant Della Mancuso, photo researchers Melissa Totten and Kate Darnton, and photographer Brian Forrest. I appreciate the careful work of copy editor Anais Scott. If there are errors in it, they are my responsibility alone.

This book would not have been possible without the assistance of Mark Burson, the executive director of the Ronald Regan Presidential Foundation, who provided a wealth of illustrations and other material. I appreciate

the help and support of Kirby Elizabeth Hanson, director of programs for the foundation. Many thanks also to Joanne Drake, the chief of staff of the Office of President Ronald Reagan, for her assistance and dependability.

Robert Kimzey and I appreciate the assistance of many people at the Ronald Reagan Presidential Library, especially R. Duke Blackwood, the director; archivist Gregory Cumming, who helped check various important details from the many thousands of documents available in the library, archivist Steve Branch, an invaluable resource on Reagan photographs, his colleague, Josh Tenenbaum, and curator John P. Langellier, who shared his knowledge of the many thousands of artifacts stored at the library. I relied heavily on my own files in writing this book; it is my intention when I am done with them to donate them to the Reagan Presidential Library, where they will be available to other scholars.

I owe a special debt to Maureen Reagan, who passed away during the completion of this book. Ronald Reagan's first daughter was deeply devoted to her father, whom she resembled in her outspoken honesty and love of life. She generously shared her insights for my books and articles, contributing to my understanding, and is sorely missed.

Last—but certainly not least—I wish to thank Nancy Reagan, her husband's loyal caregiver, for her kindnesses to the author in providing anecdotes and material for this book and for her consistent determination to keep alive the considerable legacy of Ronald Reagan.

PHOTO CREDITS

All photographs in this book are courtesy of the Ronald Reagan Library and the Reagan Family Collection. The following photographs are credited to additional sources:

1 *This is the Army*. Copyright Vitagraph Inc. All Rights Reserved.

19 Kings Row, 1942, Warner Bros. publicity still by Bert Six.

24 Ronald Reagan and Ron throwing football. *Long Beach Independent Press-Telegram*.

25 Reagan Girls. Vince Mandese Photography.

41 Talking to George Allen, the coach of the (then) Los Angeles Rams. *Long Beach Independent Press-Telegram*.

45 Ronald, Nancy, Patti and Ron Reagan on beach. *Look* Magazine.

57 With Richard and Pat Nixon (top). Mister "D".

59 With *Los Angeles Times* reporter Paul Beck (left) and San Francisco reporter Jack McDowell (wearing glasses, right). AP Photo.

61 The Reagans lived at this home in Sacramento because the old Victorian-era governor's mansion was deemed unsafe (Ronald and Ron climbing tree). Walt Zeboski, AP Photo.

66 Nancy and Ronald Reagan campaign photo. Michael Evans.

66 Nancy Reagan with Frank Sinatra. Wallace Gwynn.

67 Ronald and Nancy Reagan, the Annenbergs, and Governor and Mrs. Skafer of Pennsylvania. Rothschild Photo.

INDEX

PublicAffairs is a new nonfiction publishing house and a tribute to the standards, values, and flair of three persons who have served as mentors to countless reporters, writers, editors, and book people of all kinds, including me.

I. F. Stone, proprietor of *I. F. Stone's Weekly,* combined a commitment to the First Amendment with entrepreneurial zeal and reporting skill and became one of the great independent journalists in American history. At the age of eighty, Izzy published *The Trial of Socrates,* which was a national bestseller. He wrote the book after he taught himself ancient Greek.

Benjamin C. Bradlee was for nearly thirty years the charismatic editorial leader of *The Washington Post.* It was Ben who gave the *Post* the range and courage to pursue such historic issues as Watergate. He supported his reporters with a tenacity that made them fearless, and it is no accident that so many became authors of influential, best-selling books.

Robert L. Bernstein, the chief executive of Random House for more than a quarter century, guided one of the nation's premier publishing houses. Bob was personally responsible for many books of political dissent and argument that challenged tyranny around the globe. He is also the founder and was the longtime chair of Human Rights Watch, one of the most respected human rights organizations in the world.

. . .

For fifty years, the banner of Public Affairs Press was carried by its owner Morris B. Schnapper, who published Gandhi, Nasser, Toynbee, Truman, and about 1,500 other authors. In 1983 Schnapper was described by *The Washington Post* as "a redoubtable gadfly." His legacy will endure in the books to come.

Peter Osnos, *Publisher*